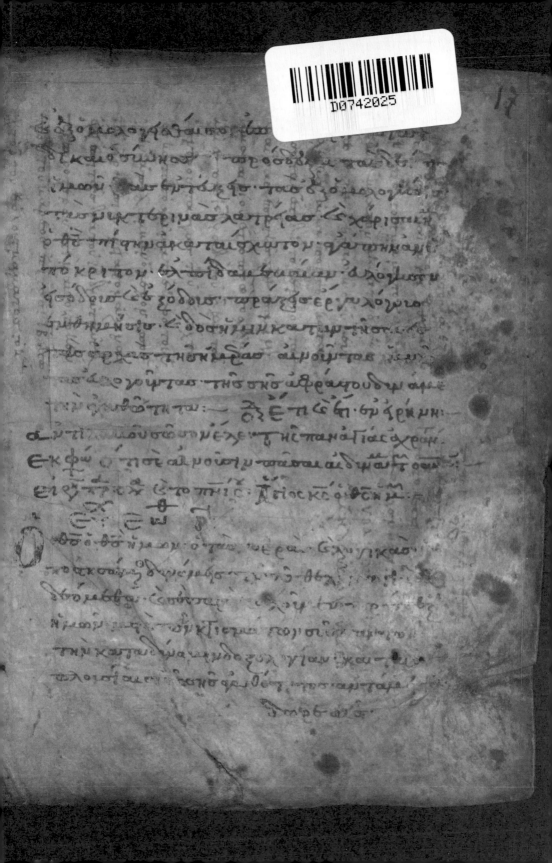

THE

ARCHIMEDES CODEX

HOW A MEDIEVAL PRAYER BOOK IS REVEALING THE TRUE GENIUS OF ANTIQUITY'S GREATEST SCIENTIST

REVIEL NETZ
WILLIAM NOEL

Da Capo Press
A Member of the Perseus Books Group

Production Services by Chris Grison for Outbox Creative Partners
Set in 11.5 point Bembo by Outbox Creative Partners

Cataloging-in-Publication data for this book is available from the Library of Congress.

First Da Capo Press edition 2007
First published in Great Britain in 2007 by Weidenfeld & Nicholson.
ISBN-10 0–306–81580–X
ISBN-13 978–0–306–81580–5

Published by Da Capo Press
A Member of the Perseus Books Group
www.dacapopress.com

Da Capo Press books are available at special discounts for bulk purchases in the United States by corporations, institutions, and other organizations. For more information, please contact the Special Markets Department at the Perseus Books Group, 2300 Chestnut Street, Suite 200, Philadelphia, PA 19103, or call (800) 255-1514, or e-mail special.markets@perseusbooks.com.

1 2 3 4 5 6 7 8 9—10 09 08 07

Contents

List of Illustrations

Endpapers: *front* The Archimedes Palimpsest, folios 16v–17r in natural light; *back* The Archimedes Palimpsest, folios 16v–17r processed to reveal the text of Archimedes' *On Floating Bodies*.

This book is dedicated to Lynn,
to Maya, Darya, and Tamara,
and to Ioannes Myronas

Preface

Nicetas Choniates, the brother of the Archbishop of Athens, witnessed the greatest calamity that ever befell the world of learning. In April 1204, Christian soldiers on a mission to liberate Jerusalem stopped short of their goal and sacked Constantinople, the richest city in Europe. Nicetas gave an eyewitness account of the carnage. The sumptuous treasure of the great church of Hagia Sophia (Holy Wisdom) was broken into bits and distributed among the soldiers. Mules were led to the very sanctuary of the church to carry the loot away. A harlot, a worker of incantations and poisonings, sat in the seat of the Patriarch and danced and sang an obscene song. The soldiers captured and raped the nuns who were consecrated to God. "Oh, immortal God," cried Nicetas, "how great were the afflictions of the men." The obscene realities of medieval warfare crashed upon Constantinople, and the hub of a great empire was shattered.

The looted city had many more books than people. It was the first time that Constantinople had fallen in the 874 years since Constantine the Great, Emperor of Rome founded it in AD 330. Its inhabitants still considered themselves Romans, and the city held the literary treasures of the ancient world as its inheritance. Among the treasures were treatises by the greatest mathematician of the ancient world and one of the greatest thinkers who had ever lived. He approximated the value of pi, he developed the theory of centers of gravity, and he made steps toward the development of the calculus 1,800 years before Newton and Leibniz. His name was Archimedes. Unlike hundreds of thousands of books that were destroyed during the fall of the city, three books containing Archimedes' texts survived.

1

Of the three books, the first to disappear was Codex B; it was last heard of in the Pope's library in Viterbo, north of Rome, in 1311. Next to disappear was Codex A; it was last recorded in the library of an Italian humanist in 1564. It was through copies of these books that Renaissance masters such as Leonardo da Vinci and Galileo knew the works of Archimedes. But Leonardo, Galileo, Newton and Leibniz knew nothing about the third book. It contained two extraordinary texts by Archimedes that were not in Codices A and B. Next to texts such as these, Leonardo's mathematics look like child's play. Eight hundred years after the fall of Constantinople, this third book, the Archimedes Codex, technically known as Codex C, walked on stage.

This is the true and remarkable story of the book and the texts it contains. It reveals how these texts survived the centuries, how they were discovered, how they disappeared again, and how they eventually found a champion. This is also the story of how patient conservation, cutting-edge technology, and dedicated scholarship brought the erased texts back to light. When they started in 1999, the members of the team working on the book had little idea of what they would uncover. By the time they finished, they had discovered completely new texts from the ancient world and had changed the history of science.

1

Archimedes in America

~

Archimedes for Sale

NEW YORK, NEW YORK

Felix de Marez Oyens. What a great name! I don't know him, but I saw him on TV once. His name and demeanor together seemed tailor-made to suggest a distinguished and international pedigree, a pedigree that quite naturally produced deep learning, refined taste, excellent judgement, and total integrity. He clearly had a vast knowledge of books, and he was extraordinarily good at selling them. That's why he was the international director of the Books and Manuscripts Department for Christie's auction house in New York.

Thursday, October 29, 1998 was an exceptionally busy day for Felix. Most of it was devoted to the auction of the final part of the phenomenal collection of books on science and medicine from the collection of Haskell F. Norman. Among the 501 lots were some treasures. In the morning, he sold Marie Curie's doctoral thesis, which she had signed for Ernest Rutherford, the man who discovered the nuclear structure of the atom; a first edition of Darwin's *On the Origin of Species*; and a copy of Einstein's 1905 publication on Special Relativity. In the afternoon, further extraordinary books were under the hammer: a copy of the first edition of James Clerk Maxwell's *Treatise on Electricity and Magnetism,* which had been won as a prize by J. J. Thompson, the man who discovered the electron; Wilbur Wright's first published account of the trial flights at Kitty Hawk, North Carolina; and Nicolai Lobachevskii's *On the Principles of*

Geometry, the first published work on non-Euclidian geometry. Great books, all of them, and a great day for Felix.

Sandwiched between the morning and afternoon sessions of the Norman sale was a separate mini-auction devoted to just one book. It was not a printed book but instead a handwritten one, and it had not belonged to Norman. In fact, the impressive catalogue that Felix had prepared for the occasion, with the splendid sale code "Eureka— 9058," didn't record to whom it did belong. It didn't even look like a great book. It was charred by fire, devoured by mold, and it was almost illegible. To make matters worse, just the day before, the Greek Orthodox Patriarchate of Jerusalem had sought a restraining order against Christie's in the US District Court, Southern District of New York, Judge Kimba Wood presiding. The patriarchate argued that the manuscript had been stolen from one of its libraries. Christie's successfully defended their right to auction the book the next day, but it was clear that the case of the rightful ownership of the book would be pursued after the sale. Even with the smart catalogue, the book itself was going to be a hard sell. Who would want an illegible manuscript, in appalling condition, with an ongoing court case attached to it? Nonetheless, at 2 p.m. on that day Felix was determined to sell it for an astronomical sum, and he set the reserve price for the manuscript at $800,000.

Felix hoped that the book would be worth that much because, barely visible underneath thirteenth-century Christian prayers, were the erased words of an ancient legend and a mathematical genius: Archimedes of Syracuse. Incomplete, damaged, and overwritten as it was, this book was the earliest Archimedes manuscript in existence. It was the only one that contained *Floating Bodies*—perhaps his most famous treatise—in the original Greek, and the only versions of two other extraordinary texts—the revolutionary *Method* and the playful *Stomachion*. You could barely read them but, as Felix was very quick to point out, there was the possibility that the most modern imaging techniques might help. There were other erased texts in the book too, but they were almost invisible. No one could read them, and no one had given them much thought. What mattered was that this book contained the extremely battered material remains of the mind of a very great man. If this was a big day for Felix, it was a huge day for the history of science.

The auction room was in Christie's offices on the corner of Park Avenue and 59th Street in New York City. The room was lined by large contemporary paintings, which provided the splendid visual setting that the manuscript could not. The manuscript itself was strapped to a book cradle and secured inside a dramatically lit cage to the right of the auctioneer's podium. Reporters arrived as the minutes before the sale counted down. They stood at the back of the room with their cameramen who trained their lenses on the book and tried in vain to make it look as photogenic as one of the paintings. The rows furthest from the podium were full, but mainly with academics like the Professor of Mathematics at West Point, Fred Rickey. He was passionate about the manuscript and deeply interested in its fate, but could not possibly afford it. The seats at the front, where one might expect the most seriously interested customers, were still alarmingly empty. Felix may have been a little worried. But Felix was lucky. His lucky number was two, because the market value of an object is always determined by how badly more than one person wants it.

One of the people who wanted the book badly was Evangelos Venizelos, the Minister of Culture of Greece. He wanted it for his country. He had publicly broadcast that it was Greece's moral, historic, and scientific obligation to acquire the manuscript. At the last minute, he organized a consortium to buy it and the Greek Consul General in New York, Mr. Manessis, was sent to the auction. He sat in the front row, together with an associate, on the left side of the room.

Just behind Mr. Manessis was a man hoping to disappoint him— Simon Finch, a high-profile book dealer from London. If your idea of a bookseller is a bespectacled and tweedy English gentleman, then think again. Finch is nothing like that. About 45 years old, he looks more like a rock star than a book man, and he sells books to rock stars quite as frequently as to libraries. Finch is the sort of man who can normally be found at book fairs wearing Vivienne Westwood suits and sporting designer stubble and disheveled hair. He actually owns a pair of blue suede shoes. Finch is a romantic and that's why he is in the book business. If you don't think that the combination of great history and supreme quality that books can provide is romantic, then he will tell you that that's because you've never turned the pages of a great book. Five minutes later, you might be a customer. When he went in to bid for the Palimpsest containing the treatises of Archimedes, Finch had more than his usual air of mystery. No one knew for whom he was acting, and no one knew quite how much that person was prepared to pay for the Archimedes Palimpsest.

At 2 p.m. the duel started, with Christie's Francis Wahlgren on the podium. The reserve price of $800,000 was quickly reached, and the auction headed over the million-dollar milestone. Every time the Greeks raised their paddle—number 176—high into the air, Finch would respond with his—number 169. The Greeks were on the telephone, taking instructions, and each time the price went up it would take them slightly longer to raise their paddle. Each time, Finch would top the new price. The Consul General answered to the call of $1,900,000 from the podium. Finch responded quickly to a call for $2,000,000. Wahlgren looked to the Consul General for a response to his request for any offers over $2,000,000. The Greeks were on the phone, desperately raising money. After what seemed like an eternity, Wahlgren brought down the hammer. "Two million dollars it is," he said. "Paddle 169." The Greeks had failed; the book had gone to Finch's unknown client. With the buyer's premium, the Archimedes Palimpsest had sold for $2,200,000.

This one book made just under half the amount of the combined total of all 501 lots of the Norman sale. No wonder its story hit the presses. The next day, Finch's role was printed on the front page of the *New York Times* to an expectant world. He was the front man, not for a university, not for a library, but for an individual. But Finch would not tell all; he admitted only that the buyer was an American citizen who was "not Bill Gates." Felix de Marez Oyens had shown the book to Finch and the buyer before the sale. Felix had called it "an old, dirty book" and took it out of a brown-paper bag in his desk. This was not Felix's usual sales pitch, but it had worked. Whoever the individual was, unlike many eminent institutions, he wanted the book badly enough to take on a national government and a religious leader. He was also prepared to pay top dollar for the privilege of owning a moldy, illegible, legally contentious old book. Was he a nutcase, intent on keeping secret knowledge to himself? Felix might have been happy, but many were outraged. If the Palimpsest's past was obscure, its future appeared dangerously uncertain.

BALTIMORE, MARYLAND

My name is Will Noel, and I am a curator at the Walters Art Museum in Baltimore, Maryland. The Walters, as it is always known, is a great American museum modeled on a Renaissance palazzo in Genoa. Think grand marble staircases and a central courtyard surrounded by columns and you get the picture. It stands together with a number of other noble edifices around Mount Vernon Place in downtown Baltimore. In the center of the square is a tall pillar surmounted by George Washington. If this were London, the square would be crowded with tourists, street musicians, and students. But, located in inner-city Baltimore as it is, Mount Vernon Place is normally quite empty of people which lends it a sense of moody suspended animation that the passing traffic doesn't quite relieve. Inside the building is the superb collection of two individuals—father and son, William and Henry Walters. In a great act of civic philanthropy the collection was given by Henry to the City of Baltimore in 1934. Few people visit it, but the museum houses fifty-five centuries of art and in many areas its holdings are truly fabulous. Thomas Hoving, the director of the Metropolitan Museum of Art in New York, said of it: "Piece for piece it is the greatest art museum in the United States." It is my job to research into, teach from, and exhibit the Walters collection of manuscripts and rare books.

They are the stuff of legend and the fabric of history. They range in date from 300 BC to 1815, from an Egyptian Book of the Dead to Napoleon's memoirs. Most of them are medieval and sumptuously illuminated with images. Among the Walters' other holdings are massive Roman sarcophagi and paintings by Hugo van der Goes, Raphael, El Greco, Tiepolo, and Manet.

Gary Vikan, the director of the Walters, is my boss. Several weeks before the sale I had told Gary about the Archimedes Palimpsest. It is part of my job to follow the New York sales and Gary has a particular interest in medieval manuscripts. It struck a chord. When I walked into work the day after the sale, he hailed me down the grand stairway of the house that was once the Walters' home and, brandishing the *New York Times*, he said, "Will! Why don't you find out who bought the Archimedes Palimpsest and see if you can get it for exhibition?"

I thought it was a bad idea. After all, the Walters is an art museum. It is concerned with what things look like. You cannot even see what is interesting about the Archimedes Palimpsest. I sent Gary a memo asking him if he really wanted me to do this. A couple of days later I got my memo back with a characteristic directorial scrawl: "NOT WORTH MUCH WORK." It was clear to me that at least I had to try. I didn't have any more leads than anybody else did. Simon Finch was the only name I had and so I asked Kathleen Stacey, the head librarian at the Walters, to find his email address on the web. This she did, and I sent Finch the following email:

Dear Mr. Finch,
   I am the manuscripts curator at the Walters Art Museum, Baltimore. The Walters has 850 medieval manuscripts, 1,300 incunables, and another 1,500 books printed after 1500. Most of these books are illustrated and Henry Walters collected them between about 1895 and 1928.
   We have an active acquisitions program, although our funding is limited. We have, for example, recently purchased a

deluxe sixteenth-century Ethiopian manuscript from Sam Fogg. In general terms, therefore, I would be most interested in receiving your catalogues and would be grateful if you would add me to your mailing list.

However, I do have a more specific reason for writing. The Director of the Walters, Dr. Gary Vikan, is a specialist in Greek material, and was fascinated (as am I) by the Archimedes Palimpsest. Dr. Vikan wondered if there was any possibility of displaying the manuscript at the Walters for a short period of time. I do not know whether the purchaser of the volume would be at all interested in this idea. But if you think he might be, I would be most grateful to you if you could pass on the suggestion.

The Walters does have an active exhibition program. We are currently putting on a show of works from the Vatican, Monet came earlier in the year, and the Arts of Georgia are coming in 1999. If the owner of the Palimpsest is interested in putting the manuscript on view, he might consider that the Walters is an appropriate place.

Please excuse this cold call. It is just a thought, but from our point of view an exciting one, given the extraordinary cultural importance of the codex. Whatever you think of this I would, as I say, look forward to hearing from you and receiving your catalogues. With many thanks for your time,

William Noel
Curator of Manuscripts and Rare Books

I moved my cursor to the top left of the screen: send. By the next minute I had dismissed it from my mind. Frankly, the chances of anything resulting from this were remote in the extreme, I didn't even much want anything to happen, and I had labels to write for an exhibition of Dutch illuminated manuscripts. Still, I had done my job.

Emails are short on ritual. There is no walk to the mailbox, no looking at the stamp, no slicing the envelope, no guessing the handwriting. They just pop up unbidden on your computer screen while you are engrossed in your daily business. Some of them, like little electronic terrorists, can blow your mind and change your life. Three days after my email to Finch this happened to me. I was happily writing an exhibition label for a book illuminated by the Masters of the Delft Grisailles when my computer went PING. You've got mail. Sam Fogg. Left Click:

> Dear Will,
>   I am writing with reference to your letter to Simon Finch on the subject of the Palimpsest. I think the buyer of the Palimpsest is very sympathetic to the idea of sending the Archimedes to the Walters. I have already suggested to him that we visit the Museum in January. Perhaps we could discuss this and the Archimedes on the telephone soon.
>   Best wishes,
>   Sam Fogg

I sat motionless in my chair—eyes shut, hands cradled behind my head, rocking gently, my stomach slowly turning to wax. Then I picked up the phone and dialed a number. It was a number I knew almost by heart. Although I hadn't been expecting to hear from him, I knew Sam Fogg well. As an unemployed postgraduate eking out an impoverished existence in Camden Town, London, I had once done some research on his behalf (for which you should read "he employed me"), and when I became a curator in America, I was in a position to acquire the odd manuscript from him. Sam is one of the art world's most colorful characters. Famous for having sold ceiling panels of Henry III of England's painted bedroom at Westminster to the British Museum; for having sold a leaf of Jan van Eyck's miniature masterpiece, the *Turin Milan Hours*, to the J. Paul Getty Museum; and for having bought a Rubens for £40,000,000. Sam is savvy, successful, and very smart. I don't remember the conversation well, but

Sam must have told me that Simon Finch had called him because I had mentioned Sam to Finch in my email.

I arranged a flight to London. Before I caught the plane I discussed strategy with Gary. He thought that Simon Finch and Sam Fogg might actually be the same person and that I was being given the runaround. I didn't think so. Two days later I could prove it: I had lunch with both Simon Finch and Sam Fogg in Brown's restaurant on Maddox Street in London. It was only at this lunch that I discovered who the owner of the Palimpsest actually was. He had in fact been present at the auction, unnoticed by the competition, and unrecognized by the press. He still likes to tell the story. Moreover, he had known exactly the liability that he was trying to buy and had bought it on the assumption that he would deposit it somewhere for conservation and scholarly study. His anonymity was important to him and hereafter he became known in any written correspondence as Mr. B. We agreed that Sam and Mr. B would visit the Walters in January.

This was just great. The trouble was I didn't really know anything about Archimedes or his book. My brother Rob had written a story about a dog-eared palimpsest once and so I had the vague, romantic notion that palimpsests could harbor secret knowledge that you could only understand if you were really smart. But that was all I could remember. I needed a few facts and a map of the Mediterranean. It was November. I had two months to learn enough not to look like a total idiot.

At about eleven o'clock on the morning of Tuesday, January 19, 1999 Mr. B and Sam arrived at the museum. I met them at the entrance. Sam was a laugh a minute, as he always is; Mr. B was completely silent. Nervous to begin with, I took them up to the manuscript room, a climate-controlled vault that serves as my office as well as the repository of hundreds of medieval treasures. I entertained Sam and Mr. B for an hour or so, before taking them to have lunch with Gary. I couldn't get a measure of the man. All I knew was that he was retiring, rich—richer than Croesus—and that he liked food. I knew he liked books too, but I wasn't learning anything more.

I had arranged to have lunch at a Baltimore institution, Marconi's, which is about four blocks from the Walters on West Saratoga Street. A slightly down-at-heel survivor of Baltimore's elegant past, it serves wonderful food in a beautifully proportioned, white wooden-paneled room. On the way, Sam walked in front with Gary, and I walked behind with Mr. B—a nervous puppy trying to come to grips with the biggest fish of my little career. I remember congratulating him on his exciting new acquisition and saying that it was extremely generous of him to even consider putting his great new treasure on deposit at the Walters. His reaction to this was my first lesson in the mind of Mr. B. He said that he had already left it on deposit with me. I did not understand. I asked him to say it again. He said that he had left it in a bag on my desk. I swallowed hard. As a museum registrar will quickly point out, this does not conform to standard museum protocols for the transportation and documentation of objects worth several millions of dollars. I went with the flow. Great, I told him, and I reassured him that I had locked the door of my office on the way out.

Lunch was cordial, but a little odd to me. As I have said, Mr. B enjoys his food, and he also likes to take his time. I wanted to go back to the museum and look at the manuscript. I was quite happy with one course; Mr. B wanted his chocolate sundae. I could barely sit in my seat, and I couldn't get Mr. B out of his. Eventually lunch was over and the check was requested. Gary tried to pay with a credit card. This is Baltimore. Marconi's doesn't take American Express. I paid cash. Back we walked to the museum. I made my excuses on the way and ducked away to buy a pack of cigarettes. I hadn't had one for three hours, and I smoked two in five minutes—pacing nervously. I caught up with them in time to turn the key to the manuscript room where my desk sits.

A lightweight blue bag was on my desk. Stamped in white on its side was a pair of scissors and, underneath them, the words GIANNI CAMPAGNA, MILANO. I unzipped the bag and pulled out a brown box.

On the spine, in gold letters, was written: "THE ARCHIMEDES PALIMPSEST." I called my colleague Abigail Quandt, who is the Conservator of Manuscripts at the Walters. We opened the box. Inside was a small, thick book. The cover was made of battered leather and was badly stained. On the upper cover there was a flash of red paint and an odd silver-looking stud. Abigail placed the book between two velvet-covered blocks of wood on the table. The blocks prevented the manuscript from opening too far and placing unnecessary strain on the binding and the pages. She opened the book just far enough so that we could see inside. She kept it open by gently draping book "snakes" over the edges of the pages. (These "snakes" are actually curtain weights that you can only get at John Lewis, a department store on Oxford Street in London; they work really well for keeping your place in a medieval book.) Mr. B, Gary, and I all peered over her shoulder. At first I saw nothing. Only slowly did my eyes adjust. And then the awesome thought dawned on me. I was looking at the unique key to the mind of a genius who had died 2,200 years earlier. I could barely see it to read it, and I would not have understood it if I could, but there it was nonetheless.

After a few minutes, I grasped the fact that the time for gawking was over. Proper looking would have to come later. The museum registrar, Joan Elisabeth Reid, prepared a receipt for the book, which I handed over to Mr. B. I took his email address. (Email was, and still remains, his preferred form of communication.) We said our good-byes at the front entrance of the museum on North Charles Street, and then I dashed back upstairs to the manuscript room where Sam was still waiting. I gave him an enormous and excited hug, forgetting for a moment that we were on live video feed and that the Walters' security staff was monitoring our every move.

Two days later I received a letter from Mr. B that contained a check made out to the Walters. It was big enough to get the institution's attention and me a pay raise.

★

Help for Archimedes

Mr. B told me that he had bought an ugly book. Since he'd paid over two million dollars for it, I took this with a pinch of salt. But no. Now that I had it in my hands, I could see that he had played it straight this time. It was ugly. It was small—about the size of a standard bag of Domino sugar. When I opened it, I saw that the pages were mottled brown in color. Matching tide lines caused by water faced each other across page openings. The pages tended to be brighter in the middle than around the edges where they were more deeply stained. In fact right on their edges the pages were black, as if they had been in a fire. Overlaid upon the brown of the pages was stitched a grid pattern of slightly darker-brown Greek letters, which were all jumbled up. The monotony of the pages was only slightly relieved by the speckled red of the odd capital letter and occasionally by purple stains of mold. When I turned pages, I could, just once in a while, make out the circles and straight lines of things that looked like diagrams that would, most inconveniently, disappear into the spine of the book from the inner margins. Compared to other manuscripts I had handled, the pages didn't flex very easily, and they were contorted. Sometimes, as I was turning a page, it would suddenly "pop" into a slightly different shape. Once in a while a whole page would just come out of the book in my hands. As I went through the book from start to finish, four pages stood out as having a certain charm because they had paintings on them, but overall it was a deflating experience. And then, toward the end, the pages looked so fragile and so moldy that I shut the book in alarm. This book, for which Mr. B had paid so much, was on its last legs.

That is not a very helpful description, so let me describe the book etymologically. It is a manuscript book or, more technically, a manuscript codex. Derived from the Latin words *manu* (by hand) and *scriptus* (written), a manuscript is entirely written by hand. It is fundamentally different from a printed book in that it is not one of a large number of books printed in an edition. It is unique. Other manuscripts might contain some of the texts in it. All I knew for sure at this point was that no other manuscripts contained Archimedes' *Method, Stomachion,* or *Floating Bodies* in Greek. Secondly, this manuscript is a palimpsest. Derived from the Greek words *palin* (again) and *psan* (to rub), this means that the parchment used to make it has been scraped more than once. As we will see, to make parchment you need to scrape the skins of animals. If you want to reuse parchment that has already been used to make a book, you need to scrape the skin again to get rid of the old text before you write over it. This palimpsest manuscript consisted of 174 folios. Derived from the Latin *folium* (leaf), a folio has a front and back—a recto and a verso—that are equivalent to modern pages. The folios were numbered 1 through 177 but, mysteriously, three numbers were missing. I hoped Mr. B knew that he was missing some folios.

The manuscript is now called the Archimedes Palimpsest, but this is a bit confusing. Make no mistake: the manuscript *is* a prayer book. It looks like a prayer book, it feels like a prayer book, it even smells like a prayer book, and it is prayers that you see on its folios. It is only called the Archimedes Palimpsest because folios taken from an earlier manuscript containing treatises by Archimedes were used to make it. But remember the Archimedes text had been scraped off. Note, too, that the scribes of the prayer book used the folios taken from several other earlier manuscripts as well as the Archimedes manuscript. At the time of the sale, nobody had a clue what was on these folios. They didn't look like folios from the Archimedes manuscript, and they didn't look as if they were all from the same manuscript. For example, while the Archimedes text was laid out in two columns, the texts on other palimpsest folios were laid out in one column; others had a different number of lines per folio; and the handwriting on the other folios, when it wasn't invisible, was sometimes very different. Mr. B had bought several different books in one. Basically, I concluded that the Archimedes Palimpsest was only called the Archimedes Palimpsest because no one could identify the other texts in the manuscript and because the Archimedes texts were considered so much more important than the prayer book that was on top of them.

But how important, really, was this "Archimedes Palimpsest?" I began to ask around and Mr. B's book got decidedly mixed reviews. Even though it had commanded $2.2 million at auction, the truth was that only three parties had put up a fight for it: the patriarchate, the Greek government, and Mr. B. None of them knew all that much about Archimedes. How come, I asked? Was there no academic institution sufficiently interested in it to enter the fray? I found out that many well-informed scholars were skeptical that we could learn much more from the book. Everybody kept mentioning that someone named Heiberg had discovered the manuscript and read it in 1906. And Heiberg, apparently, was something of a god in classical studies. They said that it was unlikely that he would have missed anything important. Mr. B, they told me, had bought a relic, not a book that would reward much further research.

Still, Mr. B had entrusted his relic to me, and I had no choice but to take his new possession as seriously as he did. His book clearly needed three things: first, since it was literally falling apart, it needed conservation; second, since no one could see the Archimedes text in it properly, it needed advanced imaging; third, if by any chance Heiberg had missed a few lines, then scholars needed to read it. I knew that Mr. B would require the best. This was good, because his book was such a wreck that it needed the best—the best conservators, the most advanced imaging, and the most highly qualified scholars. I was none of these things, and I wondered whether I was the right person to be looking after Mr. B's book. My expertise is in Latin manuscripts, not Greek ones; religious books, not mathematical ones; beautiful books, not ugly ones; and certainly legible books, for goodness sake, not invisible ones.

That Mr. B chose me, of all people, to look after his book seemed more than a little absurd, I thought. But Mr. B knew my limitations. My job, as he saw much more clearly than I did at the time, was not to do the work, but to get the right people to do it. But how was I going to do that?

THE PROJECT MANAGER

On Friday, July 16, 1999, the *Washington Post* published an article on the Palimpsest. Abigail and I received many emails in reaction to it. Some are among the most zany I have ever received. (To the unacknowledged grandson of Rasputin, I can only say that I have not yet found any corroboration of your pedigree in the Archimedes Palimpsest.) Let's concentrate on the ones we found helpful. Here's the best of them.

> Dear Drs. Noel and Quandt:
>   I read with interest the article in the *Washington Post*. Congratulations. It certainly puts our work in perspective. We in the intelligence community have equipment that may be able to help. We also have a wide range of contacts in the imaging community that could prove useful to you. If you would like to discuss this further, please do not hesitate to get in touch. Whatever the case, it sounds like a fascinating project. Good luck in your endeavors.
>   Yours sincerely,
>   Michael B. Toth
>   National Policy Director
>   National Reconnaissance Office

The National Reconnaissance Office (NRO) is not a secret any more, but it was for a long time. Mr. B told me that the only reason it was forced to become public is that people could not understand why hundreds of cars were disappearing into a small office building. The answer was that most of it was underground and that it was the unacknowledged nerve center of the US reconnaissance satellite program. Now, however, you can find details about NRO on the web.

Working with the CIA and the Department of Defense, it can warn of potential trouble spots around the world, help plan military operations, and monitor the environment. Its mission is to develop and operate unique and innovative space-reconnaissance systems and conduct intelligence-related activities essential for U.S. national security. As an avid John le Carré reader, I have always been enthralled with the world of espionage.

I phoned Mr. Toth. I was tempted to say, if he hung on just a moment, I would take the book up to the roof of the museum and if he could just fly a satellite over it, we would all be finished in a few minutes. More soberly, I invited him up from Washington to Baltimore. I was still hoping that he would have a gadget, maybe in his back pocket, maybe disguised as a watch, that could help me with my problem. Much to my disappointment, it soon became clear that no government agency could help us with the imaging of the Palimpsest. Since it was private property, the tax dollars of the American public could not be spent on it. Mike said that he would nonetheless be happy to help us as a volunteer. Deprived of his toys, I was not sure how he could, but it seemed unwise to annoy this man, and he seemed pretty certain that he would be useful.

Mike, it turned out, was an expert at managing highly technical systems, including imaging systems and particularly in assessing something called "program risk." This was an amazing stroke of fortune. Apparently, I had found someone who was professionally trained to tell me exactly the magnitude of my trouble. But, more importantly, he was willing to help me. I am a scholar who specializes in illuminated liturgical manuscripts from Canterbury, England from the early eleventh century. I have a few skills. I can, for example, recite the Book of Psalms backward and the kings and queens of England forward from Hengist through Henry VIII. But these skills are not particularly well suited to running an effective integrated project at a reasonable cost, to the correct level of performance, and on a practical schedule in order to produce value for the owner and an Archimedes text for the world. I needed someone like Mike, a technical consultant, and preferably one who, I liked to believe, had pressed the "go" button to launch a space shuttle.

Mike, like so many people who would ultimately help with Archimedes, was a volunteer. He didn't want money, and he didn't want his government service celebrated by the press. In fact, his work on Archimedes was all done through his father's company, R. B. Toth Associates, and that was how we introduced him to people. With Mike on board everybody else seemed to get a cover, too. Mr. B became the "source selection authority" (that is, he decided everything); Abigail became the "critical path" (that is, everything depended on conservation); the scholars became the "end-users" (that is, they defined what was best); and the imagers became the "value added" (that is, they made the difference). And me? I was given the very grand title of "project director."

THE SOURCE SELECTION AUTHORITY

I know the owner of the Archimedes Palimpsest. I know him very well. If you don't know him by now, you don't need to know him. To the press, I say that he's of more use to you as an enigma; to the curious I say mind your own business. To those who do know him, he is a loyal, generous, thoughtful, and enlightened man. His email style is a bit short, but you get used to it.

When the Archimedes Palimpsest was sold, some scholars were outraged that the book had returned to a private collection. But if Archimedes had meant enough to the public, then public institutions would have bought it. Archimedes did not. Public institutions were offered the book at a lower price than it actually fetched at auction, and they turned it down. If you think this is a shame, then it is a shame that we all share. We live in a world where value translates into cash. If you care about what happens to world heritage, get political about it, and be prepared to pay for it.

The practical reasons why it might have been a "bad thing" if the manuscript was maintained in a private collection are that the book might have been poorly handled and the right scholars might not have gotten to see it. Someone could have just tossed it into his or her attic. As we will learn, given the state in which the book came out of its last private collection, these were valid concerns. I hope by the end of this book, if not by the end of this chapter, to demonstrate that this manuscript has been cared for extremely well and that the right people have cared for it. Another reason why it might have been a "bad thing" is that its future was uncertain. This still remains true. When the work is done the manuscript will go back to its owner, and I do not know what will happen to it then. But the best predictor of future behavior is past behavior and over the last eight years the owner has behaved responsibly, thoughtfully, and generously.

What do I mean by this? Well, Mr. B is extremely interested in the Archimedes Palimpsest and greatly concerned with the project and its goals. He is knowledgeable about books, he cares about them, and he has a superb library. He makes all the important decisions regarding the book, but he does so after carefully listening to us and reading proposals that I have forwarded to him. And what's more, he pays for all the work that needs to be done. The project has never suffered from a lack of money. Manuscript scholars, classicists, and mathematicians owe a great deal to the owner of the Archimedes Palimpsest.

THE CRITICAL PATH

The first task was to secure the well-being of the manuscript. Whatever else happened, the manuscript had to stay safe. I didn't have to do anything and have done nothing about this since the book arrived at the Walters. Abigail Quandt has done it all. Abigail has an international reputation for the conservation of medieval manuscripts. She has worked on some of the world's most famous manuscripts, including the Dead Sea Scrolls and one of the greatest masterpieces of the Middle Ages—the *Book of Hours* of Jeanne D'Evreux. Abigail received her training in Dublin with Tony Cains, Head of Conservation at Trinity College Dublin and in England with

Roger Powell who rebound the *Book of Kells*. She has been at the Walters much longer than I have—since 1984.

Abigail was integral to the planning of Archimedes' future. In any of the decisions concerning the well-being of the manuscript—and there would be many—Abigail's voice was the strongest. I didn't just have a great colleague; I was convinced that Archimedes was in the safest possible hands—hers. I could rest assured that I wouldn't make the situation worse for Archimedes, and I was able to concentrate on other things.

THE END–USERS

I received many offers, by a variety of enthusiasts, to help with the decipherment of the Palimpsest. Some of these offers were rather forceful (this is an understatement). I tried not to be offensive while I worked out a strategy. The manuscript was so fragile that I could not let just anyone have a crack at it. I needed to get the two or three people who could best edit the texts so that they could be published. The question was which two or three?

Gary Vikan immediately advised me to get in touch with Nigel Wilson of Lincoln College, Oxford. He was an obvious choice for two reasons. The first was that he knew the book better than anyone else having just contributed a great deal to the catalogue Christie's produced for the auction. Christie's asked him to catalogue it for the same reason that I wanted him to work on it: he is without peer in scholarship on the transmission of classical texts from antiquity through the Middle Ages and his paleographical (script-deciphering) and philological (text-analyzing) skills are legendary. I wrote to him on Monday, January 15, 1999 and explained that if we were to do justice to the manuscript, we needed a distinguished scholar who knew about the subject to be our advisor. If he was willing, he was in this respect uniquely qualified to help us. Ever since then Nigel has been helping us. He has become far more than an independent advisor.

Next I phoned my very discreet friend Patrick Zutshi, Keeper of Manuscripts and University Archives at Cambridge University Library and spoke to him about my problem. He advised me to get in touch with Patricia Easterling, who was Regius Professor of Greek at Cambridge University. This was pretty grand for me, but not, I thought, for Archimedes. So I phoned her and said, "Can you please tell me who is the best person to study the Archimedes Palimpsest?" I met her in early March 1999 in the tea room of the University Library, and she suggested I get in touch with Reviel Netz who was translating Archimedes into English for Cambridge University Press. Netz, she said, would be more interested in the book than most. While many were skeptical about the discoveries that could be made from the text, all agreed that the manuscript was important for its diagrams. Netz had a distinct interest in the diagrams. (More about this later.) Netz was at the Massachusetts Institute of Technology. I wrote him an email, and then we talked in detail on the phone. Pat Easterling was right:

"Yes. I need to see the diagrams, particularly for *Sphere and Cylinder.*" I think were the first words out of his mouth. I am still not sure because he has a rather thick Israeli accent. That's a bit pushy, I thought, and I tried to put the brakes on. So I spoke slowly and painted a broad picture of what our work might be and how he might fit into it. And, if he was interested, perhaps, just perhaps, he should come to Baltimore in the fullness of time.

When I met him at the airport terminal a couple of days later, I understood immediately that his pushiness was induced by his fear and his excitement. I did my best to calm his fear: yes, the Walters was a center of excellence; no, the Palimpsest wasn't here for a passing visit; yes, he could look at it—tomorrow, even—but he had to be very careful; no, I didn't plan to show it to just anyone. By the next day, I understood where he was coming from. He knew better than anyone that the box containing the Palimpsest was a time machine to Archimedes of Syracuse in the third century BC. He explained the importance of the diagrams to me as no one else ever has. Having convinced himself that I understood the grave responsibility that was on my shoulders, he looked at me with sympathy. He knew that I was going to do my best for the book, even though I did not understand it and it would be a long, demanding task that would take me away from my own research for years. Good. He was on my side, if only because I was on Archimedes' side. Now, eight years later, we find ourselves writing this book side by side and chapter by chapter.

Unlike me, Reviel has never thought of the Palimpsest as ugly. He doesn't care about its looks; he simply regards the Palimpsest with awe. His initial reaction was to feel daunted by the task ahead of him. His doubts were gone, though, when he heard that he would be working side-by-side with a colleague of the stature of Nigel Wilson. Reviel had another suggestion, too. He thought it was important to get someone to work just on those folios of the Palimpsest that contained texts not by Archimedes. He wanted to know who kept Archimedes company in this prayer book. I thought this was a good idea. Even if the text of Archimedes was well understood, there was the chance that we could find out more about the other palimpsested texts.

The name Reviel suggested was Natalie Tchernetska, a Latvian who was doing her PhD on Greek palimpsests at Trinity College, Cambridge. Pat Easterling was her supervisor. Small world. I met her in Pat's office at Newnham College in the summer of 1999. She was helpful in assessing the images, and we will have reason to look at some of her work later. This was the core of the academic team that was going to paint an entirely new picture of the greatest mathematician of antiquity and to reveal the world's greatest palimpsest.

THE VALUE ADDED

One day in August 1999 I sat down beside Abigail in my office and faced Mike Toth. We had to find the right people to image the Palimpsest. This was intimidating. I felt overwhelmed with the thought of how much work I would have to do, but I didn't even know precisely what this work was. Mike thought that we should arrange a competition for people to image the Palimpsest. I thought this was a bad idea; it seemed like a lot of work. Mike gently insisted. It would greatly increase the number of imaging procedures that we could perform on the book and it would give the participants the incentive to reduce costs and increase performance in the hope that they would be rewarded with the commission for imaging the entire volume. This was merely sensible, he said. It sounded like rocket science to me. Then he told me for the first time about a Request for Proposals. An RFP is quite standard to me now. It is a document in which you outline the problem and ask for a solution.

Abigail wrote the RFP. It is one of a number of thorough and brilliant documents that she has written throughout the history of the project. It started with a goal: to digitally retrieve and preserve for posterity all the writings in the 174 folios of the Archimedes Palimpsest. It mentioned all the constraints: because the manuscript was very fragile, all the handling of the manuscript would be undertaken by Abigail and personnel that she designated. It outlined the phases of work: after the competitive phase, the selected contractor would image the entire manuscript in a disbound state. The whole proposal ran six pages. In response to the RFP, we received six proposals. Of the six, we submitted three to Mr. B and of the three Mr. B selected two for the competition.

One team consisted of Roger Easton, a faculty member at the Chester F. Carlson Center for Imaging Science at the Rochester Institute of Technology, and Keith Knox, who was the Principal Scientist at the Xerox Digital Imaging Technology Center also in Rochester. (He now works for Boeing in Hawaii.) Keith, together with Brian J. Thompson, had achieved fame years earlier by developing and patenting a method—the Knox-Thompson Algorithm—that recovers images from telescopic photographs that have been degraded by the atmosphere. More recently, Roger and Keith had formed a team together with the late Robert H. Johnston to image degraded texts including a palimpsest in Princeton University Library and several of the Dead Sea Scroll fragments. Their work had already been celebrated on the BBC and on American TV. They had already done some work on the Palimpsest, because Keith's sister-in-law knew Hope Mayo, who had worked with Nigel to prepare the catalogue for the Christie's sale. Some of their images are actually in the catalogue. Roger, Keith, and Bob Johnston were a known quantity and a safe bet.

The other team was from Johns Hopkins University and was, in effect, one man, William A. Christens-Barry. Bill is not an imaging scientist, still less a photographer; he is a physicist. At the time we met him, he was working at the Applied Physics Laboratory of Johns Hopkins University. APL employs nearly three thousand engineers, information technologists, and scientists. It works primarily on development projects funded by federal agencies. Foremost among these are the US Navy and NASA. Scientists at APL participate in the entire range of data collection and analysis activities of interest to its sponsors, including data from air-, ocean-, and space-borne reconnaissance and imaging platforms. Work on non-defense, non-space projects constitutes a secondary activity of the laboratory. Most of Bill's research pertained to problems in biological and medical science, particularly in relation to cancer. Impressive place; impressive guy. His proposal was full of ideas that no one else had even considered.

THE PROJECT DIRECTOR

All these people had well-defined roles, but I wondered about my role. I was to be Archimedes' factotum. I did the talking, and I did the arranging. As Mike put it, I kept an awful lot of plates spinning on their poles. And I was going to have to do it for a long time. By the end of the year, I had talked to the right people and had arranged a lot. I had a plan in place and the key players were on board. I could say what I was doing to anybody who called. I just couldn't really say why I was doing it. If you had called me up and asked me why any of us wanted to do this work, I would immediately have referred you to Reviel Netz.

2

Archimedes in Syracuse

A rchimedes is the most important scientist who ever lived. This conclusion can be reached as follows. The British philosopher A. N. Whitehead once famously remarked: "The safest general characterization of the European philosophical tradition is that it consists of a series of footnotes to Plato." This judgment may sound outrageous, but in fact it is quite sober minded. Plato's immediate followers, such as Aristotle, tried above all to refute or to refine Plato's arguments. Later philosophers debated whether it was best to follow Plato or Aristotle. And so, in a real sense, all later Western philosophy is but a footnote to Plato.

The safest general characterization of the European scientific tradition is that it consists of a series of footnotes to Archimedes. By which I mean, roughly the same kind of genealogy that Whitehead meant for Plato applies to Archimedes. As an example, we need only to look at one of the most influential books of modern science, Galileo's *Discourses Concerning Two New Sciences*. This book was published in 1638, by which time Archimedes had been dead for exactly 1,850 years—a very long time indeed. Yet throughout it, Galileo is in debt to Archimedes. Essentially, Galileo advances the two sciences of statics (how objects behave in rest) and dynamics (how objects behave in motion). For statics, Galileo's principal tools are *centers of gravity* and the *law of the balance*. Galileo borrows both of these concepts— explicitly, always expressing his admiration—from Archimedes. For dynamics, Galileo's principal tools are the *approximation of curves* and the *proportions of times and motions*. Both of which, once again, derive directly from Archimedes. No other authority is as frequently quoted or quoted with equal reverence. Galileo essentially started out from where Archimedes left off, proceeding in the same direction as defined by his Greek predecessor. This is true not only of Galileo but also of the other great figures of the so-called "scientific revolution," such as Leibniz, Huygens, Fermat, Descartes, and Newton. All of them were Archimedes' children. With Newton, the science of the scientific revolution reached its perfection in a perfectly Archimedean form. Based on pure, elegant first principles and applying pure geometry, Newton deduced the rules governing the universe. All of later science is a consequence of the desire to generalize Newtonian, that is, Archimedean methods.

The two principles that the authors of modern science learned from Archimedes are:

- The mathematics of infinity
- The application of mathematical models to the physical world

Thanks to the Palimpsest, we now know much more about these two aspects of Archimedes' achievement.

The mathematics of infinity and the application of mathematical models to the physical world are closely interrelated. This is because physical reality consists of infinitesimal pulses of force acting instantaneously. As a consequence, to find out about the outcome of such forces, we need to sum up an infinite number of "pulses," each infinitesimally small. This is surprising. We might think that the mathematics of infinity is some kind of flight-of-fancy with no practical application. After all, we might think that there is no infinity to be met with in the ordinary world. But it turns out that the mathematics of infinity is the most practical tool of science, so important that it is often called simply "the calculus." The application of mathematics to the physical world via the calculus is in a formula, modern science. Newton, in particular, used the calculus in implicit form to work out how the planets behave. It is a beautiful result and the inspiration for all later science. It is also, at its core, the application of Archimedean insights.

And so, since Archimedes led more than anyone else to the formation of the calculus and since he was the pioneer of the application of mathematics to the physical world, it turns out that Western science is but a series of footnotes to Archimedes. Thus, it turns out that Archimedes is the most important scientist who ever lived.

Archimedes' influence was not confined to the contents of his science. There is a special quality to his writings. Again and again, his readers are shocked by the delightful surprise of an unexpected combination. Elegant, unanticipated juxtapositions were Archimedes' staple. The main reason later scientists were so influenced by him was that he was such a pleasure to read. Later mathematicians, directly or indirectly, all tried to imitate Archimedes' surprise and elegance. Our very sense of what a mathematical treatise should aim to be is shaped by Archimedes' example. In the following chapters, I will try to explain not only the contents of Archimedes' works—his contributions to the calculus and to mathematical physics—but also his style. Both are equally worthy of our admiration.

I gradually came to appreciate both of these aspects of Archimedes' achievement while working on the Archimedes Palimpsest. A major discovery made in 2001 made us see, for the first time, how close Archimedes was to modern concepts of infinity. Another major discovery made in 2003 made me rethink our entire perception of Archimedes' style. Such was the work on the Palimpsest. I would laboriously pore over a manuscript page (or more often over its enhanced image on my laptop screen); the letters forming into words, into phrases; usually nothing new; occasionally discoveries, sometimes of important historical significance; and then, twice, discoveries that shook the foundations of the history of mathematics.

I never thought that I would ever find myself laboriously poring over manuscript pages. The work of editing major texts from antiquity, based on the transcription of medieval manuscripts, was mostly completed in the nineteenth century. Of course, one could always make small improvements or one could edit minor authors, but not many people do this kind of work today. This is not only because the more interesting authors have already been edited, but also because the intellectual climate today is very different from that in the nineteenth century. Nowadays, people are less interested in the dry details of texts and more interested in the syntheses based on those texts. A PhD thesis in Classics today is usually some kind of theoretical reflection upon the established texts rather than an addition to the texts themselves. "Theory" is what people want. Putting it bluntly, you're not likely to get a job if your intellectual output is made up only of textual editions. Nor is this necessarily a bad development. Nineteenth-century scholarship was very impressive, and we owe it a great deal. But it does sometimes make for very boring reading (often in Latin, at that), and it is even occasionally naive in its lack of critical and theoretical reflection. Our understanding of the ancient world was made much richer and more profound by the application of insights from cultural anthropology, for instance, or from general poetics and linguistics. My own PhD thesis, prepared at Cambridge under the supervision of Sir Geoffrey Lloyd, the doyen of Greek science, was very much part of this modern tradition. I was greatly inspired by Geoffrey Lloyd's application of anthropology to the study of Greek thought, as well as by his comparative method (where he places Greek science side by side with its Chinese counterpart). My first book, *The Shaping of Deduction in Greek Mathematics: A Study in Cognitive History,* involved specifically the application of insights from cognitive science (or the other way around: my hope was that cognitive scientists would find something to learn from what historians had to tell them). My objective throughout was to uncover the mathematical experience: how does it register in the mind's eye? To get a sense of this, I was persuaded, one must first be able to read the mathematics in accurate translation, which carefully follows the author's formulations, because they convey to us how the ancients themselves thought about their science. The most important of them all was never translated into English. For Archimedes there existed only T. L. Heath's poor paraphrase published in 1897, which simply ignores Archimedes' mathematical language. I, therefore, decided to produce a new translation with a commentary that incorporates my own theoretical angle on Greek mathematics.

I was going to do more than just translate Archimedes. I am one of a number of scholars who have, only recently, begun to pay attention to the visual aspect of science. I mentioned earlier that nineteenth-century scholarship may appear, in some respects, outdated, and here is one respect having to do with the editing work itself. The scholars who edited mathematical texts in the nineteenth century were so interested in the *words* that they ignored the *images*. If you open an edition from that era, the diagrams you find are not based upon what is actually drawn in the original manuscripts. The diagrams represent, instead, the editor's own drawing. I was shocked to realize this and began to consider whether I should produce, for the first time, an edition of the diagrams. I knew that this would involve travel to the major libraries housing Archimedes' various manuscripts. I researched where those manuscripts were located. It turned out that they were in Paris, Florence, Venice, and Rome. Well, why not? I decided it was a good idea.

This was a very ambitious project and not an altogether likely one. There are some 100,000 words of Archimedes to be translated. Difficult 100,000 words. Worse, as friends kept pointing out to me— what was I going to do when the text was uncertain? How was I going to decide, given that the most important manuscript was *no longer available?*

Because, you see, there it was—the Archimedes Palimpsest, the unique source for *Floating Bodies, Method,* and *Stomachion* and a crucial piece of evidence for most of the other works—and no one knew where it was. It had been studied at the beginning of the twentieth century and then it disappeared. Nor did I expect it to resurface, which was my reply to my friends: since the manuscript is likely to remain unavailable, let us just proceed as if it did not exist, otherwise we will never do anything regarding Archimedes.

Pat Easterling, the Regius Professor of Greek at Cambridge and an expert on Greek manuscripts, closely followed my project, teaching me the basic skills of paleography. One day I received a letter from her. The letter said that Christie's was asking permission to photograph a certain leaf kept at Cambridge University Library, because this leaf was believed to have been taken out of the Archimedes Palimpsest, a manuscript that they were about to sell.

I mentioned this casually to my colleagues in ancient science, assuming they had known about this all along. No one did. This letter from Pat Easterling was a bombshell. The news of the imminent sale broke in the community of Archimedes scholars, and the rest is history. Will has already mentioned his own meeting with Pat Easterling and his email to me. As for my reaction to this email, that is, my own wild, childish, embarrassing cries of jubilation; of this I prefer not to speak. Let us speak of Archimedes.

Who Was Archimedes?

The Second Punic War (218–202 BC) was, to antiquity, much like World War II was to the modern era. It was a cataclysmic catastrophe of unprecedented proportions, turning the geopolitics of the Mediterranean upside down. For a moment, it appeared as if Hannibal might conquer Rome. Yet, Rome survived, triumphant, and so powerful at the end of the war that the entire Mediterranean was at its mercy. The independence of Greek states was gone; the civilization that Archimedes represented was humbled. One of the major turning points of the war came as Syracuse fell. This, the leading Greek city in the western Mediterranean, had made the wrong strategic decision of allying itself with the Carthaginians. In 212 BC, following a long siege, its defenses—set up by Archimedes and undefeated in battle—succumbed to treachery. We do not know how, but Archimedes died.

The above, in point of fact, sums up what we know about Archimedes as a historical figure. It should be stressed that we are lucky to know even that; indeed we should be amazed that we can date events in antiquity at all. After all, no one in antiquity jotted down: "Archimedes died in 212 BC!" The way ancient dates are derived is fundamentally as follows. We are lucky to possess several historical documents from antiquity arranged as annals. These documents detail events year by year. (The Roman author Livy is a famous example.) Their dating system was different from ours, but occasionally such authors provide us with astronomical data, eclipses, in particular. We can then apply Newtonian physics to calculate the date of those events, and with the results of such calculations, we gain footholds into ancient chronology, constructing the basic equivalencies between ancient dates and modern ones. Without such astronomical data, no chronology could be fixed with any certainty. Even calculating the date of Archimedes' own death is based on his science.

The siege of Syracuse was a major event etched into ancient memory. It was listed in all the annals, and we know very well when it ended. The figure of Archimedes, as the chief Syracusan engineer, was of great fascination to his contemporaries, and he appears again and again in ancient accounts. (This, once again, is a little like World War II: think of the way in which Einstein was etched into the public imagination as "the father of the atom bomb.") It is safe, therefore, to assume that the date of his death is correct. But other pieces of evidence are much less reliable. Archimedes' dates are often reported in encyclopedias as 287–212 BC. We know where the date 212 comes from. But what about 287? This is based on a Greek author who mentions that Archimedes died "as an old man, 75 years old." Unfortunately, the author in question, Johannes Tzetzes, lived in the twelfth century AD! What he has to say about Archimedes comes from a gossipy, fanciful poem. This is also the main source for the story about Archimedes inventing mirrors that burned enemy ships. Surely, Archimedes' contemporaries would have reported such a thing had it happened and Tzetzes was a Byzantine, whose navy was famous for its ship-burning feats. In short, Tzetzes' story is just that—a story—and he makes his Archimedes an old man just for literary effect. Probably Archimedes was quite old (so says the reliable Polybius), but nothing more is known.

Here is the problem. Archimedes was so famous that legends clung to him. And now, how are we to separate history from legend? This is the historian's problem. Up until the nineteenth century it was common to accept ancient stories as reality. Since then, skepticism has reigned. Perhaps historians today are too cautious, but we tend to dismiss nearly everything that is said about Archimedes. Did he cry *"Eureka"*? I doubt this myself, and let me explain why. Let's take the most famous version of this story (also the earliest) told by Vitruvius—the date and author already give room for doubt. Vitruvius writes some two hundred years after Archimedes' death and, in general, is not a very reliable historian (his book is a manual of architecture, which he spices up with historical anecdotes).

Here is the story. Archimedes is lost in thought contemplating the problem of a crown. The crown is supposed to be made of gold, but is it pure? Then Archimedes notices the water splashing out of his bath . . . and immediately he runs out crying *"Eureka, eureka."* Eureka what, precisely? According to Vitruvius, *eureka* is the observation that the volume of water displaced by a body immersed in it is equal to the volume of the body itself: so place the crown in water, measure what may be called the "splashed" quantity—and you have the volume of the crown. Compare this to an equally heavy mass of gold: does it make the same splash? The heavier it is, the smaller the splash it makes. So now you can conclude whether the crown has the specific gravity of gold or not. The method is sound, but it is based on a trivial observation. Essentially, the observation is "bigger things make bigger splashes." This is so trivial that it was not even mentioned in Archimedes' treatise on *Floating Bodies*.

To me it appears that Vitruvius or his previous source knew that Archimedes discovered something about bodies immersed in water. They were also familiar with some trivial, pre-scientific observations such as "bigger things make bigger splashes." They invented the story to tie the two together. Vitruvius clearly knew nothing about

Archimedes' science. This is the pattern with all of the stories dealing with Archimedes, from Vitruvius to Tzetzes. They appear to be urban legends. Sorry.

Some pieces of real evidence can be put together, providing us with the outlines of a fascinating story. As we will see again and again throughout this book, the pieces of evidence are extremely minuscule and often call for lots of interpretation. This holds for the most important piece of biographical evidence that we have about Archimedes. This piece of evidence is an aside made in the course of one of Archimedes' more surprising works, the *Sand-Reckoner*. In this treatise, Archimedes notes various estimates that were offered for the ratio of the sun to the moon: Eudoxus, for instance, said that the sun was *nine* times bigger and, as the manuscript reads, "Pheidias Acoupater" said the sun was *twelve* times bigger. There is no such name or place as "Acoupater." The text reads literally *pheidia tou akoupatros*. You must bear in mind that, until late in the Middle Ages, Greek was written without spaces between the words. This gives rise to the following conjecture. If we separate the words differently, which is permitted when interpreting ancient Greek texts, and change just one letter, the gibberish "acoupater" makes perfect sense. The reason we are allowed to make corrections such as these is that mistakes were certainly made by scribes as they copied their texts; our manuscripts are full of such scribal errors. So the suggestion was made, by several editors in the nineteenth century, to reread it with the "*k*" changed to "*m*," and space inserted as follows: *pheidia tou amou patros*. This translates to "Pheidias, my father." You can see that this is a thin thread, but a very robust one. The text *has* to be corrected, and the correction offered is so elegant and straightforward that it seems as if it *has* to be true.

On this thin thread hangs the entire family biography of Archimedes, which should give us a sense of how important—and how difficult—the detailed study of manuscripts is. All of our knowledge of the ancient world is derived from the patient, laborious piecing together of jigsaw puzzles. The previous example does not seem like much, but it does tell us that Archimedes' father was an astronomer and that his name was Pheidias.

This is a fact I find very meaningful. I have studied the name "Pheidias" in antiquity, and I ask you to bear in mind two facts. Art, as well as craftsmanship in general, were not highly appreciated by ancient aristocrats (who generally speaking looked down on anyone dirtying their hands). And, Pheidias is the name of the most famous artist in antiquity—the master sculptor of the Parthenon in the fifth century BC. Now, with these two facts in mind, I ask you to consider the following observation: *elsewhere when we determine what a person named "Pheidias" did, it typically turns out that he was an artist of some sort.* The conclusion is quite simple. The name Pheidias would be bestowed upon your son—as a proud prophecy—only in artists' families. Otherwise, why give a name that had the lowly associations of craftsmanship? So let us note this fact, as well: Archimedes' grandfather was an artist.

We have not yet exhausted the quarry of names. What about the name Archimedes? This is, in fact, unique—and uniquely appropriate to Archimedes. As is very often the case with Greek names, it is comprised of two components: *arche* or "principle, rule, number one," and *medos* or "mind, wisdom, wit." The name means, if read from the beginning to the end, "the number one mind," which is a very good description of Archimedes. But it was probably meant to be read from the end to the beginning, as is more often done with Greek names. It is a unique name, but it has a parallel in another name, Diomedes, with "Dio" (a variant of "Zeus") instead of *arche*. The name Diomedes means "The Mind of Zeus," and therefore the name Archimedes means "The Mind of the Principle," which sounds a bit strange but makes perfect sense. Greek philosophers in the generations before Archimedes, starting with such figures as Plato, gradually evolved a kind of monotheistic, scientific religion in which they worshipped not so much the anthropomorphic gods of Greek religion but rather the beauty and order of the cosmos, its "principle." The name Archimedes suggests that Archimedes' father, the astronomer, subscribed to such a religion and worshipped the beauty and the order in the cosmos. So we can tell quite a bit about Archimedes' background from tiny pieces of evidence and lots of interpretation. The grandfather was an artist; the father was a scientist, more specifically an astronomer who turned to the new religion of beauty and order in the cosmos; and the son who created works in which art and science, beauty and order, all worked together in perfect harmony.

Those works are of course the key to understanding Archimedes. The stories may be urban legends, but the works exist for us to read and the surprising thing is that, dry mathematical pieces as they might seem to be, they actually burst with personality. In his pure science, Archimedes keeps splashing out of the bath. Art and science, beauty and order: let us begin to see how they come together in Archimedes' works.

Science before Science

When we say that "Archimedes was a scientist," we may be tempted to imagine him wearing a white coat, contemplating vials with purplish liquids. Well, this is not what he did. He was wearing a tunic, contemplating diagrams drawn on sand. We may also be tempted to imagine him as a very earnest man, dedicated entirely to the cause of impersonal truth. This, would be as wrong as the purplish vials. Archimedes was not a modern scientist. His was a different kind of science; a science from before our own professionalized, capital letter "Science."

Perhaps the best introduction to the man is what he tells us in the introduction to one of his treatises, *On Spiral Lines*. The introduction is presented as a letter to a colleague, Dositheus, and Archimedes begins by reminding Dositheus of previous letters. You will recall, says Archimedes, that I put forth a number of mathematical puzzles. I announced various discoveries and asked for other mathematicians to find their own proofs of those discoveries. Well—(notes Archimedes, somewhat triumphantly)—no one did! And now, continues

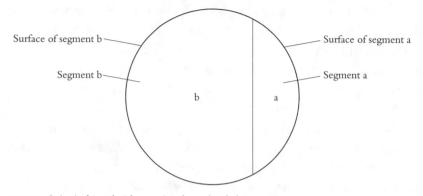

FIGURE 2.1 *Archimedes' hoax: A sphere divided into two segments*

Archimedes, it is time to reveal a secret: two of the discoveries were "poisoned." For example, Archimedes had announced his "discovery" that, if a sphere is cut into two segments, and the ratio of the surfaces is a:b, then the ratio of the volumes is $a^2:b^2$ (see fig. 2.1).

I wish to stress that there is no doubt, on the internal evidence of his own writings, that Archimedes was indeed aware, from early on, that these two claims were false. He is not trying to save face retroactively. He really did send out "poisoned" letters hoping to trap his fellow mathematicians. As he puts it, he did this "so that those who claim to discover everything, producing no proof themselves, will be confuted, in their assenting to prove the impossible."

Archimedes, you should note, did not have a gentle character—nor did he have an earnest one. "Playful" is one term that comes to mind, "sly" is another. It is not for nothing that historians keep debating the precise meaning of Archimedes' discoveries: he *meant* for his readers to be puzzled. So, incidentally, he would most likely have thoroughly relished the future history of his writings. That the effort to read him is so tantalizing, so difficult; is precisely as Archimedes wanted.

The entire structure of scientific activity during Archimedes' time was radically different from anything we are familiar with. There were no universities, no jobs, and no scientific journals. It is true that, about a century before Archimedes' death, a number of "schools" were founded in Athens, but these, too, were quite different from modern scientific institutions. They were more akin to present-day clubs, where like-minded people come together to discuss issues of importance to them (usually philosophical rather than scientific). In Alexandria, the Ptolemaic kings set up a huge library. There were other libraries, as well, but they were not part of research institutions, instead simply marks of enormous wealth and prestige. So, quite simply, there was no career in science. Nor was there much glory in it. After all, few people could even read science. The real path to glory was then—as always in the pre-modern world—via *poetry*. If you wanted to make a name for yourself, to win some kind of eternity, you would write poems—which, after all, was what everyone read (starting, in early childhood, with the *Iliad* and the *Odyssey*).

How would one become a mathematician? You would have to be exposed to it by chance—say, by your father if he happened to be an astronomer . . . And then, you were hooked. This was a rare affliction. I once estimated that in the entire period of ancient mathematics, roughly from 500 BC to AD 500, there were, perhaps, a thousand active mathematicians—one born every year, on average. I should make clear right now that earlier figures, such as Pythagoras and Thales, were not mathematicians at all. The name "Pythagoras' theorem" is a late myth. Mathematics began in the fifth century BC—the age of Pericles and of the Parthenon—but very little is known about the authors. Perhaps the most important was Hippocrates of Chios. (This should not be confused with the doctor of the same name, from Cos). All we know of such authors comes from late quotations and commentaries. In the fourth century BC not much more is known: Archytas was Plato's friend and a great mathematician, but only a single proof survives by him. Even that does not survive from Eudoxus, later in the century; but Archimedes mentions him twice, with admiration. Apparently Archimedes considered Eudoxus to be his greatest predecessor; but the works of this predecessor are now all lost.

This is not so with the works of Euclid, writing, perhaps, early in the third century. They survive in plenty. However, Archimedes wouldn't think very highly of them, as they consist mainly of basic mathematics. Archimedes was an advanced mathematician, writing for people who knew much more than just the contents of Euclid's *Elements*. And there must have been very few of these. I believe that Archimedes may have had an "audience" consisting of a few dozen mathematicians at most, spread throughout the Mediterranean, many of them isolated in small towns, impatiently waiting for the next delivery of letters from Alexandria (the exchange center)—is there anything new from Archimedes?

When Archimedes' introductions start with a letter sent to an individual, this should be understood in a very literal way. They *were* private letters—sent out to people in Alexandria who had the contacts to deliver the contents further. Everything depended on this network of individuals. Archimedes keeps lamenting in his introductions the death of his older friend Conon (who was an important astronomer). He was the only one who could understand me! In most of Archimedes' letters there is a faint note of exasperation. There was no one to write to, no reader good enough. (There would be, in time. Archimedes would eventually be read by Omar Khayyam, Leonardo da Vinci, Galileo, and Newton; these were Archimedes' real readers and the ones through whom he has made his real impact. He must have known that he was writing for posterity.)

Many of the works are addressed to Dositheus, of whom very little is known. We do know one thing, which, yet again, is based on his name alone. It turns out that practically everyone in Alexandria at that time named Dositheus was Jewish. (The name, in fact, is simply the Greek version of Matityahu or Matthew.) This is very curious: the correspondence between Archimedes and Dositheus is the *only* one known from antiquity between a Greek and a Jew. It is perhaps telling that the arena for such cross-cultural contact was science. In mathematics, after all, religion and nation do not matter. This, at least, has not changed.

Squaring Circles

And what mathematics it was, sent to Dositheus! First came a treatise on the *Quadrature of the Parabola*. Then two separate books on *Sphere and Cylinder*. Then a book on *Spiral Lines*. (The one in which the hoax was revealed.) And, finally, a book on *Conoids and Spheroids*. There might have been more, but these are the five books that survive. The five works form a certain unity, as together they constitute the cornerstone of the calculus. However, this is probably not how Archimedes would have thought of them. To him, they were all variations on squaring the circle. That is: time and again, Archimedes takes an object bounded by curved lines and equates it with a much simpler object, preferably bounded by straight lines. Apparently this task—squaring, or measuring, the circle—was, for Greek mathematicians, the Holy Grail of their science.

The very idea of measurement depends on the notion of the straight line. It is not for nothing that we measure with *rulers*. To measure is to find a measuring tool and apply it successively to the object being measured. Suppose we want to measure a straight line. For instance, suppose we want to measure your height, which is really saying that we want to measure the straight line from the floor to the top of your head. Then what we do is take a line the length of an inch and apply it successively, well over a sixty times, but probably less than eighty times to measure your height. Since this is very tiresome, we have pre-marked measuring tapes that save us the trouble of actually applying the length successively, but, at the conceptual level, successive application is precisely what takes place.

When measuring area, we do the same successive application, but instead of a straight line, we use a square. This is why floor plans are literally measured by square feet. Cubes similarly measure volume. Of course, not all objects come pre-packaged in squared or cubed units.

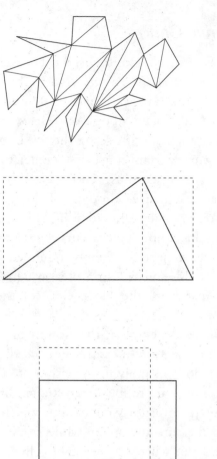

First, any area – however complex in shape – is easily divided up, as in the picture, into triangles.

Second, every triangle – no matter its shape – is exactly half the rectangle enclosing it, as a consideration of the two symmetries in the figure serves to show.

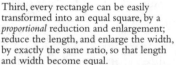

Third, every rectangle can be easily transformed into an equal square, by a *proportional* reduction and enlargement; reduce the length, and enlarge the width, by exactly the same ratio, so that length and width become equal.

FIGURE 2.2 *How to measure an area bounded by straight lines*

However, Greek mathematicians from very early on came up with three important discoveries (see fig. 2.2):

- Every area bound by straight lines can be divided into triangles.
- Every triangle can be made equal to half a rectangle.
- Every rectangle can be made equal to a square.

The combination of these three facts means that it is possible to measure any area bounded by straight lines as a sum of squares. The

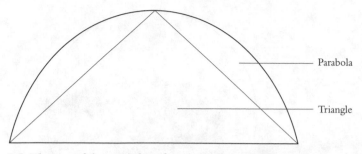

FIGURE 2.3 *The area of the parabola is four-thirds the triangle*

same, analogously, holds for solids divided into pyramids, which are then made equal to cubes. It is all this straightforward. Take any object bounded by straight lines. It can be conceptually difficult—a Rubik's cube or a many-spangled snowflake—but its measurement always follows the same principle and it is truly straightforward. Take, instead, an object as apparently simple as a baseball—just the most ordinary sphere—and measurement suddenly breaks down. It is impossible to divide the baseball into any finite number of pyramids or triangles. The baseball has an infinitely complex, infinitely smooth surface. Archimedes would measure such objects again and again, pushing the most basic tools of mathematics.

In the *Quadrature of the Parabola,* Archimedes measured the segment of a parabola: it is four-thirds times the triangle it encloses (see fig. 2.3). A very striking measurement, given that the parabola is a curved line, so this is rather like squaring a circle. He also, in the same treatise, introduced a certain daring thought experiment: to conceive of a geometrical object as if it were composed of physical slices hung on a balance.

The two books on *Sphere and Cylinder* directly approach the volume of the sphere. It turns out that it is exactly two-thirds the cylinder enclosing it. What is its surface? It turns out it is exactly four times its greatest circle (see fig. 2.4). This recalcitrant object—the sphere—turns out to obey some very precise rules. In the second book, remarkable tasks are achieved. For instance, finding the ratio

43

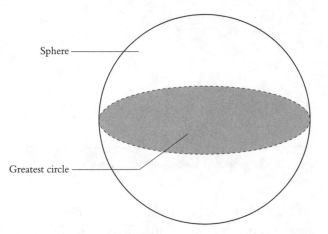

FIGURE 2.4 *The surface of the sphere is four times the area of its greatest circle*

between spherical segments, which was the substance of the hoax mentioned previously.

In both *Spiral Lines* and *Conoids and Spheroids,* Archimedes is not content to measure known objects. Instead he invents a new curved object—a complex, counter-intuitive object—and then measures it. The spiral line—invented by Archimedes—turns out to enclose exactly one-third the area enclosed by the circle surrounding it (see fig. 2.5). As for conoids, which are hyperbolas or parabolas turned around so as to enclose space, and spheroids, which are ellipses turned around in similar fashion—these have more complex measurements. All were obtained, with precision, by Archimedes (see figs. 2.6, 2.7).

This is a major feature of all of his works. Archimedes starts out promising to make some incredible measurement, and you expect him to fudge it somehow, to cut corners. How else can you *square the circle?* And then he begins to surprise you. He accumulates results of no obvious relevance—some proportions between this and that line, some special constructions of no direct connection to the problem at hand. And then, about midway through the treatise, he lets you see how all the results build together and, "By God!" you exclaim, "he is actually going to prove this precisely, no fudges made!"

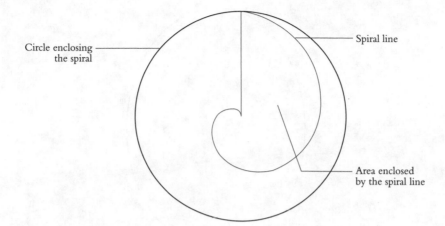

Circle enclosing
the spiral

Spiral line

Area enclosed
by the spiral line

FIGURE 2.5 *The area of the circle is three times the area enclosed by the spiral*

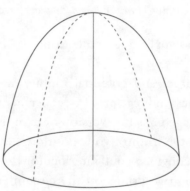

FIGURE 2.6 *A conoid is a solid created by rotating a parabola or a hyperbola on its axis*

Each of these works was of a completely different order of origi-nality and brilliance from anything ever seen before. In all of them Archimedes was furthering the mathematics of infinity.

Imaginary Dialogues

In his measurements Archimedes adopts a surprising, circuitous route, which was always his favorite way of approaching things. The general

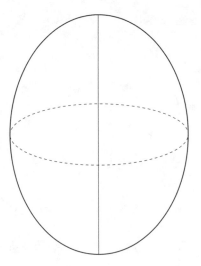

FIGURE 2.7 *A spheroid is a solid created by rotating an ellipse on its axis*

plan is as follows: apply a combination of "indirect proof" and "potential infinity."

Both indirect proof and potential infinity are best considered as imaginary dialogues. Indirect proof is easier to understand, and you have probably engaged in some version of it yourself. You try to convince someone of the truth of your position. Let us say, for instance, that you want to convince your interlocutor that, when you draw a straight line joining two points on the circumference of a circle, all the points on this straight line must fall *inside* the circle. Everything you tell him about this line fails to persuade him. And so you resort to indirect proof. You assume the opposite of the truth, as if pretending to agree with your interlocutor.

"Let us assume that some point E falls outside the circle," you concede (see fig. 2.8). And now you follow the logic of this situation, until you draw the following conclusion: line DZ is both smaller than DE and bigger than it. But a line cannot be at the same time both smaller and greater than the same given line. "See," you now turn to your imaginary interlocutor, "I have conceded your claim, but the result was an absurdity; therefore your claim must be false. I have now

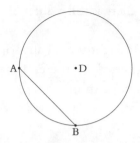

The line AB must never get out of the circle.

Imagine it does, as the 'line' AEB.

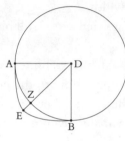

DE is greater than DZ, because it contains it: **DE > DZ**. DZ is equal to DB (both are radii of the circle), while DB, in turn, is greater than DE. (This is because in a triangle such as

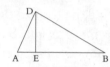

the external side DB is greater than the internal line DE.) As a consequence, DZ is greater than DE: **DZ > DE**.

Both DZ > DE and DE > DZ ⟶ Contradiction!

FIGURE 2.8 *Indirect proof: Why does a line never get out of its circle?*

proved this *indirectly.*" This type of argument is one of the hallmarks of Greek mathematics.

Archimedes did not invent potential infinity, but he made it his own in a series of original applications. You remember the fundamental problem with measuring a curved object: it could not be fully divided into triangles; with any finite number of triangles in it, there is always some piece of the curved object "left out." Now let us concentrate on the size of this piece that is left out. What Archimedes does is develop a certain mechanism, capable of indefinite extension, of packing triangles (or their like) into the curved object. This is best seen, once again, as an imaginary dialogue between Archimedes and his critic.

Let us say that he has packed the curved object in such a way that a certain area has been left out, an area greater than the size of a grain of sand.

A critic comes along and points out that there is still a difference—the size of a grain of sand.

"Is that right?" exclaims Archimedes. "All right then, I shall apply my mechanism successively several more times." By the end of this operation the area left out is smaller than the grain of sand.

"Wait a minute," says the critic, not yet satisfied. "The area left out is still greater than a hair's width."

Archimedes, unfazed, applies the mechanism once again, with the area left out becoming smaller than a hair's width.

"No, no!" the critic squabbles again; "the area left out is still bigger than an atom."

The critic may think he has had the last word, but Archimedes just goes on applying his mechanism. "See," he returns now to the critic, "the area left out is now even smaller than the atom." And so it goes on, the difference always becoming smaller than any given magnitude mentioned by the critic.

This dialogue could go on *indefinitely*. This is what philosophers refer to as *potential infinity*. We never go as far as infinity itself in this argument. There is no mention, at any point, of an area which is *infinitesimally* small, merely of areas that are *very, indefinitely* small. But we allow ourselves to go on *indefinitely*. And this, taken together with indirect proof, allows Archimedes to measure the most incredible objects.

Squaring the Parabola

Three times in his career Archimedes proved that the parabolic segment—a certain curved object—is exactly four-thirds the triangle it encloses. This was his favorite measurement. Later on we shall see his most spectacular measurement, which transcends geometry itself. But before we can follow such flights of imagination we must first acquaint ourselves with Archimedes' geometrical method, which is based on the combination of indirect proof and potential infinity. It is an extraordinarily subtle argument, one that even professional

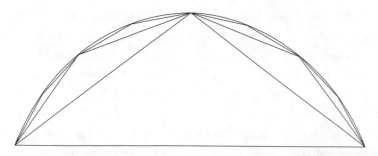

FIGURE 2.9-1 *The parabola encloses a jumble of triangles. This can be made to approach the parabola as closely as we wish. We assume its difference from the parabola is less than a grain of sand*

mathematicians have a hard time unraveling. It is like an affirmation based on a double double negation. And this is how it works.

Since what we are going to prove is that the area of the curve is four-thirds the triangle, how shall we start? By assuming, of course, that the area of the curve is *not* four-thirds the triangle! This, after all, is how indirect proof works. Let us assume that the curved area is greater than four-thirds the triangle, by a certain amount:

1. The curve is greater than four-thirds the triangle, by a certain amount. Let us say, it is greater by a grain of sand.

For exactly such occasions, Archimedes has a special mechanism up his sleeve. He fills up the curve with triangles so that the difference between the triangles and the curve is *smaller* than a grain of sand!

We therefore now have two objects side by side. One is a curve. The other is the product of Archimedes' mechanism—a complex jumble of triangles whose difference from the curve is known to be *smaller* than a grain of sand:

2. The curve, with a grain of sand removed, is smaller than the jumble of triangles (see fig. 2.9-1).

At this point Archimedes leaves aside the results obtained so far. The following piece of reasoning involves, instead, a separate piece of geometrical ingenuity. Remember that the jumble of triangles is an object bounded by straight lines. Four-thirds the enclosed triangle is also an object bounded by straight lines, i.e. both are objects that can be precisely measured by ordinary means. It is therefore not a surprise that through the application of geometrical ingenuity one can determine a definite measurement comparing the jumble of triangles and four-thirds the enclosed triangle. What Archimedes would come up with—applying his geometrical ingenuity—is as follows:

3. The jumble of triangles is smaller than four-thirds the enclosed triangle (see fig. 2.9-2).

Now, recall result 1. It was: "The curve is greater than four-thirds the triangle, by a grain of sand." Or, putting differently:

4. The curve, with a grain of sand removed, is equal to four-thirds the triangle.

Put this alongside result 2: "The curve, with a grain of sand removed, is smaller than the jumble of triangles."

The same object is *equal* to four-thirds the triangle, but is *smaller* than the jumble of triangles. In other words, the jumble of triangles is the greater. It is greater than four-thirds the triangle, which we can put as:

5. The jumble of triangles is greater than four-thirds the enclosed triangle.

This makes no sense if we put it side by side with result 3: "The jumble of triangles is smaller than four-thirds the enclosed triangle."

Results 5 and 3 directly contradict each other. There is no way to reconcile them. The jumble of triangles cannot be both smaller and greater than four-thirds the enclosed triangle. In other words, we are left with only one option: concluding that our original assumption was wrong. The curve is *not different from* four-thirds the enclosed triangle. The curve *is* therefore four-thirds the enclosed triangle. The

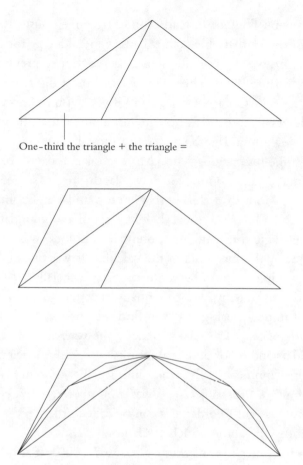

One-third the triangle + the triangle =

The jumble of triangles is smaller than
four-thirds the enclosed triangle.

FIGURE 2.9-2

result is therefore obtained. Indirect proof and potential infinity
together have brought us the answer.

Beyond Potential Infinity

Now let us put this into historical context. In the seventeenth century,
mathematicians found a way to apply this technique of Archimedes in

a more general fashion. Instead of finding, ingeniously, this or that strategy for this or that object, they had a general recipe for measuring all curves. This was the calculus, which, as mentioned previously, is the foundation of modern science. The persons most directly responsible for this were Newton and Leibniz, and if you wish to know which of the two deserves more credit, you are not alone. The battle for priority between Newton and Leibniz was the most famous—as well as the ugliest—in the history of science. Most scholars today think it should be considered an honorable draw. Both, in a sense, followed Archimedes. More than this, both Newton and Leibniz managed to bring the calculus to a great height—on shaky foundations. The underlying logic of handling potential infinities was not clearly worked out by the inventors of the calculus. It was put in order only at the beginning of the nineteenth century, especially by the French mathematician, Cauchy, who essentially reverted to the Archimedes method of implicit dialogue ("You find me an area X; I'll find you a smaller difference."). In every step along the way, our calculus, as well as our understanding of potential infinity was Archimedean. So much for potential infinity. As for *actual* infinity, the contemplation of an actual infinite set of objects, it was not mastered by Newton or Leibniz, but was put in order, if it can be called order, in the late nineteenth century by authors such as Cantor.

And here comes the shocking surprise. In 2001, it was discovered for the first time—against all expectations—that Archimedes knew of *actual* infinity and used it in his mathematics. This was discovered through the Palimpsest and it is, without any doubt, the most important discovery made through its reappearance.

Proofs and Physics

The new discovery was made by reading a passage of Archimedes' *Method* that had never been read before. This work, the most fascinating of all the works by Archimedes, survives in the Palimpsest alone. It is his most fascinating work because, more than anywhere else, he brings together his *two* interests: the mathematics of infinity, which we have seen already, and the combination of mathematics and physics, statements of pure geometry with those of the physical world. It all comes out of the balance. Archimedes was the first to prove, mathematically, the law of the balance: objects balance when their weights are exactly reciprocal to their distances from the fulcrum. In the *Method*, he pushes forward a surprising technique. He takes geometrical objects and creates a thought experiment in which they are both arranged on a balance. He then uses their weights (that is, their lengths and areas) and their distances from the center, to measure some purely geometrical properties. The law of the balance becomes a tool of geometry instead of physics.

This work was not among the series sent to Dositheus. This may be because Archimedes valued it so highly. It was instead sent to the most influential intellectual of Archimedes' time—Eratosthenes. This polymath wrote on everything from Homer to astronomy, from prime numbers to Plato. As a result he was nicknamed "Beta," because he was the number two on everything . . . Archimedes, who clearly saw himself as number one in his field, approached Eratosthenes with great apparent respect, but he almost seems to be teasing him, as if saying "See if you can catch me!" The work is so interesting, in part, because it is the most enigmatic. Archimedes suggests that he has discovered a method of finding mathematical results which is very powerful, but which does not quite constitute a proof. Yet he never explains what this method actually is or how it falls short of actual proof. He leaves it as an enigma to be worked out by the reader—first Eratosthenes and then, since the discovery of the *Method* in the twentieth century, every historian of ancient mathematics. Everyone has a theory about the *Method*. We will return to this enigma, perhaps to understand it better, based on the new readings of the Palimpsest.

Of course, Archimedes' claim to be the founder of mathematical physics does not rest on the *Method* alone. Of his studies in this field, two major works are still extant—*Balancing Planes* and *On Floating Bodies*. In *Balancing Planes*, which we will examine later, Archimedes finds the center of gravity of a triangle, which is one of the key results of the science of statics. *On Floating Bodies* sets the stage for another science—hydrostatics. This work provided the foundation for Vitruvius' nice but silly story about Archimedes' splashing in the bath. He may have splashed, he may have run naked; but he certainly did not cry *Eureka* over such a trivial observation as "bigger things make bigger splashes." The deduction in *On Floating Bodies* is much more subtle and sophisticated.

This is it. In a stable body of liquid, each column of equal volume must also have equal weight otherwise the liquid would flow from the heavier to the lighter (this is why the face of the sea is *even*). The same must hold true even if a solid body is immersed within such a column of liquid. In other words, if we have a column of liquid with a solid body immersed in it, the aggregate weight of the liquid and the body must be equal to that of a column of liquid of the same volume. It follows that the solid body must lose some of its weight. Archimedes performs a complex calculation that demonstrates that it must lose weight equal to the volume of water it has displaced.

This explains why we feel lighter in the bath. Indeed it tells us precisely by how much we *should* feel lighter in the bath. Now that's something to cry *eureka* about! Because, you see, by the power of pure thought alone, Archimedes is capable of saying what must happen in the physical world! This power of mind over matter is what is so fascinating about Archimedean science. This is what Galileo and Newton tried to imitate and, incredibly, succeeded in doing. In this way, ultimately Newton discovered, by the power of pure thought—as well as by the calculus—*how the planets must move*. And, with this Archimedean achievement, Newton set the stage for all later science.

Puzzles and Numbers

Newtonian science was sober-minded; Archimedes' science was not. Archimedes was famous for hoaxes, enigmas, and circuitous routes. These were not some external features of his writings; they characterized his scientific personality. Science is not—mathematics is not—dry and impersonal. It is where one's imagination is allowed to roam freely. And so, Archimedes' imagination roamed to childs' play, and to a puzzle called the Stomachion or Bellyache (because of the difficulty of solving it). The game consists of a tangram puzzle of fourteen pieces made to form a square. Archimedes wondered: what was the underlying mathematics of this puzzle?

This, in fact, was a puzzle to modern scholars, as well. Since 1906, we have known that Archimedes wrote about this Stomachion puzzle. But just what was he trying to do? We had available to us only a single bifolio of the Palimpsest and it was one of the worst preserved. Heiberg had made little sense of the Greek and none of the mathematics. Digital technology finally allowed us to make further readings and, in 2003, I was finally able to offer an interpretation of the Stomachion—the first ever in modern times. I argued that Archimedes was trying to do the following: calculate how many ways one can form the square given the original fourteen pieces. There is more than a single way, as figure 2.10 illustrates. In point of fact, there are 17,152 distinct solutions.

The most striking thing about this interpretation is not the very big number itself, but something else. If true, and most historians think I am probably right, then this would make Archimedes the first author, ever, on *combinatorics*—the field of mathematics calculating the number of possible solutions to a given problem. This was the second important discovery made through the Archimedes Palimpsest.

The field of combinatorics is at the heart of modern computer sciences, but it had no such application in Archimedes' time. It is very different in character from the kind of geometrical study we see so often in Greek mathematics. Indeed, the Stomachion appears like a pure flight of fancy. You look for a number because you know it is there. Along the way you generate a fantastic array of complicated calculations. Archimedes, after all, was a master of this game—this hunt for big numbers and surprising combinations. In the *Sand-Reckoner*, he calculated how many grains of sand it would take to fill the universe.

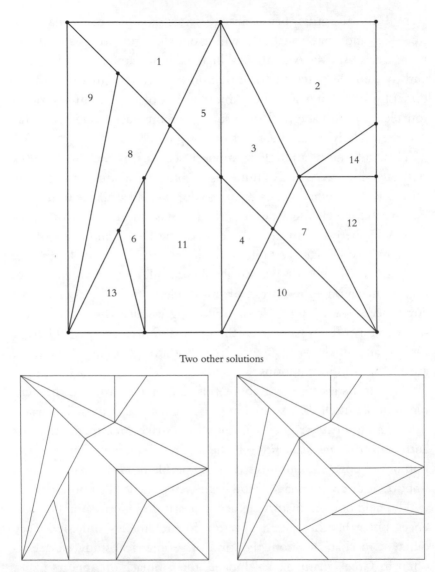

Two other solutions

FIGURE 2.10 *The Stomachion*

(For this, you recall, he needed an estimate of the size of the universe and he mentions his father's estimate.) And then again, most famously, he offers a fantastically precise approximation of the ratio of a circle to its diameter, which is known today as the number pi. He managed to

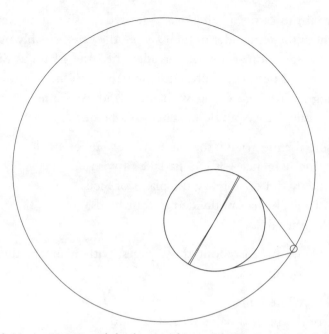

FIGURE 2.11 *A ninety-six-sided polygon within a circle. The inner circle shows a magnified detail of the ninety-six-gon within the outer circle.*

determine that this ratio is smaller than that of 14688 to 4673½, but greater than that of 6336 to 2017¼. He then simplified it, losing a tiny bit in precision but gaining much more in clarity, to the ratio of less than three and a seventh and greater than three and ten-seventy-oneths! This amazing calculation is based on a method not unlike that of the treatment of potentially infinite series, but, in the case of the circumference of the circle, precise calculation is impossible so approximation works best. So Archimedes calculated not the circumference of a circle but the circumference of a polygon with ninety-six sides, which, to sight, is nearly the same (see fig. 2.11).

Perhaps the most strikingly playful calculation made by Archimedes is that of the cattle of Helios. His readers would have known the context from their memories of Homer's *Odyssey*. In book twelve Odysseus' crew reaches the island of Thrinacia, which was sacred to Helios. Against Odysseus' advice, his crew members slaughtered the cattle of Helios and feasted lavishly for seven days. Throughout the remainder of the *Odyssey*, they are horribly punished for this transgression. Tradition has identified the island as Sicily, so the story could be turned into a poetic tribute to Sicily's power and a warning against interfering with the island. Archimedes created a riddle—a calculatory puzzle couched in a poem:

> Measure for me, friend, the multitude of Helios' cattle,
> Possessing diligence—if you partake of wisdom:
> How many did once graze the plains of Sicily,
> The Island Thrinacian divided in four herds,
> In color varied . . .

The text goes on for about three pages, with many mathematical constraints for instance:

> . . . The white bulls
> Were of the black a half and then a third
> And then the whole of yellows, friend, do know this . . .

In short, Archimedes constructed an arithmetical problem with eight unknowns (four herds: black, white, yellow, and many-spangled, each divided into both bulls and cows); seven equations (for example, the one above, [white bulls] = 5/6 [black bulls] + [yellow bulls]); and two complex conditions in which the solutions were integers (there are no half-cows). To try and solve this problem, it turns out, is a transgression as fateful as the original slaughter. Do it at your own peril. Modern mathematicians have proved that the smallest solution involves a number written out in 206,456 digits.

This was a game. For you see, the presentation above, with its short, metrical lines, was not whimsical on my part. *Archimedes wrote out this problem in verse.* A poet-mathematician! The thought seems absurd, but it was natural for Archimedes whose entire science was based on a sense of play and beauty, on hidden meanings. In this case, the hidden meanings were, among other things, political. Archimedes was trying to suggest that one should not interfere with Sicily. Many did, in his time, and he did his best to stop them. And here, finally, we return to the historical facts of Archimedes' life.

Death and Afterlife

Syracuse was the leading city of Sicily—the pivot between the eastern and western Mediterranean. Previous invaders had tried to conquer it. Most famously, in the year 415 BC, Athens tried to force the outcome of the Peloponnesian War by gaining the riches of Sicily. The crashing failure of that expedition marked the end of the Athenian Empire.

So it was with some realistic hope that the Syracusans were waiting, in 214 BC, for the Romans to come. For a generation Syracuse, nominally free, had been tightly enmeshed within the Roman sphere of influence. Undoubtedly Archimedes—like most of his fellow citizens—was eager to shake off this indirect Roman control. Hannibal's recent victories over the Romans appeared to make this finally possible. Syracuse openly sided with the Carthaginians. Unless the Romans could contain and reduce this city, their own fate would be sealed. Through Sicily, Hannibal would receive fresh supplies. The Romans, their power depleted, would not be able to withstand the siege for years on end. So the fate of the Mediterranean rested on this question: could Syracuse take it for long enough?

The previous century had seen a military revolution. From the wars of hoplites clashing on the battlefield a new kind of warfare had evolved—the siege. In the ancient world's version of an arms race, all cities were building up their walls and all the military powers were building up their arsenals of catapults—the machines that drove the military revolution. In principle, a catapult is no more than a huge spring that, once released, serves to propel a rock to smash into walls or people. It can be surprisingly effective, knocking down, in time, very sturdy defenses. But one needs to get the catapult within range of the walls where it will also be within range of the catapults from inside—and so on, with the arms race.

59

The Romans fully expected the Syracusans to spring rocks on them. Yet they were in for a surprise. I now quote from Polybius, a very sober historian who wrote not long after the events described and the best source for Archimedes' life. Here is the surprise sprung by Syracuse on its invaders:

> But Archimedes, who had prepared machines constructed to carry to any distance, so damaged the assailants at long range, as they sailed up [the first attempt was by sea] with his more powerful catapults as to throw them into much difficulty and distress; and as soon as these machines shot too high he continued using smaller and smaller ones as the range became shorter and, finally, so thoroughly shook their courage that he put a complete stop to their advance . . . [The Romans gave up the assault, and so Polybius sums up:] Such a great and marvelous thing does the genius of one man show itself to be . . . The Romans, strong as they were both by sea and land, had every hope of capturing the town at once if one old man of Syracuse were removed; but as long as he was present, they did not venture even to attempt to attack . . .

What did Archimedes do? After all, catapults were well known before him. What seems to have taken the Romans completely off balance was the careful sighting and ranging of the catapults. There were no "blind spots," which is a crucial consideration. "Blind spots" gave the attackers safe spaces. They could jump from one to the other, largely disabling the scheme of defense.

How do you avoid blind spots and sight your catapults? This is a formidable problem, not at all capable of solution by means of simple trial and error. There had to be some principle of *constructing a catapult to order*. That is, one which would allow a catapult, positioned at a given point, to cover a precise range.

At the most basic level, this involves a deep problem of geometry. The propulsive power of a catapult is roughly equivalent to its mass, which determines the physical force it exerts. This, in turn, is roughly equivalent to its volume. Now, how do we measure volume? The same way we measure surfaces: by multiplying the dimensions (two in the case of surfaces, three in the case of volumes). Since a solid has three dimensions, its volume is equivalent to the cubic power of its linear dimension. So, let us say, that you have a catapult whose length is a yard, and you wish to transform it into another catapult that is twice as powerful. Making it two yards long would be wrong. A two-yard-long catapult would be not twice as powerful, it would be eight times more powerful. How do you create a catapult that is twice as powerful, then? For this, we must find the *cubic root of two* (which is roughly 1.26) and extend the length, as well as all the other linear measurements, by that ratio. The finding of cubic roots is not an easy task. In fact, it calls for very powerful mathematical techniques. Greek mathematicians had already tackled the problem, but there were few solutions allowing any practical application. None appear in Archimedes' name, but there is no doubt that he had found a technique and applied it in the year 214 BC.

However, I suspect more than this. Here is a pure flight of fancy on my part. Archimedes could tell *where a missile would land* by following in his imagination the curve traced by that missile. So, why wouldn't he concentrate his attention on the problem of *representing projectile motion as a geometrical curve*? Wouldn't he have found the curve—his beloved parabola—and used it to place his catapults in position? After all, Archimedes' pupils Galileo and Newton did. They based their ideas on mathematical techniques not so different from those used by Archimedes. Galileo traced the motions of projectiles and Newton traced the motions of planets using parabolas. Archimedes would have had interesting problems to ponder, surely, constructing those machines!

And so legend has it: picture Archimedes in the year 212 BC, pondering his problems. The Roman siege is nearly defeated, Archimedes' genius triumphing over Roman power. Complacency has set in. The Syracusans are celebrating a festival and a deserter informs the Romans that the sentries, drunk, have deserted their posts. The

Roman general, Marcellus, quickly dispatches a group of soldiers to occupy positions on the wall and, as ever in this kind of warfare, once a breach is made the game is up. Soon the city is overtaken by the Romans. They have little reason to be merciful. Syracuse had been counting on Rome's downfall and now Rome could thoroughly relish the reversal of its fortune. The looting is unprecedented in scale, even for the Romans, who now take away everything that can be removed.

We are told that the booty included a huge planetarium, a marvel of science, produced by Archimedes. We are also told that Marcellus wished to capture and bring home Archimedes in person, but with the pillage came a spree of senseless murder. The legend is famous and reported by Plutarch:

> He was by himself, working out some problem with the aid of a diagram, and having fixed his thoughts and his eyes as well upon the matter of his study, he was not aware of the incursion of the Romans or of the capture of the city. Suddenly a soldier came upon him and ordered him to go with him to Marcellus. This Archimedes refused to do until he had worked out his problem and established its demonstration, whereupon the soldier flew into a passion, drew his sword, and killed him.

So much for the legend. (Plutarch himself reviews several other alternatives, and the truth is likely be different still.) But it is an appropriate legend. Several ignorant hands nearly brought an end to Archimedes' heritage by destroying a scientific legacy that they did not understand. Yet Archimedes survived.

For we may conclude with sober historical fact, instead of legend. Let us follow Cicero in the year 75 BC. Archimedes has been dead for 137 years. Sicily is a Roman province, part of a Mediterranean that has been thoroughly subdued. Cicero himself is a quaestor, a high official, on the island. He is also a cultivated man, with deep respect for the Greek scientific heritage. He knows about the old tomb of Archimedes and is capable of finding it again, despite its having been lost for all those years. And on the tomb the old engraving (requested by Archimedes himself) is still there: a sphere, and a cylinder exactly enclosing it.

Archimedes did prove that the first was always two-thirds the second—a masterpiece of reasoning that got him as close to squaring the circle as is humanly possible. The diagram on this tomb was immortal. Archimedes did find the first deep, revolutionary truths. In time, they would give rise to our science. But first, his works had to survive—to cross the seas of history so that, on the other shore, modern science could be born.

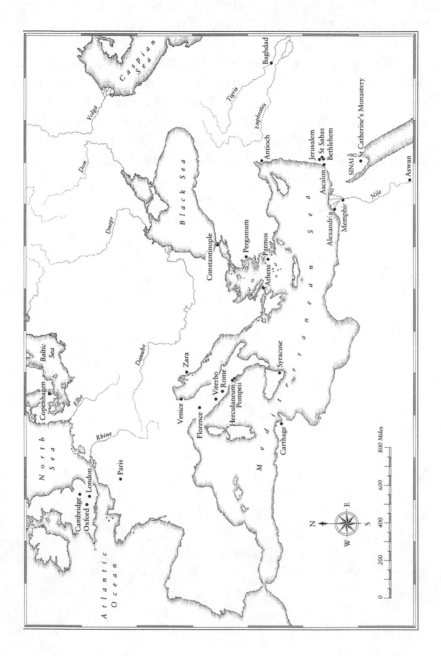

3

The Great Race, Part 1
Before the Palimpsest

M r. B sent me another letter, but it wasn't a check this time. It contained transcripts of the court case concerning the Palimpsest, which continued after the sale. In the transcripts, the lawyer for Christie's said that plans for an exhibition of the manuscript were already being explored through a major museum in Baltimore. Clearly, Mr. B had the idea of an exhibition even before I did. Since the book would not have made much of an exhibition by itself, I decided to make a film that explained why it was so important. I got in touch with John Dean, a filmmaker and now a dear friend. He bought the airplane tickets, and we flew around the Mediterranean making the movie, with John singing and making friends along the way. We had to pack the story of 2,200 years into two weeks of filming.

The film told the story of the book as if it were taking part in a race. The race lasted for centuries and took place all over the Mediterranean world. It was a race for survival, and it was an epic. Archimedes rode on a donkey—the concern of the scholar and the care of the scribe. Arrayed against Archimedes were the mighty thoroughbreds of destruction: war, indifference, and the second law of thermodynamics. If his works were to survive, Archimedes would have to stay ahead of his opposition throughout the race; his treatises had to be rewritten more times than they were destroyed. Ancient authors were all in the same race and facing similar odds. But for most of them, thanks to the printing press of Johannes Gutenberg, the race was effectively over by the end of the sixteenth century. From 1454 onward, these authors dismounted their donkeys and climbed onto Pegasus, the winged horse. Even destruction's thoroughbreds found it difficult to overtake the printing press. But Gutenberg's invention was still 1,666 years away when Archimedes died. By a series of truly fantastic circumstances, Archimedes' race is not even over in the twenty-first century, and the final lap is still being run in the New World.

A Letter Is Written

You might think of it as a soccer ball kicked by Italy. But Sicily isn't a sphere; it's a triangle. And that's how the ancients thought of it. John Dean and I landed in Palermo, which is on the western angle of the triangle. We drove through its center at Piazza Armerina, then down toward the south-east angle, leaving Mount Etna on our left. We then arrived at Archimedes' home town—Syracuse. John and I might have stayed in Winston Churchill's favorite hotel, but we walked the streets that Archimedes trod, sat in the theater where he watched plays, visited the altar at which he worshipped, and followed the city walls that he defended. High above the city, on the Epipolae Plain, the impressive remains of the Euryalus fortress still stand. In April 1999, it looked stunning with its white ramparts emerging from a sea of wild flowers. The view was magnificent, and we could see the port below us to the east.

From Syracuse, before the Second Punic War, Archimedes had written a letter to a friend. The letter began:

Archimedes to Eratosthenes: greetings! Since I know you are diligent, an excellent teacher of philosophy, and greatly interested in any mathematical investigation that may come your way, I thought it might be appropriate to write down and set forth for you a certain special method . . . I presume there will be some among the present as well as future generations who

by means of the method here explained will be enabled to
find other theorems which have not yet fallen to our share.

It is easy to accept recorded history as a full account of the past.
However, it really isn't. If we think of it this way, we not only misun-
derstand what history is but also miss marveling at what it is that we
know. Nothing is inevitable about the fact that we know that a great
man in the third century BC wrote a private letter to a friend; it is
absolutely extraordinary that we know this. Amazingly, we also know
a lot of what he wrote in the letter and even what it looked like.

The letter was made of papyrus sheets and wrapped around a
wooden core. In other words, it was a roll. Papyrus is a fibrous plant
that used to grow plentifully in the Nile delta, and papyrus rolls were
the stationery of choice in the ancient Mediterranean. Strips taken
from the lower stem of the plant were laid down parallel and slightly
overlapping each other. Then another set of strips was laid down at
right angles to the first. The two layers were bashed with a mallet and
they would stick together to make an excellent writing surface.
Sections could be glued together to make rolls of different lengths.
The rolls were made in Egypt and distributed throughout the ancient
world from the greatest trading port at the time—Alexandria. To
write on the roll, Archimedes used a reed pen and wrote on just one
side of the sheet—the side on which the papyrus leaves were laid
horizontally. He wrote in narrow columns of capital letters, not down
the length of the roll but instead down its width. He did not leave
spaces between his words, and there was virtually no punctuation as
we understand it today. His diagrams, which he regarded as integral
to his text were placed within the columns of his text, following the
text to which they referred.

Once he finished his letter, Archimedes took it to the port and
arranged for it to be shipped to its destination. He was sending his
roll on a perilous sea voyage right back to where it had come from—

Alexandria. If he kept a copy of what he sent—and this was standard practice—then no trace of that copy survives. Perhaps it was destroyed, along with Archimedes himself, in the siege of 212 BC. Once the boat left the harbor, the fate of his letter was no longer in his hands. It was no ordinary letter; it was his *Method*.

In the Library

The town of Aswan, in Egypt, lies on the Tropic of Cancer. This means that at noon on June 21 the walls of its buildings cast no shadows. The walls of Alexandria, about 485 miles farther north, do. At the same date and time a small shadow lines their walls' northern edges. Even though the walls of both towns are vertical, and the sun's rays are nearly parallel, the walls stand at different angles to those rays. The vertical walls of Aswan are at a seven-degree angle from the vertical walls of Alexandria. It was obvious to Eratosthenes that the surface of the Earth itself, the ground upon which the walls of both towns stood, was curved. By measuring the distance from Aswan to Alexandria, which accounts for 7 of the 360 degrees of a sphere, one can estimate the circumference of the Earth. Eratosthenes thought this through in the third century BC and came up with the value of 250,000 stadia, in which 1 stadion is 125 paces or about 625 feet. This was astonishingly close to the value accepted today—24,900 miles. A smart calculation, and because of feats like this Archimedes addressed the *Method* to Eratosthenes. It may have been because Eratosthenes also knew a lot about a lot of subjects that he was appointed director of the library at Alexandria in 235 BC.

Alexandria was a young city in Eratosthenes' day. It was founded on April 7, 331 BC by Alexander the Great, and it soon replaced Memphis as the capital of Egypt. From 305 BC it was ruled by Ptolemy I Soter, of Greco-Macedonian ancestry, and the dynasty that he founded was to rule Egypt until Cleopatra's suicide in 30 BC. Under the Ptolemies, Alexandria became a great center of Greek culture. By 280 BC a Temple to the Muses—the world's first museum—had been created. Built in the palace complex, it was a set of buildings, including a large dining hall, a covered walk, and an arcade with recesses and seats for the use of a scholarly community. It was there that Eratosthenes and other scholars spent their days, pacing the covered walk, speculating on such subjects as the circumference of the Earth, and occasionally receiving letters from their friend Archimedes. Their library constituted the greatest collection of texts in the ancient world. It had grown rapidly in the previous fifty years, because scholars had set out to systematically record the sum of world learning as it then existed. In the middle of the third century BC a catalogue of the library was attempted by Callimachus of Cyrene, entitled "Catalogues of the Authors Eminent in Various Disciplines." It was a monumental achievement. It took up 120 rolls. It was divided into categories, and within each category authors were discussed alphabetically based upon the first letter of their name.

It would not have taken more than a couple of weeks for the ship bearing Archimedes' letter from Syracuse to arrive at the port of Alexandria, because it had a tail wind. After making a sacrifice to Poseidon for a safe voyage, someone would have taken the roll to its intended recipient—the safest of all hands, the learned and responsible lover of rolls—Eratosthenes. Eratosthenes probably placed his letter from Archimedes in a section of the library devoted to science texts, and it rested there beside other rolls containing different treatises by the same author. It is more than likely that Eratosthenes had copies made of the letter. Judging by Archimedes' hope that later generations would read the letter, this was most certainly his expectation. One of the copies may have been stored nearby in the precincts of the Temple of Serapis. The scrolls in the Serapeum, as it was called, were copied from those in the museum and were available not only to scholars leading their sequestered lives but also to members of the public. Eratosthenes lived to be about 80 years old. In his later years, he was blind and it is believed that he committed suicide by voluntary starvation. But he had done all he could for Archimedes, and it was enough—just.

We know that Archimedes' letter to Eratosthenes arrived in Alexandria only because we know that it was read there. In the first century AD someone retrieved a copy of it. We even know the name of this person—Hero. Hero wrote a treatise, *Metrica*, which mentions the *Method*. "The same Archimedes shows in the same book [the *Method*] that if in a cube two cylinders penetrate whose bases are tangent to the faces of the cube, the common segment of the cylinders will be two thirds of the cube. This is useful for vaults constructed in this way . . ."

Hero was interested in Archimedes' treatise because it could help in the construction of a groin vault, which consists of cylindrical spaces carved out of rectilinear masonry. This was a specialty of Hero's, and he also wrote a treatise on vaulting. We will see again and again, while tracing the survival of Archimedes' treatises, that they were of interest to people who wanted to apply his knowledge to real-world technical problems.

Note, however, how thin the trail of evidence is by which we can trace the history of Archimedes' works. Hero's *Metrica* survived only in one manuscript, and we can place him in Alexandria in the first century AD only because the Sun, the Moon, and the Earth have extremely regular movements in relation to one another. In another treatise, *Dioptra*, Hero gave an eyewitness account of an eclipse of the Moon, which he states took place on the tenth day before the vernal equinox beginning at Alexandria in the fifth watch of the night. Otto Neugebauer, the great figure of ancient mathematical astronomy, observed that this corresponds to an eclipse in 62 AD and to no other eclipse for centuries on either side of this date. And for centuries on either side of this date, we hear nothing further of the *Method*.

A Change of Medium

Nothing is more dangerous for the contents of old documents than an information-technology upgrade, because mass data transfer has to take place and somebody has to do it. The transition from the roll to the codex—the book format we know today—was a revolution in the history of data storage (see fig 3.1).

The introduction of codices was gradual. It started in the first century AD yet was only more or less complete by the end of the fourth century. To me, the great surprise is that it took so long. The genius of the codex is that it contains knowledge not in two dimensions, like a roll, but in three. The roll has height and width; the codex has height, width, and depth. Because it has depth, it doesn't need to be nearly as wide. A codex with 200 folios (400 pages), 6 inches wide, has the same potential data-storage area as a roll of the same height that is 200 feet long. Since each leaf of a codex is so thin, you save an awful lot of width for a very small increase in depth. What's more, to access data on a roll you have to travel through the width dimension. To access data in a codex, you only

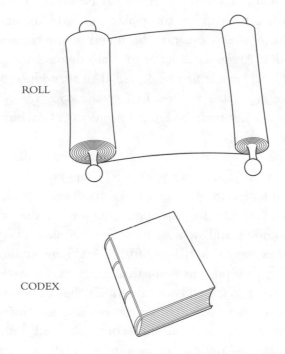

ROLL

CODEX

FIGURE 3.1

have to travel through the depth dimension, which is just a couple of inches thick. There is a big difference between "unrolling" and "thumbing through." If you are consulting a catalogue listed alphabetically getting to Archimedes is not a problem. But what about Zeno? With a codex you could just flip to the folios at the end and then close the codex. You would have to unravel nearly the whole roll in order to find a few lines about Zeno. This did not happen, of course. If the catalogue were of any length, this literally could not have happened. This is why Callimachus' catalogue consisted of 120 rolls. If Callimachus' rolls were ever transcribed into codices, there would have been a lot less than 120 of them.

Ancient texts that didn't make the transition from roll to codex simply disappeared. The ancients shunned their rolls for the same reasons that we neglect our 78 rpm vinyl records: they had become an outmoded storage system. Only decades ago, 78 rpm records were the preferred medium for music recordings. Now they are more often found in trash cans than on turntables. Similarly, the fragmentary remains of ancient texts can now be found in the trashcans of the ancient world. If Archimedes' letter to Eratosthenes had stayed in its roll, it would have been at first neglected, then abandoned, and finally it would have crumbled to dust. In fact, the copy (or copies) that stayed in rolls did just that, though no fragments of Archimedes have been found in trash cans.

Just because Archimedes was famous, it doesn't mean that his works were an obvious priority in the IT upgrade. In truth, even though he was legendary, Archimedes was hardly ever read. The most important of his results, like his approximation for the value of pi, became well known and well used, but few people actually read his arguments. They were simply too difficult. And here Archimedes was at a particular disadvantage compared to other great thinkers in antiquity. The Homers, the Platos, and the Euclids of this world were recognized at the time as not only great but also fundamental. They were frequently used and, in due course, copied into codices. Archimedes was too difficult to be fundamental; very few people could understand him. His genius actually worked against him. His texts were very often left unrolled, and they were always going to have had a tough time getting into codices. Three hundred years after Hero another mathematician, Pappus, discussed a treatise by Archimedes on semi-regular polyhedra. Of this treatise no trace remains. Perhaps it never made it into a codex. It lost the race against destruction right there.

The person who did more than anyone else to ensure the survival of Archimedes' treatises through this decisive period was named Eutocius. Eutocius was born in Ascalon, Palestine in about 480 AD. He didn't just read Archimedes' treatises; he researched them and explained them. Eutocius traveled widely among the great centers of learning at the time, including to Alexandria, where he must have met a teacher named Ammonius. Eutocius dedicated his first work on Archimedes, a commentary on *Sphere and Cylinder I*, to Ammonius, and clearly held him in high regard. In his preface, Eutocius says that he would write commentaries on other treatises by Archimedes if Ammonius approved of this one. Ammonius must have approved, because Eutocius went on to write three additional commentaries— on *Sphere and Cylinder II*, on the *Measurement of the Circle,* and on *Balancing Planes.* Eutocius had to struggle to find Archimedes' writings. Regardless of whether they were already in codices or still in rolls, there weren't very many of them. At one point in *Sphere and Cylinder II,* Archimedes promises to prove a mathematical point but never does. Eutocius therefore went on a search. He writes: "In a certain old manuscript (for we did not cease from the search of many manuscripts) we have read theorems written very unclearly (because of the errors), and in many ways mistaken about the diagrams. But they had to do with the subject matter we were looking for, and they preserved in part the Doric dialect Archimedes liked using, written with the ancient name of things." Eutocius then included an account of this text in his commentary.

Eutocius' treatises survive together with the works of Archimedes that they comment upon. And this is an important point. Eutocius, like everybody else, clearly saw the advantages of the new IT and exploited it. Just as a CD can store a great many more Bach cantatas than a 78, so a single codex can contain many more of Archimedes' treatises than a roll. Eutocius, it seems, prepared an edition of several of Archimedes' treatises, together with his commentaries, and had them bound within wooden boards. From the sixth century onward, we should imagine a treatise by Archimedes inside a handy parchment codex, placed safely within wooden covers, and nestled comfortably with other letters of a similar nature.

The Gathering Storm

Archimedes' letter to Eratosthenes might have been comfortable in codex form, but it was by no means safe. Times were changing, and they were not changing to Archimedes' advantage. One by one the great cities of the ancient world, which held the ancient schools of learning and the books upon which they depended, were pillaged by invaders. Rome was sacked by the Goths in 410 AD, Antioch by the Persians in 540 AD, and Athens by the Slavs in 580 AD. There may have been many copies of Archimedes' letters outside of Alexandria in the third century AD; there were hardly any by the end of the sixth. Things were not much better in Alexandria. In about 270 AD, Emperor Aurelian, during his war against Zenobia, damaged a large portion of the palace complex, which contained the Museum. In 391 AD, Theophilus, the Archbishop of Alexandria, destroyed the Serapeum, the sister library of the Museum. In 415 AD, the distinguished female mathematician Hypatia was torn to pieces by a fanatic and ignorant Christian mob. Archimedes' letters had to get out of Alexandria before they suffered a similar fate.

As the ancient world disappeared, its gods went with it. And as Christianity became the official religion of the Roman Empire, many classical texts, if they were not condemned as dangerous, were dismissed as irrelevant. It is not that Christians willfully destroyed them very often; they just ceased to copy them. Scribes put their energies into Christian texts. The Christian curriculum did include some ancient authors—Homer was necessary for Rhetoric and Euclid for Geometry. But Archimedes was not included in the curriculum of Salvation. Fewer people than ever before had the resources to read him, and even fewer would have read him, if they could.

In the fifth and sixth centuries, for every donkey that Archimedes could ride on, there were hordes of thoroughbred barbarians. The race against destruction for all classical texts was getting increasingly desperate. The only question was where could they run? The only answer was Constantinople.

Into the Ark

John Dean and I flew to Constantinople, present-day Istanbul, in search of Archimedes. The city was founded on the Bosphorus by Constantine, the first Christian Emperor, on Monday, May 11, 330 AD. He founded it specifically as the capital of the eastern Roman Empire. Constantinople was a relative newcomer to the Mediterranean world of learning. Successive emperors poured the resources that only they could marshal into making the city worthy of the empire that it inherited. Certainly the emphasis was on Christian works. Constantine ordered fifty complete copies of the Bible to be written. But the classics were also a concern in Constantinople. On Wednesday, January 1, 357 AD, in an address to the Emperor Constantius, the philosopher Themistius described a plan to guarantee the survival of ancient literature. He proposed a scriptorium—a writing center—for the production of new copies of the classics. This would ensure that the new capital of the empire would become a center of culture. The plan may have actually been put into effect. In 372 AD, an order was issued to the city prefect, Clearchus, to appoint four scribes skilled in Greek and three in Latin to undertake the transcription and repair of books. In 425 AD, the Emperor Theodosius II established an imperial foundation for literary and philosophical studies. Even more importantly, in 412 AD he built massive walls around the city.

John Dean and I didn't have to look far to find Archimedes. His geometry is indelibly stamped on Constantinople. Between 532 AD and 537 AD, the Emperor Justinian crowned the "New Rome" with one of the greatest buildings the world has ever seen—the Church of Hagia Sophia. This is how a contemporary, Procopius describes it:

> A construction of masonry rises from the ground, not in a straight line, but gradually drawing back from its sides and receding in the middle, so as to describe a semi-circular shape which is called a half-cylinder by specialists, and this towers to a precipitous height. The extremity of this structure terminates in the fourth part of a sphere, and above it another crescent-shaped form is lifted up by the adjoining parts of the building . . . On either side of these, columns are placed on the ground, and these, too, do not stand in a straight line, but retreat inward in a half-circle as if making way for one another in a dance, and above them is suspended a crescent-shaped form.

Hagia Sophia is an astonishing building on many levels, but the important point is that it was designed with diagrams and by numbers. It was the work of mathematicians. One of them was Anthemius of Tralles. Anthemius wrote texts on *Burning Mirrors* and *Remarkable Mechanical Devices*. The second architect was somewhat younger than Anthemius. His name was Isidore of Miletus and he wrote a commentary on Hero of Alexandria's treatise on *Vaulting*. Anthemius and Isidore were masters of Archimedes' discipline and the plan of Hagia Sophia might well resemble the figure that was inscribed on Archimedes' tomb.

The mathematical world was small in the sixth century, and it was getting smaller all the time. It is not surprising that Anthemius and Isidore were well acquainted with Eutocius. Eutocius dedicated his commentaries on the works of Apollonius of Perga to Anthemius. Isidore knew Eutocius' works on Archimedes extremely well. The text of Eutocius' commentary on *Sphere and Cylinder I* is preserved because it was copied by one of Isidore's students. When he had finished his copying, this student wrote: "The commentary of Eutocius of Ascalon on the first book of Archimedes *On the Sphere* and the *Cylinder*, the edition being collated by the Milesian mechanical author, Isidore, our teacher." Thus, Isidore was preparing an edition of Archimedes' works, together with Eutocius' commentaries, in Constantinople.

Archimedes made it to Constantinople in the nick of time. For three hundred years after the time of Isidore, his writings, like most of the classics, disappear from recorded history. The empire became embroiled in internal strife about holy images and was subject to external threats from barbarians and Arabs. When texts were read, they were read only to bolster particularly contentious aspects of Christian doctrine. Constantinople did the one thing it had to do for Archimedes, and for so many ancient authors—it survived. It was the only city of the ancient world of any consequence to survive unmolested into the Middle Ages. Constantinople served as the ark for ancient literature, and the Noah of the classics was the Emperor Theodosius. A hundred years before Isidore built his great church, Theodosius had already constructed the city's massive walls to weather the Dark Age storm.

The Byzantine Renaissance

On Saturday, July 26, 811, Krum, the Bulgarian Khan, slew Nicephorus, the Byzantine Emperor, at the battle of Pliska. The Khan turned the Emperor's skull into a wine cup. Not a good start to the ninth century for Constantinople. On the surface, things didn't look much better thirty years and six emperors later when Michael III, "The Drunkard," ascended the throne. But, in fact, the intellectual climate was improving, and it got even better when Basil I assassinated Michael in 867 AD. Under Basil I, Constantinople quickly became the capital of the greatest empire in the Mediterranean world. The Macedonian dynasty that he founded could boast both scholarship and mettle. While Constantine VII wrote a book on the administration of the empire in 1014 AD, Basil II took 14,000 Bulgarians prisoner and blinded ninety-nine out of every hundred; the lucky one got to guide his comrades home. Constantinople had entered a golden age, if not an enlightened one.

The famous Byzantine "rebirth" of the ninth and tenth centuries produced impressive buildings and consummate works of art. John and I could still see and film the Imperial Palace, and when we got back to Baltimore we could still photograph Henry Walters' fabulously illuminated Byzantine manuscripts. But the most important thing about this cultural revival was that as scholars started reading the classics that had been lying neglected in their libraries, they started copying them again. The most voracious reader of them all was a distinguished civil servant, and twice the Patriarch of Constantinople, Photius. His *Bibliotheca* was a compilation of works that he had read; it contained a summary of the contents, style, and biography of each author. As Nigel Wilson describes it, Photius had invented the book review. The *Bibliotheca* is invaluable for many reasons, but prominent among them is that it gives us a good idea of the extraordinary variety of classical texts that were still extant in Constantinople in Photius' day. Admittedly, scholars have thought that some of Photius' claims were a bit much. He claimed, for example, to have read works by Hyperides, an ancient Greek orator. Since no one else in Constantinople even mentioned whole texts by Hyperides, and since none survive in codex form, this is considered unlikely. Nonetheless, the statistics gleaned from Photius are impressive. For example, of the thirty-three historians that he discussed, the works of twenty are now unknown.

When ninth-century scribes copied classical texts they wrote in a fundamentally different script from that used in Isidore's day. Before the ninth century, texts were written in capital letters, technically called majuscules. Generally speaking, after the ninth century, they were written in a new script, technically called

FIGURE 3.2 *Majuscules (left) and Minuscules (right)*

minuscule, whose letters could be joined up in order to take up less space (see fig 3.2).

The origins of minuscule script were probably in the letters, documents, and accounts of the civil service based in Constantinople. Minuscule script was faster to write, its letters were easier to form, and more words could fit on a folio. By the middle of the ninth century, it was also used for religious and scientific texts. Many codices, written in capitals during and before the sixth century, were systematically transcribed into lowercase script. This change in how texts were copied was just as important of a hurdle for Archimedes' texts as the transition from roll to codex. So few majuscule codices from the fifth and sixth centuries survive, because many ninth-century scholars may have destroyed their majuscule manuscripts after they made minuscule copies. The majuscule codices may have been increasingly difficult to read, and after they had been transcribed, there was no need for them. The texts of nearly all the ancient Greek authors were dependent on just a few minuscule manuscripts copied in Constantinople during the ninth and tenth centuries. Archimedes was no exception. He was actually dependent on three manuscripts.

And this is the fundamental point. All that stuff that Reviel has talked about, and will go on to talk about, survives because of just three physical objects, of which the codex on my desk is one.

The ABC of Archimedes

These three objects are called Codex A, Codex B, and Codex C. They had some texts in common. All three contained *Balancing Planes*; A and B contained *Quadrature of the Parabola*; A and C contained *Sphere and Cylinder, Measurement of the Circle,* and *Spiral Lines*; and B and C contained *On Floating Bodies*. Codex A was the unique witness to *Conoids and Spheroids* and *Sand-Reckoner*; Codex C is the unique witness to *Method* and *Stomachion*.

It seems very likely that all three codices were the fruit of a revival of interest in Archimedes' texts early in the ninth century. When a scribe finished copying Archimedes' *Quadrature of the Parabola* in Codex A, he wrote a little note of adulation, but not to Archimedes. He wrote: "Leo the geometer, may you flourish—May you live many a year, dear friend of the Muses." This Leo was almost certainly the Leo who was giving private instruction in Constantinople during the 820s. Known as Leo the Philosopher, he was evidently a talented teacher. In 830, the Arabs captured one student, who had read Euclid under his supervision. His report of Leo's learning was sufficient to cause the Caliph to invite Leo to Baghdad. Thankfully, Leo did not go. Leo was clearly something of a polymath and a practical one at that. He built fire signal stations between Constantinople and the border of the empire. If there was an emergency on the border north of Tarsus, a message could reach the capital in less than an hour. In the late 850s, Leo's skills were rewarded. He was appointed director of a school in the Imperial Palace. He must have played a prominent role in choosing the other professors. One of them was Theodore, a geometer. We are safe to assume that Archimedes was being studied and copied in the school of the Imperial Palace, and that the texts in Codex A were copied in that school. The accession of Basil I in 867 ensured that Archimedes' treatises could be studied in safety, at least for the time being.

We will trace the histories of the three manuscripts that contained Archimedes' treatises in more detail later. But for now, it is important to know that Codices A and B survive no longer. We have only copies and translations of them. As a result, Codex C is not only the unique source for the *Method* and *Stomachion* and for *Floating Bodies* in Greek, it is also the oldest surviving manuscript of Archimedes' treatises in Greek by over four hundred years. Codex C is on my desk, and now it is time to see how it was made.

Codex C

Codex C, like most medieval manuscripts, is not written on paper; it is written on the backs of animals. The skin of an animal is such a refined product of natural selection that it is hard to see how it could be used for much else. But skin has two great qualities: it is supple, enabling movement, and it is tough, allowing animals to sustain all types of knocks. Skin is well suited to life on earth outside of fire and too much water, and, with some treatment, the same properties make it an excellent, durable writing surface. With that treatment, it is called parchment.

Parchment was invented at Pergamum in Asia Minor—or so legend has it. King Eumenes II wanted his library to match that of Alexandria, so the Ptolemies put an embargo on the export of papyrus from Egypt at the beginning of the second century BC. Parchment was Eumenes' home-grown substitute. With the introduction of the codex, parchment came into its own. While papyrus certainly had tensile strength, it fractured more easily than parchment when it was folded. Since codices consisted of folded sheets, those made of parchment survived better than those made of papyrus.

81

Parchment is more durable than paper, which is why certificates and awards meant to last are sometimes still inscribed on sheepskins.

Making parchment is not everybody's idea of fun. Certainly not Reviel's; he's a vegetarian. This is what you do. Kill the animals and drain the blood from their veins. Flay them; slit their underbellies; cut off their extremities; and peel back the skin. Place the skins in a vat containing a weak solution of lime, which you can make by heating limestone. The lime solution is destructive to organic tissue, so it breaks down the epidermis and the subcutaneous fat and weakens the bonds that attach the hair to the skin. The inner layer of the dermis alone remains intact. This layer is mainly made up of collagen. Collagen is a protein made up of three chains of amino acids that spiral around an elongated straight axis. The chains are staggered and the resulting fibers have no definite terminal limits. Collagen is the crucial constituent of parchment; it is what makes it tough. After several days, remove the skins from the vat, place them over a beam, and scrape them down with a dull blade. Once you have removed the worst of the fat and the hair, attach the skins to wooden frames. As they dry they will contract and become taut. Once they are taut, scrape them again, this time with a very sharp half-moon-shaped blade. Cut them from their frames, and you have produced parchment.

Imagine a set of newspapers stacked in a pile, sandwiched between wooden boards, the whole lot stitched together, and you actually have a good first impression of the physical construction of a tenth-century Byzantine manuscript. The newspapers, called quires, usually consisted of four nested double sheets called bifolios (see fig. 3.3). This makes up eight sheets of a newspaper (sixteen pages). Remember that manuscript people call the sheets folios. Since you could get two bifolios out of each sheep, twenty-four sheep were needed to make enough bifolios for the surviving parchment in the Archimedes manuscript. To make the quires you had to cut the skins to size, rub them with a pumice stone to raise a nap, and give them a transparent glaze mainly consisting of egg white. This was the support that housed the texts of Archimedes and the others.

FIGURE 3.3 *A Quire*

And now to the ink. This is more fun to make. You start with a solution of gallic acid. Gallic acid is present in oak galls, which are growths on oak trees resulting from infections from insects and mites. It is made up of carbon, hydrogen, and oxygen, and it has the power to contract organic tissues such as collagen. This allows the ink to etch into the parchment and remain in place. Crush the galls and boil them in water. To this solution add ferrous sulphate, which is sometimes called green vitriol or copperas. This will supply most of the color to the ink. It is a compound of iron and sulphuric acid that you can frequently find together with pyrite. You then need to add a thickening agent to this solution. By a process called gummosis, trees belonging to the Fabaceae family, produce gum from their bark if they are under attack. Gum Arabic is produced by the acacia tree, which grows in Africa. Gum tragacanth, produced by several shrubs of the genus *Astragalus*, principally astragalus gummier, can be found in Asia Minor. If you are making a manuscript in Constantinople, you might find it easier to get hold of gum tragacanth. It is still used today to coat pills. To produce it in a quantity sufficient to satisfy the pharmaceutical industry, incisions are made into the bark and wooden wedges are driven into the incisions. The chemical makeup of gum is complicated and varied, but it contains carbon, hydrogen, oxygen, and metals such as calcium, magnesium and potassium. Since the resulting mixture darkens slowly as it oxidizes on the parchment, you might want to add carbon black to it. This way you will be able to see what you are writing as you are writing it. Combine the ingredients and give them a good shake, and you have the ink that the scribes used to write their texts.

And so, about a hundred years after the death of Leo, a scribe prepared himself for a job. We can imagine this scribe, because pictures of scribes writing survive from this period. When we see him, he has already gone through familiar procedures. Guided by a ruler, he has made lines on the parchment to help him keep his columns of text straight, he has sharpened his reed pens on a stone, and cut the nib down the middle to help the ink flow. He has prepared his ink and placed the inkwell on his table, and he has beside himself a knife so that he can refine his pen or scrub out a mistake should he make one. He has prepared the tools of his trade, the mystic implements of the human voice. We picture him seated in his chair, ready to write. He doesn't have a writing table, but then he doesn't need one. He is going to write on his lap, resting the parchment on a board. In front of him, on a stand, is a codex. This is the codex that he is going to copy.

Before we look at what he wrote, let's think a bit about the codex on that stand in front of him. Did the codex on the stand look like the codex that the scribe was about to make? Was it a sixth-century codex from the time of Isidore or was it written in minuscule? Was it one codex containing the same treatises in the same order or should we be thinking about several codices sequentially placed upon the stand? We do not know enough about the parent manuscript (or manuscripts) that our scribe used. Judging from the text, he did not copy any of his treatises from Codex A. It is certainly possible that he copied a sixth-century manuscript, but the evidence is not conclusive. This is perhaps the most important unanswered question about our manuscript.

Be that as it may, the scribe did his job and wrote his text. Each folio that he wrote measured about 12 inches by 7.5 inches. He wrote his text in two columns and wrote thirty-five lines in each column. He made a codex with generous margins, so together the columns were 9.5 inches high and 5.5 wide. Of course, Archimedes' letter to Eratosthenes—the *Method*—was just one of the texts he copied. The manuscript currently starts toward the end of *Balancing Planes* and is followed by *Floating Bodies* and the *Method*. The *Method* is followed by *Spiral Lines, Sphere and Cylinder, Measurement of the Circle,* and finally by one folio of *Stomachion*. Our scribe was an expert, writing in a minuscule script characteristic of the third quarter of the tenth century. Nigel Wilson says that his handwriting is similar to that in a manuscript, with the date 988, which is now in the Monastery of St. John the Theologian on the island of Patmos. The scribe didn't understand what he was copying but, as Reviel will explain later, this was a good thing. We can assume that he worked for no longer than a few months. We can only guess at the true extent of the original codex, because we are now missing the beginning, the end, and several chunks of the middle. In fact, it is perfectly possible that the manuscript originally contained more of Archimedes' treatises.

The codex our scribe wrote was actually a typical product of the Byzantine Renaissance of the ninth and tenth centuries. As with most Byzantine manuscripts, we do not know who commissioned it or even who read it. In fact, judging by the lack of marginal comments, it does not seem to have been used very much. But none of this matters. It is the unique source for the *Method, Stomachion,* and *On Floating Bodies* in Greek. If our scribe did nothing else in his long life, his was a life well spent.

This is a story of survival, achieved against all the odds, through an extravagant process by which creation just managed to outrun destruction. Many rolls have crumbled and many codices have burned. I have brought you to the earliest surviving text of Archimedes—the thoughts of Archimedes preserved in a highly ordered arrangement of flesh and iron. But it was made in the tenth century, closer to our own time than to the time of Archimedes. Tenth-century parchment codices look nothing like third-century BC rolls. As Archimedes' letters were copied, they were transformed and the treatises that survive no longer look anything like the letters that Archimedes wrote. Archimedes would not have recognized them, and could not have even read them. This is important, but to explain why, we need again to consult the expert.

4

Visual Science

There is a lot one can learn from manuscripts. For one thing, we can pick up what's written in them. We can find out what thoughts Archimedes had, in Syracuse, in the third century BC. We can find out how such thoughts came to influence all of later science.

And we can do more: we can use manuscripts to find out not just what thoughts past scholars had, but also how they came to think such thoughts. How did Archimedes think through his mathematics? How did his readers? Such questions are raised by a recent cognitive turn in science studies. To answer such questions we must turn to manuscripts, because they provide us with the unique source of evidence for this fundamental question: how does science register in the mind's eye?

In fact, we all have, nowadays, a rather clear image of science in our mind's eye. Let us consider the following experiment. In fig. 4.1, I show two pictures of open pages from books. Take a look for a minute: even though the illustrations are too small to be read comfortably, they allow us immediately to make certain judgments. We just *know* that the left-hand page is scientific. It is, in fact, from an introductory text in the calculus (the subject pioneered by Archimedes, to which we shall return). The right-hand page is from James Joyce's *Finnegans Wake* (and is, incidentally, much more difficult to read than the left-hand page).

When publishers say they are afraid of publishing popular science that "looks technical," what they mean is that they want their pages to look like the right-hand, not the left-hand page. What are readers afraid of ? They are afraid of *equations*. With good reason: they were force-fed

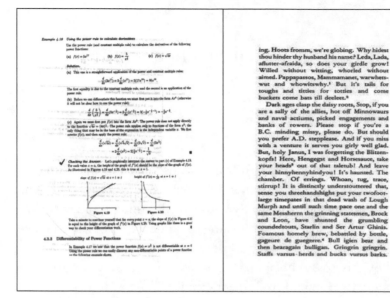

FIGURE 4.1

such equations for several terrible years of their childhood and adolescence. The result is that we tend, first, to hate equations and, second, to consider them to be the natural format of science. Both assumptions are wrong. Equations are a great invention—they should be respected, if not loved—and they are not natural. Instead, they are a historical invention whose origins lie in such documents as the Palimpsest. The Greeks did not use equations. Archimedes did not use equations. Their science looked nothing like the left-hand page in the figure.

Before Equations

Equations make logic visible. Suppose you say: "The first together with the second is equal to the third; therefore the first is equal to the third minus the second."

Give it a moment's thought and you see why this is true. But that's the trouble: you must give it a moment's thought; meanwhile your attention has wandered away and the thread of the argument may have been lost. Write instead:

A + B = C, therefore
A = C − B

and it works effortlessly: we *see* how the argument runs. Now no attention is thrown away, and we can go on following the argument with great ease.

We see how the same information acts differently through its different interfaces. The different media are important not only for the survival of science but also for its very nature. Indeed, we can hardly understand Greek science without first understanding its essential interface. This, however, was not the equation. It was the diagram.

Greek Mathematics Was a Visual Science

The starting point, as always, should be at Syracuse. In particular, we begin with the story recounted by Cicero: the tomb of Archimedes. We recall Cicero finding, after much effort, a desolate, neglected slab of stone and on it the message that Archimedes chose as his symbol— a diagram showing a sphere and a cylinder. This was the self-chosen symbol of science. Once again, we make the inevitable comparison to Einstein. What was Einstein's symbol, the emblem that immediately comes to mind? No, I don't mean the protruding tongue; I mean this:

$$E = mc^2$$

You have seen this emblem endless times. It has become a kind of symbol not only of Einstein but also of science in general. And it is, of course, an equation. So here is the starting point, in a nutshell: modern science is a science of equations; ancient science was a science of diagrams.

In the ancient exact sciences—not only mathematics but also astronomy and mechanics—and in many other fields, such as music theory, diagrams always occupy center stage. The text is made of individual "propositions," each making a point, proving that so-and-so is the case. The late British historian of Greek mathematics David Fowler used to say that each proposition is "drawing a figure and then telling a story about it." Everything is about those figures and done for the sake of those figures.

Diagrams, of course, are also used in modern science; but there is a big difference. In modern science diagrams serve as a kind of illustration; they are there to make the experience of learning science somewhat less traumatic for the student, but they are not part of the logic of the argument itself. In modern science it is considered crucial to make sure that no information depends on the diagram, otherwise one could end up with a false argument such as is demonstrated in figure 4.2.

The area of a triangle is the product of its two sides, divided by two.

Proof: we draw a triangle ABC. The two smaller sides are AB, BC. On the longer side AC, we apply another triangle, exactly identical to the triangle ABC, namely the triangle ACD. The result is a rectangle ABCD. The area of this rectangle is obviously the product of the two sides AB, BC. The triangle ABC is obviously exactly half the rectangle ABCD (after all, the two triangles ABC, ACD are identical). So, the area of a triangle is the product of its two sides divided by two, QED.

What is wrong with this proof? Well, it assumes something just on the basis of the diagram, even though there is no basis in the text for making such an assumption. In the diagram we happened to have

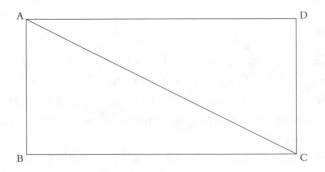

FIGURE 4.2 *The right-angled triangle ABC*

drawn a right-angled triangle. In a right-angled triangle the claim of the proof follows. But, it does not follow in other triangles (see fig. 4.3, where the product of the two sides AB and BC is clearly more than double the area of the triangle!). In short, we thought we were talking about triangles in general, but inadvertently we slipped into only talking about right-angled triangles, all because we had taken the diagram on faith. And so modern philosophers and logicians are adamant: do not rely on diagrams!

The logical and philosophical issue is deep: language is general, but a diagram is a particular thing. You see, you cannot draw a diagram without it having some particular properties. Suppose I wanted to draw a triangle so that its angle is neither right-angled, nor acute-angled, nor obtuse-angled, but just a "general" angle. How would I do that? I can't do it. On the page, I have some definite triangle drawn, and because it is a definite triangle, it also has some definite angle. Language, on the other hand, is more forgiving. I can say, "Let there be a triangle," and because I did not say which triangle—just "a triangle"—I am allowed to think of it as right-angled, obtuse-angled, or acute-angled. And so the modern philosophers and the logicians insist: to make sure the logic of the proof works in its full, most general form, we must rely on the language alone and never on the diagram.

FIGURE 4.3

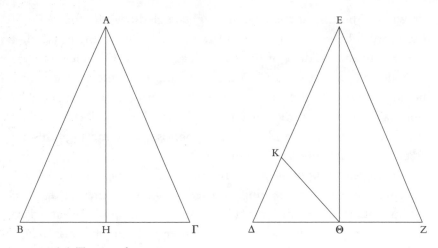

FIGURE 4.4 *Two isosceles cones*

This is precisely what Greek mathematicians did and, incredibly, without making any logical errors. It is one of the great puzzles of Greek mathematics: it is thoroughly diagrammatic and also thoroughly precise. The Greek mathematicians never made mistakes, such as the trivial one mentioned above, not even in subtle and indirect ways. Greek mathematics is as precise as modern mathematics. How? In a few pages, I shall try to provide an answer.

First of all, let us see how Greek mathematicians did in fact rely on the diagram. The following is from the first book on *Sphere and Cylinder*—the work eternalized on Archimedes' tomb. As already mentioned, Archimedes had a sly manner of writing—clever and playful, always hiding the main point of attack from the reader until the last moment. It should therefore come as no surprise that, until late in the book, spheres and cylinders are hardly mentioned. Instead, Archimedes keeps referring to *cones*. Here, for example, is proposition 17 (see fig. 4.4):

Let there be two isosceles cones ABΓ, ΔEZ; let the base of the cone ABΓ be equal to the surface of the cone ΔEZ; and let the height AH be equal to the perpendicular KΘ drawn from the center of the base Θ, on one side of the cone (such as ΔE). I say that the cones are equal.

The proposition makes its claim in terms of the diagram. This is the only place where the points and lines of the proposition are provided with meaning. This is done through alphabetic labels in exactly the same way as we do it today. In fact, in this sense we follow a Greek invention. (The Chinese had a different method—each line was labeled as if it had a different color. But then again, their alphabet is very different.)

Now, one of the most difficult things for a scholar is to notice those things that are obvious. The things that lie "under our noses" are often the most difficult to see, but when you notice them they may be the most rewarding. I had one such moment when considering such simple passages as these in Greek mathematics. I made this observation in the first chapter of my PhD thesis and, quite frankly, it is the one thing most of my peers know about my work. I will probably die and still be mentioned as "the guy who made that observation on Greek diagrams," which I find quite annoying, seeing that this was just about the first thing I ever did as a scholar. (I do like to think it was not all downhill from there!) Still, it is an important observation because it definitely shows that Greek mathematicians did not work the way modern philosophers and logicians wish that they had. They most certainly relied on the diagram.

For example, in an expression such as "the cones $AB\Gamma$, ΔEZ" we may easily guess that the points $AB\Gamma$, ΔEZ each stand for the vertices of a triangle cutting through the cone (see fig. 4.4). But how are we to know the individual distribution of the letters? In each cone, two letters must stand on the base and one on the top, but which is which? This is what makes this observation so difficult. Visual information is so powerful that the moment we are in front of a diagram we immediately "read off" the information and establish that $B\Gamma$, ΔZ are bases and A, E are tops; and we even fail to notice that *the text said no such thing*. In fact, this is the general rule throughout Greek mathematics: the identity of objects is not established by the words but by the diagrams. The diagrams are there not as some kind of illustration to make the reading experience more pleasant; the diagrams are there to provide us with the most basic information. They tell us the who's who of the proposition—which letter stands next to which object. Ancient diagrams are not illustrative, they are informative; they constitute part of the logic of the proposition. And so, Greek science was a visual science.

How did it come about, then, that Greek mathematicians did not make trivial mistakes based on the information in the diagram? How did they keep their logic perfect? The reason has to do with a very special interface used in Greek mathematics: the subtle, clever way in which diagrams are used.

The Sands of Syracuse

What did Archimedes' diagrams look like? As we can see, following Will's explanation of the history of manuscripts, this is a question for which we have only very indirect evidence. The earliest evidence we have, in fact, is in the Palimpsest itself. One's first reaction might be that of despair. If our evidence is so far from the original, what chance do we have of ever getting there? How can we realistically hope to know what ancient diagrams looked like? Indeed, this is a difficult question. In principle, nothing guarantees that we can answer it. It could be that medieval scribes simply invented their own diagrams instead of faithfully copying their ancient sources. After all, modern editors very clearly do just that: they invent their own diagrams. When I set out on my study of the medieval diagrams of Archimedes, I couldn't tell whether the medieval scribes did the same or not. My greatest fear was that I would get to Paris, Rome, Venice, and Florence, and each time, open an old book and find a completely different diagram. If this had been the case, my conclusion would have been that the ancient diagrams just could not be reconstructed.

Instead, city after city, page after page, and diagram after diagram—I opened books and they all showed effectively the same figure. Errors crept in here but not there. Corrections were made in some manuscripts, but not in others (suggesting the original might have contained an error detected by some scribes). But it was clear that the diagrams were related. They were copied, not invented. In short, one could apply *the philological method*. To do so, we take separate manuscripts and compare them. If two separate manuscripts possess the same text or diagram, this means that there must have been a common source for both. This allows us to go back and infer an earlier form. And while we can never be sure that this earlier form dates all the way back to Archimedes, it is still very important to try to push our evidence back as far as possible.

Now this must be stressed. Readers are sometimes dissapointed to hear that not all of Archimedes' works are represented by the Palimpsest alone. Some of the works are represented in the Palimpsest and also in the various descendants of Codex A. This is not some kind of blemish on the value of the Palimpsest. To the contrary, for the philological method, it is of the utmost importance to have *more than one* source. Taken alone, the Palimpsest can only tell us about the year AD 975. But when we can compare it to other independent medieval sources, it suddenly tells us much more. Whenever both the Palimpsest and another independent medieval manuscript tell the same story, we can push back the dates probably to a source from Eutocius' time or before, following which the two traditions diverged. And this already makes us much closer to the world of Archimedes himself.

This work is of a complex character. After all, Codex A itself is no longer extant, so we have to apply the philological method twice over. My original project of studying the Archimedes manuscripts involved the descendants of Codex A alone. (The Palimpsest, remember, was not available when I started my work.) So I looked at those manuscripts.

There are some 250 figures in the works of Archimedes, but let us review one example. In fig. 4.5, we can see the various variants of the diagram for *Sphere and Cylinder I*, proposition 38. On the basis of

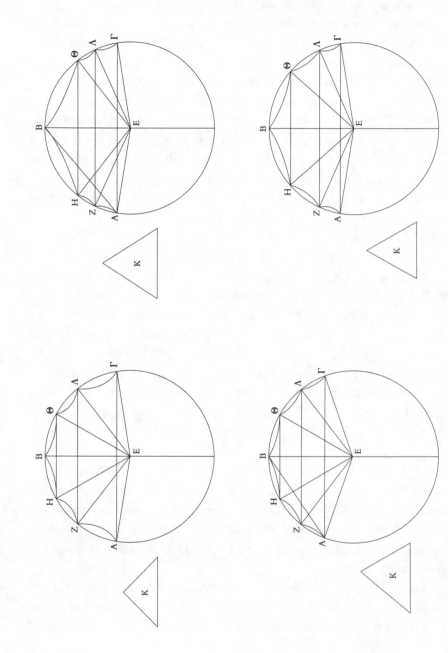

FIGURE 4.5 *Variants of diagram for Sphere and Cylinder 1, proposition 38*

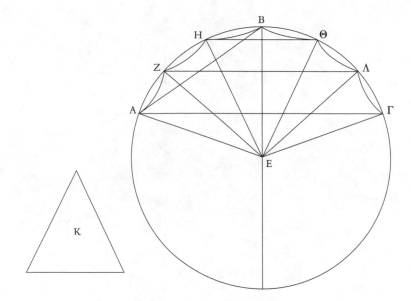

FIGURE 4.6 *Lost diagram of Codex A*

these variants, I was able to reconstruct the lost diagram of Codex A (fig. 4.6). You can see that the similarity between the various descendants is such as to make my reconstruction quite safe. There is only one point of detail—two of the codices have a line AB drawn and the others drop it. Since the line AB is not required by the text, I can guess that it was in the original figure. The more alert scribes simply did not copy it. Two of the scribes did not think about what they were doing and just copied what they had in front of their eyes. For this reason, they are the more trustworthy witnesses. This is a well-known paradox of the philological method, known as *lectio difficilior* ("the more difficult reading"). A bad piece of text is likely to be the original one.

Now, this in itself involves a fair amount of time travel. The descendants of Codex A are from the fifteenth and sixteenth centuries, while Codex A itself (like the Palimpsest) probably derived from the tenth century. The philological method has already gained us some 500–600 years. I had traveled from the Renaissance to the Middle Ages. But I wanted to continue my time travel. I needed a time machine to get me from the Middle Ages to antiquity.

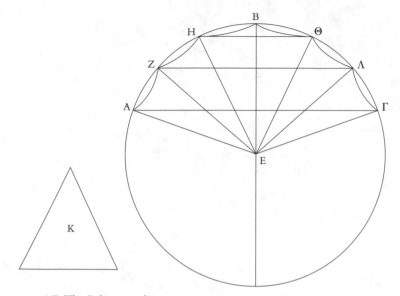

FIGURE 4.7 *The Palimpsest diagram*

The email from Will Noel, inviting me to look at the Palimpsest, offered me just that. This is why I was so excited. I just had to look at the diagrams. Here, once again, was a crucial deciding point. Either the figures would be largely identical to those of Codex A, in which case I could reconstruct ancient diagrams, or they would be different, in which case my quest for "the original Archimedes" would abort at around the year AD 975. Byzantine scribes—it might turn out—merely invented their diagrams and did not copy them from their originals. What I saw at Baltimore during my first visit—faintly, but the traces were familiar enough—was the same figure. Indeed, with digital imaging I reconstructed it with confidence. I took the reconstructed figure from Codex A and put it side by side with the figure from the Palimpsest (see fig. 4.7). I could see that they are nearly identical. This discovery was among the most important ones made through the Palimpsest. It is the cornerstone to the reconstruction of the figures of Archimedes.

Let us continue to follow the philological method. The Palimpsest does not include the line AB, and it adds a letter A at the bottom of the circle. Now, it is easy to see how a scribe can, in haste, forget to copy a single letter. I therefore chalk the absent letter A in Codex A down to scribal error and assume it was present in the common archetype. As for line AB, this is less clear. It is there in error, and since there is only a single manuscript bearing this error—Codex A—it may well be only the error of the scribe of Codex A. Of course, it could also be an earlier error, that was corrected by the scribe of the Palimpsest, but not by that of Codex A. But then again, I now know enough about the scribe of the Palimpsest to tell you that he did not, in general, correct geometrical errors. He clearly understood nothing of mathematics, judging from some absurd errors he made. In other words, I believe that the line AB was not there in front of his eyes; it was not part of the common archetype of the two codices, A and the Palimpsest. And so, having completed my philological detective work, I argue that the Palimpsest preserves the ancient diagram of Archimedes' *Sphere and Cylinder I*, 38 in fig. 4.7. Thus, we can go all the way back to Syracuse. I now move on to consider the deep conceptual significance of this.

The Logic of Greek Diagrams

Look at the diagram again. I just noted that I believe it is identical to the one drawn on the sands of Syracuse by Archimedes himself. And I believe it represents the most crucial fact about Greek diagrams— one that holds the key to their great success as cognitive and logical tools. It explains why ancient diagrams did, indeed, contribute to the proof, against everything said by modern philosophers and logicians.

I need first to tell you something about the lines AZHBΘΛΓ. In the diagram as it stands, the lines appear like a sequence of arcs, very much like the rounded edges of the drum of an ancient column. But what do they represent, geometrically? They represent a polygon—a sequence of straight lines. Indeed, in figure 4.8 you can see how the modern editor has chosen to represent the same figure. Instead of arcs he has used straight lines. He has preferred to call a spade a spade. If it's a polygon, let it appear like a polygon. This is not so with

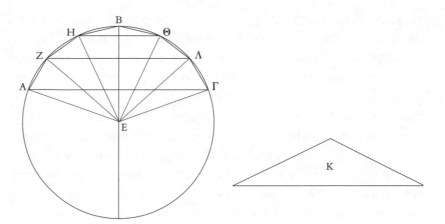

FIGURE 4.8 *A modern editor's representation of the same figure*

Archimedes, whose position appears to be that one may well draw a series of circular arcs to show a polygon—who cares how it looks?

This is not an isolated example. We can compare the diagrams that we could reconstruct, for example, for proposition 30 (see fig. 4.9). There are altogether fourteen examples of the same type of figure in this treatise. The circular arcs form a principle of the drawings in this treatise. And it is of deep significance.

First of all, I believe no one would dare introduce such a radical convention against the manuscript authority. Suppose you were a scribe and paid to copy diagrams from the original. The original has polygons. Well, you would copy them as polygons. You would not invent circular arcs instead. And this reason—that no one would introduce such a convention against the source—can be repeated again and again for each stage of the transmission. The only way to account for such a convention is to assume that it is due to the author himself. And so, this convention brings us to the shores of Syracuse—face to face with Archimedes. Let me confess: this thought does inspire me with awe. There is something particularly "tangible" about diagrams. Words are conceptual, but drawings are physical—they are bodily. This is how he, Archimedes, traced his figure, turning a stick in his hand. If indeed I am right, and I have succeeded in reconstructing

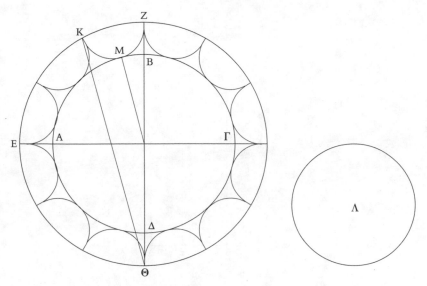

FIGURE 4.9 *Diagram for proposition 30*

the diagrams of Archimedes, then I have reconstructed some kind of extension of his body. Those are the traces left by him, personally.

And now, we progress to the next conceptual point. What does the convention of representing polygons by circular arcs mean? It is part of a very wide phenomenon I can identify in the diagrams of Archimedes (and in other diagrams in medieval manuscripts). Namely, the diagrams are *non-pictorial*. You draw a polygon, but you do not make your drawing look like one. Instead of being a *picture*, the ancient diagram is a *schematic representation*.

Here is another example, once again using figures from both the Palimpsest and the modern edition. This time we need to look at a figure for which the only contemporary evidence is from the Palimpsest—the first figure of the *Method*. It is in some ways the most important piece of visual evidence contained in the Palimpsest. Of course, since we only have a single source, we can no longer apply the philological method. We cannot compare this figure to those of other medieval manuscripts and in this way derive an original source. However, by looking elsewhere, we have already gained confidence

101

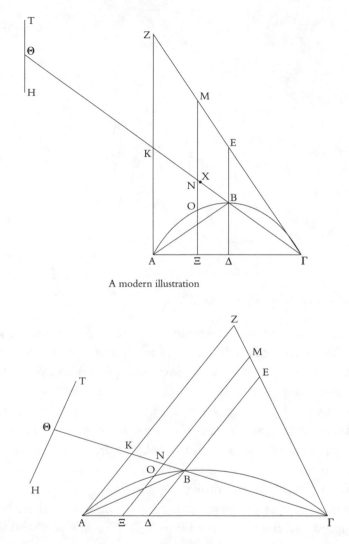

A modern illustration

The Palimpsest diagram

FIGURE 4.10 *Archimedes' Method 1*

in the Palimpsest. We have seen that, whenever it can be compared to other sources, the Palimpsest contains diagrams that appear to be authentic. And so our best guess is that the diagram here, too, is close to Archimedes' original spirit.

Finally, we need to compare the two drawings in figure 4.10. The modern one is "correct." The lines TH, ZA, etc. should indeed all be exactly parallel; line ZA should be exactly bisected at point K; and ΘΓ should be exactly bisected at the same point K. The curve ABΓ should indeed be a subtly curved, parabolic segment. In short, it is a pictorial diagram—one that is true to the object. The figure of the Palimpsest, on the other hand, is schematic. The line ZA is not exactly bisected at point K, nor is line ΘΓ. The curve ABΓ is drawn freehand as a kind of circular arc. Such are schematic drawings: they merely suggest the object without drawing it precisely at all.

Why did Greek mathematicians produce non-pictorial drawings? Why did they find the schematic satisfactory? Now, do not think for a moment that this was because ancient draftsmen were in any sense deficient. They could very well draw spectacular pictorial representations. The great discoveries of the Renaissance masters—perspective and illusion—were already made in antiquity. We know this mostly in a roundabout way. When the Romans pillaged such cities as Syracuse, they gained an appetite for Greek art, and they did their best to imitate it. In such lost cities as Pompeii, wall paintings tell us a lot about the level of ancient art, and they show a clear understanding of the geometrical principles of draftsmanship. Take for instance the rendering of depth and foreshortening in figure 4.11. The vanishing points are in place; the illusion is compelling. On a wall in Pompeii—and there were hundreds of such walls in Pompeii alone—one can admire the Greek understanding of the optical principles of painting. And there is no doubt that such an optical understanding existed in antiquity. We have extant several treatises in optics, one of which by Euclid even contains a theorem specifically on pictorial foreshortening—a wheel, seen from the side, looks like an ellipse and not like a circle! In other words, the wheels in the wall painting from Pompeii go back to knowledge shared by Euclid himself.

Yet, paradoxically, nothing of this splendid draftsmanship is in evidence in Greek mathematical diagrams. Greek mathematicians chose

FIGURE 4.11

to avoid the pictorial on purpose and instead preferred "free," schematic figures that do not represent their object. Why is that?

The reason is that those strange, counter-intuitive diagrams were the solution found by Greek mathematicians to the philosophical problem of using diagrams within proofs. This is a subtle, deep point. It deserves our close attention and admiration.

Remember what the philosophical trouble was with diagrams: namely, that they were particular. Your objective is to make a general point about triangles in general (how are triangles in general measured?). However, you can't draw a triangle in general; you must draw a particular triangle. If you happen to draw a right angle, then you might be misled into believing that the area of a triangle, in general, is the product of the smaller sides divided by two. You come to rely on the particular properties of that particular diagram.

But is it really necessarily the case that a particular diagram suggests a particular property? This is the subtle point. I could draw a green triangle, a blue circle, and a red square. But if I wanted to make a geometrical argument about them, I wouldn't refer to their color. In the Western tradition, we do not think of colors as geometrically significant. The color appears to be merely incidental; it is not part of the drawing at all as far as the geometry is concerned. It is there merely because it is impossible to draw a triangle without choosing some kind of color. Usually, of course, we use black. But this does not make our geometry "the geometry of black figures." Color is simply irrelevant.

Now imagine a tradition where the same is true for such properties as the size of an angle. So that, for instance, a polygon may be represented by a series of circular arcs and no one thinks that there is anything wrong. Because, you see, such properties as the precise angles are simply irrelevant. This is not what a geometrical figure represents. The precise angles are rather like the color. So that, when we draw a right-angled green triangle it is no more right-angled than it is green. Of course, it *happens* to be right-angled just as it *happens* to be green, but both the color and the precise angle are irrelevant and are discarded by the sophisticated reader. Only a naive child would see a "green" triangle. And only a naive modern reader—untrained in ancient diagrams—would see a right-angled triangle.

To put this in the most general terms: ancient diagrams are schematic, and in this way they represent the broader, *topological* features of a geometrical object. Those features are indeed general and reliable; a diagram represents them just as well as language represents them. And so, ancient diagrams can form part of the logic of an argument which is perfectly valid.

We have learned, therefore, something crucial and surprising about Archimedes' thought process, about his interfaces. He essentially relied on the visual; he used schematic diagrams that can be used in perfect logical rigor without danger of error based on visual evidence. When Archimedes gazed at his diagrams along the Syracusan seashore, he saw figures largely similar to those that we can reproduce today based on the Palimpsest. And I know that what he saw there was a crucial part of his thought process—one of the most basic tools that made Greek science so successful.

Mathematics Is Beautiful

It was for good reason, then, that Archimedes had a diagram put on his tomb. His reasoning inherently involved diagrams. And those diagrams were used in a clever, subtle way—very different from that of

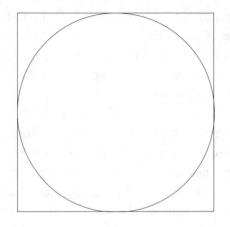

FIGURE 4.12

modern illustrations—so that they could serve as part of the logic of the argument.

Indeed, I think I may have a guess concerning the shape of Archimedes' tomb. I think it was very simple. Greek geometrical diagrams avoid the complex effects of perspective and three-dimensional illusion. How to represent a sphere and a cylinder, then? Simply by a square enclosing a circle. I believe this may have been all that there was (perhaps with the statement, inscribed underneath, that the cylinder was one and a half the sphere). A simple, austere figure. The ancients often inscribed epigrams—short, suggestive poems of farewell and regret—upon their tombs. This diagram served as such a succinct, effective visual epigram. Perhaps it was something such as figure 4.12.

Beautiful visual epigram that it was, it would have been resonant with meaning. It would have suggested many other objects, many other discoveries. The same figure of a square enclosing a circle would first of all bring to mind Archimedes' achievement of the measurement of a circle—his remarkable approximation of Pi. And the square and the circle could equally have suggested rectangles and parabolas, referring to Archimedes' many important discoveries concerning parabolas and other conic sections in the *Quadrature of the*

Parabola, On Conoids and Spheroids, On Floating Bodies and, of course, in the *Method* itself. Indeed, a circle within a square would quite directly represent the theme common to most of Archimedes' works—his obsession: measuring curved objects. Of course, I offer merely a guess. Yet I find this reconstruction of the tomb attractive. It combines simplicity of form and complexity of meaning, a visual epigram and a work appropriate to the subtle storytelling genius of Archimedes. It is in this sense that Archimedes' science was beautiful.

Of course this is not the only kind of beauty one can imagine. Greek mathematical diagrams were austere. Other ancient pictures— we can once again remind ourselves of Pompeii (see fig. 4.11)—were quite the opposite. The beauty of Pompeian paintings was lavish—as no doubt was that of many mansions in Syracuse in the year 212 BC. Nor is mathematics necessarily austere. In the seventeenth century, for instance, Archimedes took a very different form. Rivault's edition of Archimedes—incidentally the one used by Newton—was produced in Paris in 1615, and it represented the rich tastes of French monarchs (to whom it was dedicated). The figures of the sphere and the cylinder were lavishly executed with the aid of three-dimensional perspective. The images of Rivault are ravishing, but they have little to do with the mathematical significance of the works of Archimedes. Indeed, by suggesting that diagrams are precise illustrations, Rivault destroys the specific achievement of ancient diagrams—their austere, abstract precision as topological, schematic drawings.

The beauty inherent in such austere drawings can be quite compelling, purely on visual grounds. Archimedes' study *Spiral Lines* is very markedly visual in this respect. Almost all of its figures are arresting and one has the impression that Archimedes studies the spiral partly because of an aesthetic, visual fascination. The Palimpsest figure of proposition 21 (see fig. 4.13) is one of the most beautiful. (It is, of course, partly obscured by the prayer-book writing.) It is deeply austere, deeply non-pictorial. Look carefully, and you will notice that the spiral is not drawn as a true spiral, smoothly curved, but rather as a sequence of arcs of different circles.

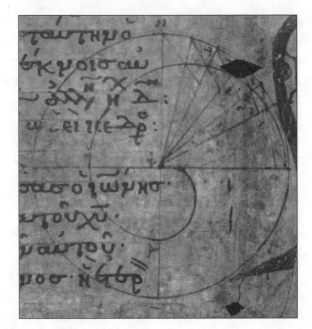

FIGURE 4.13

The small straight lines are especially telling. They form, indeed, the exact analogue to the curved polygons we saw in *Sphere and Cylinder*. Once again, we see the non-pictorial character of Greek diagrams. Those small straight lines each stand for a small arc. (In *Sphere and Cylinder* arcs are drawn to represent straight lines, and in *Spiral Lines* straight lines are drawn to represent arcs.)

This, of course, is Archimedes in the year AD 975. It is largely faithful to the ancient Archimedes, I believe, not only in its diagrams, but in its entire visual impact. The narrow columns, for instance, are significant: they hark back to the writing on papyrus rolls (which were written in a sequence of very narrow columns). As mentioned, we have no exact parallel to compare them with from antiquity itself, but there are, of course, a number of scientific works that have survived in papyrus form. They are not as important as those by Archimedes or by Euclid, but still they tell us a lot about the appearance of ancient science. The earliest of them all is a very minor astronomical text known as the *Ars Eudoxi*, which is extant in Paris. It is kept at the Louvre Museum, where it is known simply as "Pap. Gr. 1," i.e. Greek papyrus number one. It is a very ancient piece of papyrus indeed—from the late third century BC. Possibly, this piece of papyrus could have been inscribed while Archimedes was still alive. Its narrow columns, rough, schematic figures, and clean, yet unornamented, writing are all suggestive of what we have since learned about the manuscript tradition of Archimedes himself. I believe this is what ancient science looked like.

It would not have been in book form, of course. As Will Noel has mentioned, this is the major difference from the Palimpsest. Ancient writings took the form of a roll, not a book. Instead of leafing through Archimedes, you would roll him out. Will has pointed out how inconvenient this is for extracting information from, say, a dictionary. But I think the roll is, in fact, quite handy for the continuous reading of geometry. The reason Will is right is that, at about the time people were making the transition from roll to codex, they were also making the transition from a culture where continuous reading mattered most, to one where extraction of information was paramount. This was the world of the ultimate reference work—the Bible.

The roll is more convenient for geometry, as the following consideration suggests. Have you ever read a piece of geometry that extended beyond a couple of pages? You will recall the experience, then, of leafing back and forth while you were reading, from text to diagram and back, forgetting the diagram while reading the text and then forgetting the text while reading the diagram. The roll in this respect is a much better interface. (I say, books on geometry should be printed on rolls!) You roll out the book so that you have in front of your eyes, perfectly, the entire text together with the figure. Such was the ancient mathematical roll—a polished piece of spare design. Think of it as the equivalent of an elegant Italian coffee machine—simple lines joined together to make a perfect product.

The simplicity would be not only in the drawings but also in the writing itself. This is a major consideration in the history of writing—not only for mathematics but for any writing whatsoever. In time, writing diversifies. Ancient writing was simpler than ours. Instead of the many fonts we use, and especially instead of the division we have between uppercase and lowercase characters, the ancients knew just one font, just one case—effectively, the upper one. THIS IS WHAT ANCIENT WRITING LOOKED LIKE. This is what the *Ars Eudoxi* looks like, and this is how Archimedes' original writings looked. Which is simple and elegant, in its own way.

As writing gets diversified, the interface changes. In the Middle Ages—i.e., in the Palimpsest—the writing used to copy Archimedes would already have been different. And this, too, is important for the history of mathematical interfaces. I have already said that, today, the emblem of mathematics is the equation, the arrangement of symbols. And this is the product of a long historical process whose roots lie in the Middle Ages. Once again, let us turn to the Archimedes Palimpsest.

The Medieval Origins of Mathematical Symbols

The Palimpsest is an important piece of evidence not only for the year 225 BC but also for the year AD 975. The scribe who copied the works of Archimedes perhaps did not do much to advance the concepts of mathematics. He was no Archimedes. In fact, I am sure the scribe knew no mathematics at all. But he did make a contribution to the history of the *interfaces* of mathematics. His choices in the manner of writing down the words, arranging them on the page, and putting the works together all made a contribution to the way Archimedes would be read by later mathematicians. This is true throughout history, all the way from Archimedes in Syracuse down to the present day. Scribes, typesetters, and publishers make a silent contribution to the history of science, sometimes as important as that of the scientists themselves.

Silently, scribes have invented the mathematical symbol. By doing so, they paved the way for the modern equation—the most powerful tool of modern science. While faithfully copying Archimedes' dia-

FIGURE 4.14 *Sphere and Cylinder II: A phrase from proposition 2*

grams, the scribe from the year 975 AD was already preparing the way for the equations of today's science.

Let us look at a passage from the Palimpsest. Figure 4.14 is from the second proposition of the second book on *Sphere and Cylinder.* Just as we saw with the Greek diagrams, the writing in the original Greek produced by Archimedes had no frills at all. ARCHIMEDES WROTE LIKE THIS, or, more precisely, ARCHIMEDESWROTE-LIKETHIS (word division, too, is a medieval invention). In particular, Archimedes' text had no abbreviations: he spelled every word out fully.

A scribe's work is very tedious—copying, word after word, character after character. It just makes so much more sense to abbreviate. If a word is repeated often, why not invent a symbol to represent this word directly, instead of copying it again and again? Of course there are aesthetic disadvantages to it. With too many abbreviations the text may no longer look like Greek and begin to look like stenography. With a work of poetry, for example, produced for a high price, you would not use many abbreviations. But for a technical work, such as mathematics, which was probably not very highly paid, you might. The Archimedes Palimpsest is an example of a fine, polished piece of scribal craftsmanship, but it is not a luxury manuscript. No one would have stopped the scribe from using scribal abbreviations.

And so we go back to the text of *Sphere and Cylinder*. Here is a translation of his text:

> (1) Therefore as the [line] ΚΘ to the [line] ΘΕ, the [line] ΘΕ to [the line] ΕΓ, and therefore as the [square] on ΚΔ to the [rectangle contained] by ΚΘΔ, the [square] on ΑΓ to the [rectangle contained] by ΑΕΓ

You will notice first of all that my English translation takes up much more space than the Greek text in the manuscript. There are two reasons for this, one due to Archimedes, the other due to the medieval scribes. The first is the square brackets. Archimedes did not write in such words as "line," "square," "rectangle," letting the reader infer them from the context. In this way, he was capable of writing a very spare text. The language used by Archimedes was a piece of polished, minimalist design on par with his skeletal, polished diagrams. He used very few words, because the readers already knew what kinds of things he was talking about (just as the readers could "read" the minimalist diagrams correctly, because they could understand their nature as *mathematical* diagrams). Since Archimedes used only uppercase letters and no word division, his text looked like this:

(2)THEREFOREASTHEΚΘTOTHEΘΕTHEΘΕTOEΓ ANDTHEREFOREASTHEONΚΔTOTHEBYΚΘΔ THEONAΓTOTHEBYΑΕΓ

This, indeed, is somewhat challenging as an interface.

Medieval scribes, at this point, took some crucial steps in the invention of more effective typesetting interfaces. The use of several cases—an uppercase alongside a lowercase—is of great value. It allows us to separate the letters referring to the diagram (which remain in uppercase) from the rest (which is now in lowercase). Word division was another major invention. The two together bring us to a text that is more familiar to us:

(3) Therefore as the KΘ to the ΘE, the ΘE to EΓ, and therefore as the on KΔ to the by KHΔ, the on AΓ to the by AEΓ

At this point the medieval scribes introduced yet another major invention—their own contribution to making the text compact—abbreviations. They did not do this because of any deep, sophisticated mathematical reason. They did this because they were *lazy*. Instead of copying out the word *pros* (the Greek for "to") time and time again, they simply inserted a symbol that looked somewhat like our capital sigma, Σ. There are other abbreviations or symbols, such as for "as" (a bit like ω), for "and" (a bit like *K*), and "therefore" (a bit like ε), all marked in figure 4.14. So this is what the text finally looks like:

(4) ε ω the KΘ Σ the ΘE, the ΘE Σ EΓ, *K* ε ω the on KΔ Σ the by KΘΔ, the on AΓ Σ the by AEΓ

Note also that the Greek word "the" can often be written out in one or two characters (it changes according to gender and case), instead of the three characters used in the English "the." I represent this by an abbreviation, *t'*, to allow us to get the full flavor of the original writing:

(5) ε ω *t'* KΘ Σ *t'* ΘE, *t'* ΘE Σ EΓ, *K* e ω *t'* on KΔ Σ*t'* by KΘΔ, *t'* on AΓ Σ*t'* by AEΓ

This, too, may well appear rather confusing, and you may even prefer the full form of example (1) above to the abbreviations in example (5). You may feel that example (5) is written out in hieroglyphics. But this is all a matter of habit: one simply needs to learn this particular notation just the way we learn our own modern notations. For instance, a modern mathematician may well put down the same text as follows:

(6) KΘ:ΘE::ΘE:EΓ
→ KΔ^2:KΘ*ΘΔ::AΓ^2:AΓ*EΓ

which is exactly as hieroglyphic as example (5). Archimedes himself would have had no idea what example (6) was talking about, just as a modern reader, faced with example (5), has no idea what it's about. One has to learn the notation and then the hieroglyphs make perfect sense as a symbolic rendering of the contents.

For this is the deep point. All the examples—from (1) to (6)—contain *exactly* the same meaning, merely with a change of packaging. The difference is in the interface. But what a difference an interface makes! Indeed, the invention of abbreviated notations is one of the key steps in the growth of modern science.

The history of this invention still needs to be charted. Scholars have only very recently started to look at medieval manuscripts, not as containers of information about antiquity, but as interesting documents in their own right. How did scribes come to invent a system such as that in example (5)? We still do not know the full answer; we are still collecting the evidence. As the earliest extant manuscript of Archimedes, the Palimpsest will form one of the key pieces of evidence for this research.

The broad outlines of this history—the history of the scientific interface—are, however, clear. The transition was made from the science of diagrams to the science of equations. Indeed, these may be seen as two different ways of utilizing human visual skills within this highly conceptual field of mathematical thought. From one kind of visual science—the Greek one based on the diagram—we have made the transition to another kind of visual science—the modern one based on the symbol and the equation.

The Archimedes Palimpsest stands midway: as the best evidence we can gain, indirectly, on the old science of diagrams; and as a major piece of evidence for the new (nascent) science of symbols and equations.

The Mathematical Experience

Everything I have referred to—the nature of the mathematical diagram, the beauty of the mathematical page, the invention of mathematical symbolism—leads to a single point: mathematics is a matter of experience. Of course, mathematics is a highly conceptual, abstract discipline. But even an abstract content has to be mastered by a human person, somehow. It has to be sensed through the eyes. As humans, we are capable of understanding abstract concepts, but we can only understand them via our experience. The most abstract concepts must have some sensual packaging, in the sounds of language and in the artifacts of vision. For humans, to understand is, first of all, to see and hear.

In recent decades, this is the emerging consensus among philosophers, logicians, historians, and cognitive scientists: cognition and logic, the abstract and the concrete, are ultimately inseparable. Which, in a sense, is something paleographers—the scholars of ancient writing—knew all along.

In the study of ancient manuscripts one is used to questions like: How is the text written? What are the visual tools invented by the scribe? How is the page meant to work? When studying a manuscript, one is led to a study of both content and form. The ideas conveyed by the text may be abstract, but their physical form is not. This is indeed a physical object—as Will Noel calls it, Archimedes' brain in a box. This is the purpose of it all: by the study of the cognitive history of diagrams and symbols and of pages and manuscripts, we may gain an understanding of Archimedes' own brain as it worked back then, at Syracuse.

Only, when I met Will Noel in the spring of 1999, one could barely glimpse any of this evidence. The manuscript made in 975 AD had been nearly obliterated by the millennium separating us from Byzantium's heyday. It is time to rejoin John Dean and Will Noel in their journey across the Mediterranean in order to understand how this came to pass—how this manuscript was changed beyond recognition; and yet, time and again, managed, against the odds, to survive.

5

The Great Race, Part II
The History of the Palimpsest

Disaster Strikes

Back in Constantinople, John Dean and I climbed up the Galata Tower and looked out. Beyond the Golden Horn, the glorious panorama of Constantinople was spread before us. Hagia Sophia and the Blue Mosque dominated the view. The mosque was a reminder that Constantinople fell to the Ottoman Turks in 1453. This is often heralded as a great tragedy, - but the really disastrous sack of Constantinople had already happened 250 years earlier. It was perpetrated by Christians from Western Europe.

In 1204, the Fourth Crusade, sanctioned by Pope Innocent III, had to get from Europe to Egypt and from there, in theory, to the Holy Land. The problem was how to get to Egypt. The Doge of Venice was prepared to provide a fleet for 4,000 knights, 9,000 squires, and 20,000 foot soldiers, but at the price of 86,000 marks. The crusaders agreed, but they were 34,000 marks short when they were ready to sail. So they agreed to recapture the Dalmatian city of Zara for the Venetians and their portion of the loot would make up the difference. The crusaders trashed Zara, but after they had pillaged the town their loot was still not enough to pay the debt. The crusaders could not, in honor, default on their debt to the Doge. There was an imperative to recover it. How to do this? Politics supplied the answer. Isaac II, Emperor of Constantinople, had been ousted by Alexius II in 1195, blinded and thrown in a dungeon. Isaac's daughter was married to Philip of Swabia, and his son, Alexius Angelus, was also at Philip's court. Alexius Angelus agreed to pay the crusaders and the Doge of Venice 200,000 marks if they would install him on the throne of Constantinople. The Pope would be happy because Alexius Angelus agreed that the city would become Catholic; the Doge would be happy because he would get his money and trading privileges, and the powerful Philip of Swabia would have a puppet on the throne of Constantinople. Even modern politics doesn't get much grubbier than this.

The realities of medieval conquest do. The crusaders succeeded in toppling Alexius II. Alexius Angelus was made co-emperor of Constantinople with his father Isaac II. But with their puppet in place, the crusaders' debt still remained. Constantinople was in no position to pay the money that Alexius had promised. While the crusaders were waiting for their money, a few of them started attacking a mosque. A fire broke out in the chaos that followed. It spread quickly and soon great tracts of the city stood in flames. The fire lasted for eight days killing hundreds and destroying a strip three miles wide running right through the middle of the ancient city. Still the money was not forthcoming. Alexius, not surprisingly, lost the support of Constantinople's beleaguered inhabitants. He was strangled and his father Isaac II died of grief. Hostilities broke out again. On Monday, April 12, 1204, the crusaders breached the ancient walls of Theodosius. That same night another great fire broke out. The next day Constantinople surrendered. But it was only then that the full horror—the horror recorded first hand by Nicetas Choniates—began. As a result, the cash went into the coffers of the Doge, the city went into the hands of the crusaders, the Catholic faith was imposed upon the Orthodox, and the classics went up in flames.

This was truly a cataclysmic event for the texts of the ancient world. The ark of the classics was burned. This is how and when twenty of the thirty-three historians discussed by Photius disappeared. Who knows how many copies of Archimedes' treatises? The future of these treatises was not in Constantinople. The copies that survived in the thirteenth century would be found elsewhere. Codices A, B and C were flotsam upon the waters of the Mediterranean world. Let's see where they washed up—first Codices A and B, and then C, the book on my desk.

Archimedes in Italy

In 1881 a scholar named Valentin Rose came across a manuscript in the great Vatican Library. It was written by William of Moerbeke, a Franciscan friar and a great translator of Greek texts including several works of Aristotle. This particular book was his translation of the works of Archimedes from the Greek into Latin. He finished writing the book on Tuesday, December 10, 1269. Since William became a chaplain and penitentiary of Pope Clement IV at Viterbo, Italy, some time in the 1260s, and was still there in 1271, he must have translated Archimedes' treatises there.

But from which manuscripts did William translate, and where did he get them? There were two of them, and they were listed in a catalogue of manuscripts belonging to the Pope at Viterbo in 1311. They were the manuscripts that today we call Codex A and Codex B. Number 612 was Codex A. Even in 1269 it couldn't have been in great shape because it was already missing its cover. In the catalogue, the codex is recorded as Angevin. This probably means that Charles I of Anjou gave it to the Pope after the Battle of Benevento in 1266. Number 608 was Codex B. Since Codex A did not contain *Floating Bodies*, we can assume that William must have translated this treatise from Codex B.

So Codices A and B washed up in Italy. Codex B, however, didn't last very long. It has been missing since 1311. Codex A, on the other hand, became one of the most highly sought after codices of the Italian Renaissance. In 1450 it was in the possession of Pope Nicholas V who commissioned Jacopo of Cremona to translate it again. In 1492 Lorenzo de Medici—Il Magnifico—sent

Politian on a search for texts that he didn't have in his own library. Politian found Codex A in the library of Giorgio Valla in Venice, and he had a copy of it made. This copy is now housed in Michelangelo's architectural masterpiece, the Laurentian Library, in Florence. Valla thought Codex A was so precious and rare that he would not permit it to leave his library. He even declined a request to borrow it from Ercole d'Este, Duke of Ferrara. Alberto Pio of Carpi bought Giorgio Valla's library. When Pio died in 1531, the manuscript became the possession of his nephew Ridolfo Pio, who died in 1564. No one has seen Codex A since then.

Even though they disappeared, Codices A and B did their job: they transmitted Archimedes to the modern world. The reception of Archimedes has been meticulously documented in the monumental work of scholarship by Marshall Clagett, *Archimedes in the Middle Ages*. Whether it was directly through Codex A or through the Latin translations by William of Moerbeke and Jacopo of Cremona, Archimedes' treatises came into the hands of the most talented men of the Renaissance. The Renaissance was, of course, well disposed to receiving the works of this great man.

The Archimedes of legend had already become a byword for brilliant inventors and mathematicians. Filippo Brunelleschi, for example, was heralded as a "Second Archimedes" after building the magnificent dome of Florence Cathedral early in the fifteenth century. Renaissance figures soon learned that the Archimedes of the treatises far surpassed the legendary figure. Leon Battista Alberti, the great Florentine author, architect, and painter knew about *Floating Bodies* and utilized it in his exposition of the "*Eureka*" story. More impressively, as James Banker showed in 2005, Piero della Francesca, whose paintings reveal astonishing subtleties of geometry, had actually transcribed the full text of Jacopo of Cremona's translation. Regiomontanus, the German mathematician whose work was so important to Copernicus, also copied Jacopo's translation after the Pope had given it to Cardinal Bessarion. By hook or by crook the great artistic and mathematical minds of the Renaissance got their hands on Archimedes' treatises. In 1544, the first edition of the works of Archimedes was printed in Basle. For many of Archimedes' treatises, the race against destruction was over, and they had won. Galileo and Newton would read them, and modern science would be born.

The Book Leonardo Never Knew

It might strike you that I have neglected one of the greatest minds of the Renaissance—Leonardo da Vinci. We have established that from Hero onward, Archimedes was of interest to the foremost mathematicians and architects of the day—intellectuals who had not only mastered higher mathematics but who also wanted to apply their knowledge. It is, therefore, no surprise to learn that Leonardo was also anxious to obtain copies of Archimedes' works. In his notebook he writes: "A complete Archimedes is in the hands of the brother of the Monsignor of Santa Giusta in Rome. He said that it had been given to his brother who was in Sardinia. It was first in the library of the Duke of Urbino but was taken away at the time of Duke Valentino." Somehow Leonardo must have succeeded in acquiring some Archimedes manuscripts. His notebooks reveal knowledge of the *Measurement of the Circle, Spiral Lines, Sphere and Cylinder, Floating Bodies,* and *Balancing Planes.* The last named of these treatises particularly fascinated Leonardo as it dealt with finding centers of gravity. Leonardo used it to demonstrate how to find the center of gravity of a triangle. (In the next chapter, with Reviel, you will be doing the same.) Being Leonardo, however, he did not stop with what he discovered from Archimedes. He used Archimedes' work as a platform for his own calculations. In *Balancing Planes,* Archimedes had only discussed how to find the center of gravity in plane figures. Leonardo went beyond this. Applying Archimedes' techniques, Leonardo attempted to find the centers of gravity in solid ones, too. He ended up developing a theorem for finding the center of gravity in a tetrahedron. It was a remarkable achievement by this Renaissance giant and an example of the way that Renaissance scholars built on the work of Archimedes.

However, there was one treatise that Leonardo did not know about. Consequently, he could not have known that Archimedes had gone way beyond him 1,700 years earlier. In the *Method*, Archimedes had already found the centers of gravity for much more complicated solids than the tetrahedron—solids with curved surfaces. In his letter to Eratosthenes, Archimedes had calculated the center of gravity for a paraboloid, a spherical segment, a segment of an ellipsoid, and even a segment of a hyperboloid. It's not that Leonardo researched his subject inadequately; Leonardo couldn't have known about this text. It wasn't part of Codex A or Codex B, the only two Greek manuscripts by which Archimedes was known during the Renaissance. It was part of Codex C. Or rather, it had been.

A Write-off

A thirteenth-century scribe prepared himself for a job. He had gone through the procedures many times before. He had already prepared his reed pens, his ruler, and his knife. He sat down in his chair. Beside him was a small table with an inkwell filled with black ink. He took the first sheet of parchment from a stack nearby. With a hard point, he incised lines on the parchment upon which he would shortly write his letters. The parchment now rested in his lap on top of a board. In front of the scribe on a stand was the codex that he was about to copy. He was poised to write. Are you experiencing déjà vu? Excellent. Look at the scene again. This time we are not particularly interested in the codex on the stand. It is the parchment that the scribe is about to use that should be the object of our curiosity. The parchment was going through a process it had been through before.

You have guessed it, of course. This scribe's parchment was Codex C, the Archimedes manuscript from *Balancing Planes* to *Stomachion, Method* included. It had been taken apart and its folios erased of text. The scribe had more prayers to write than he had Archimedes

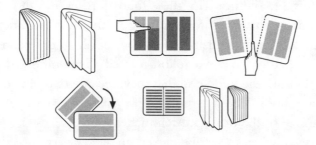

FIGURE 5.1 *How to make a palimpsest*

parchment to write on, but this didn't stop him. He simply reused parchment from other codices as well—at least four of them.

The palimpsesting of Archimedes and of all the other unidentified texts in the prayer book was a ruthless operation. The manuscripts were taken from their shelves, their bindings were cut off and discarded, and the stitching between their quires was undone. This was quick and easy to do. Once the codex was in pieces, the bifolios were scrubbed with some kind of natural acid. There are no Greek texts telling us how this was done, but Theophilus, writing *On Various Arts* in Western Europe in the twelfth century, suggests that by using orange juice and a sponge it is quite easy to erase the letters perfectly. There is no doubt that some kind of acidic mixture was used, but the operation on the Palimpsest was much more severe than the one prescribed by Theophilus. Abigail found holes on the edges of the Archimedes bifolios that appear to have been made by nails, which held the pages under tension. This would be consistent with damp bifolios being tacked down to a board to prevent shrinking as they dried out. Abigail further noticed that there were scratch marks on top of the Archimedes text. After the bifolios had dried, it appears that they were further rubbed with a pumice stone. It's done. Archimedes is gone. The skins on which his texts had been written were removed from their wooden frames and stacked in a corner.

The first thing the scribe did upon picking up an Archimedes bifolio was to cut it in two down the fold, thereby separating it into two folios. He did not trim these folios further and this is lucky for us; on each surviving folio none of the residual traces of the Archimedes text were trimmed by the maker of the palimpsest. The scribe then took the two folios, rotated them ninety degrees, and folded them in the middle so that they became two nested bifolios in the prayer book. The folios of the prayer book are therefore exactly half the size of the original Archimedes folios.

However, when the scribe picked up separate Archimedes bifolios, the bifolios were already highly disordered, so different bifolios of the Archimedes text are now found widely separated from each other in the prayer book. They are also found interspersed with palimpsested parchment of the other manuscripts that the scribe used. The Archimedes manuscript formed the overall skeleton of the Palimpsest; the parchment of other manuscripts fleshed it out.

It was standard practice in making palimpsests for the scribe to cut the bifolios in half and rotate them, and it made good sense. The great advantage of the procedure was that the scribe did not have to contend with the distracting remains of a palimpsested text because he was writing at right angles to it. It is far easier to write over a text at right angles than it is to follow its path. Of course, the scribe could have rotated the scrubbed bifolios without cutting them down the middle and simply folded them in half the other way. But, the result would have been an extremely tall, thin, and unwieldy codex. The procedure followed by our scribe was carefully designed to produce new codices effectively and economically. For this reason, palimpsested codices are nearly always half the size of the codices from which they were made. Of course, since a folio of the Archimedes manuscript became a bifolio of the prayer book, it could, and often did, constitute both the first and last folio of a quire in the new manuscript. As a result, the middle of each of the old Archimedes folios passes right through the spine of the prayer book.

If he knew what he was about to copy over, the scribe did not even give it a second thought. The first piece of parchment in his new codex contained *On Floating Bodies*. He covered it with a blessing for loaves at Easter. Further into the codex, he wrote over a different section with a prayer for repentance. He wrote over the beginning of the *Method* with a prayer of marriage. Over a later section of the *Method,* he wrote a prayer recited at the foundation of a church. And, note this, over Archimedes' critical proposition 14, he wrote a prayer for the dead.

For a short section of the prayer book our scribe worked with a colleague. He was probably glad to get the help because it was a long job. Indeed it was so long that the Archimedes manuscript could not by itself supply all the necessary parchment, and other codices had to be used too. Since no one who had investigated the Archimedes Palimpsest was very interested in these codices, it is entirely appropriate that over a folio of one of them the scribes wrote a prayer for those unreasonably excluded.

It may have made good sense to them, but the scribes of the prayer book had really stitched up Archimedes. Think about it. If some odd duck ever wanted, for some strange reason, to read any one of the palimpsested texts, it would be great fun to watch them try. For example, if someone was interested in the text of *Method,* proposition 14, they would have trouble finding it. It starts on column 1 of folio 110 recto of the Palimpsest. To read it, they would need to turn the codex ninety degrees and read through the prayer book text—the prayer for the dead—to decipher the erased text beneath. Very soon they would get stuck, because the column disappears into the gutter. They would then need to find where it reappears. In this case, it appears five folios further back on folio 105v. On this folio, they would not be able to read at least two of the lines of text hidden in the gutter. If they persisted, they would have to read the second column of text too. Now things get yet more complicated. They would have to rotate the codex 180 degrees and read column 1 of folio 110v and then rotate it 180 degrees to read the bottom of this column on folio 105r. To finish this folio, they would have to repeat this operation to read the second column. Having read as much of this folio as they could, they would then need to find the next folio of Archimedes text. It could be anywhere in the codex. Actually it is on folio 158, more than fifty folios further along in the prayer book. Then the whole process would start all over again. A truly interactive user experience. But nobody would ever do this, would they? I mean, it's a mug's game.

So what was the name of the Christian scribe who did this? And what, if any, are the mitigating circumstances that the defense can summon up before we pass judgment on him for obliterating Archimedes? Having no idea how to answer these questions, I roundly condemn an anonymous medieval scribe and move on. The book moved on, too, and when we can trace it next, it is three hundred years later and on a different continent.

Buried in the Desert

John Dean and I left Constantinople behind and flew to the Holy Land. We arrived in Tel Aviv, hired a car, and headed for Jerusalem. We went to the Wailing Wall, which is the foundation of Solomon's Temple. We saw the Dome of the Rock where the prophet Muhammad ascended to Heaven and met with Allah. We visited the Church of the Holy Sepulcher where Christ was buried. The next day we headed south from Jerusalem, through the West Bank security checkpoint, and into a different world. We drove to Bethlehem and got lost. We missed our turn, and we couldn't speak Arabic. John's smile was a sign of friendship and my agitation an international signal of distress. The combination persuaded a very patient Palestinian to get us back on the right road.

We turned left, to the east, and into the desert. The road ended and we got out of the car. It was the early evening and the sun was low in the sky, but it was still extraordinarily dry and hot. To our left a boy on a donkey passed us, whacking his stick, and driving his goats back to the village. Apart from the bells around the necks of the animals, it was silent. We could see for miles across the Judaean desert. The sky was blue over Jordan; the land, everywhere, was burnt ochre. Below us, about a mile down a gravel path, I could see two towers. I had seen them before in a black and white nineteenth-century print above the desk of my friend, Patrick Zutshi, in Cambridge. They looked exactly the same, and I knew them to be the towers of the Monastery of St. Sabas.

The print I knew was by the Royal Academician David Roberts. He had arrived at the Monastery on Thursday, April 4, 1839 with the Reverend George Croly. They had initially approached the monastery from a different angle, from the east. Croly records:

> The immediate approach to the convent is striking . . . It was
> night when after having descended into the bed of a ravine,
> where the Kidron passes to the Dead Sea, and arriving at the
> foot of the Mountain of St. Saba, we saw the convent above us,
> by the uncertain light of the moon. It looked a lofty and colossal
> structure, rising in stories and terraces, one above another, against
> the sides of the mountain to its summit, and there crowned with
> clouds. An old white-bearded monk, leaning on his staff, was
> toiling up the side of the hill leading a long procession of
> devotees. Below, apparently growing out of the rock, was a large
> palm tree said to have been planted by the hands of the Saint in
> the fourth century. History, and probably legend, contributed its
> share to the effect. In a chapel behind an iron grating in one of
> the grottos was a pile of skulls. The tradition of the convent said
> they were those of hermits who, to the amount of several
> thousand, had been slaughtered by the Osmanlis [i.e. Ottomans].
> We ascended the flight of steps, climbed up a ladder, crept
> through a small door only large enough to admit one at a time,
> and found ourselves in an antechamber, surrounded by above a
> hundred Greek pilgrims . . . It was Passion Week. The monks
> receive strangers with courtesy, and they not merely permitted
> the artist to sketch their chapel, but as their service was
> beginning before he had finished his design, they would not
> suffer him to lay aside his pencil.

John and I went through the main door, which was in a round archway and painted deep blue. We were received warmly by the only monk in the community of thirteen who admitted to speaking

English. His given name was Lazarus, and he had come to the monastery from San Francisco. He showed us around the complex including the cell of St. Sabas and the chapel of St. Nicholas where the skulls of the departed members of the community are indeed housed. It is still the most extraordinary, beautiful, and spiritual place despite the political upheavals that constantly surround it. Everything was exactly as Croly had described it. It was as if time had melted away. Brother Lazarus had found peace at St. Sabas. He missed the Grateful Dead, but he was reminded of them by the insistent ringing of the semantron, a crescent-shaped metal bar by which a fellow monk, even at that moment, called him to prayer. Before he left us, he pointed to the taller of two towers that crowned the assemblage of churches and cells. St. Justinian's Tower, he said, contained the library. John and I had reached our destination. In 1834, there were more than 1,000 manuscripts in the library of St. Sabas. One of them, one of the least prepossessing, was the Archimedes Palimpsest.

We only know that the Archimedes Palimpsest was at St. Sabas because a Greek scholar, Papadopoulos-Kerameus, described the manuscript in 1899. He said there was a paper quire in the book, which was added in the sixteenth century, and in which there was an inscription indicating that the book belonged to the monastery. The manuscript doesn't have this quire any more and this inscription no longer exists. It is only thanks to Papadopoulos-Kerameus that we know how the Archimedes Palimpsest survived the centuries.

The Palimpsest contains prayers that the brothers in the monastery would have used on an almost daily basis. It includes a prayer said when something unclean falls into a vessel of wine, oil, or honey; there is St. Gregory's exorcism for unclean spirits; and John Chrysostom's prayer for Holy Communion, to name just a few of them. The Palimpsest shows every sign of frequent use. The codex is charred at the edges, as if has been scorched by the desert heat or even burned in a fire. Many of the folios are covered with wax droplets, which would have fallen on the manuscript as its prayers were recited by candlelight. There are many emendations and addi-

THE HISTORY OF THE PALIMPSEST

tions to the text and in some places the prayers have been traced over in order to make them more legible. Moreover, either through damage or because the prayers were no longer considered relevant, approximately sixty folios from the manuscript went missing while it was at St. Sabas. That is about a third of the entire codex.

The Monastery of St. Sabas provided a temporary respite for John and me and a more permanent sanctuary for Brother Lazarus. But, it was a tomb for Archimedes. The monks had every reason to read the prayers in the Palimpsest, but absolutely none to read what was beneath them. Abstract mathematics is not a priority at St. Sabas. Archimedes was effectively buried at the monastery for at least three hundred years. Unlike the texts in Codices A and B, those unique to Codex C remained unknown to the Renaissance and the Scientific Revolution. Somehow, like Brother Lazarus's biblical namesake, the Archimedes of the *Method* and *Stomachion* would have to be raised from the dead.

Signs of Movement

One of the last stops on my journey with John Dean was Lincoln College, Oxford to see a great scholar and a gentleman, Nigel Wilson. I have already spoken of Nigel, but it was only when I met him in Oxford that I got to know him. The first thing that struck me was that he was honored to meet us. This was only in part impeccable civility. It was mainly because I bore responsibility for the Palimpsest, work on which he would later describe as "one of the most fascinating scholarly projects imaginable." The Palimpsest really mattered to Nigel and this accounted for his remarkable patience when we filmed him over and over again in the college library repeating some of the simplest statements that he has ever contrived to utter. One sound bite he gave us was: "Constantinople was the one place in the ancient world with an unbroken tradition of copying and studying ancient texts." Another was: "I went to Cambridge, saw the leaf and said, 'That's it; that's Archimedes.'"

In truth, in 1971, acting on the suggestion of his friend G. J. Toomer of Brown University, Nigel set out from Oxford to

Cambridge to see a palimpsest fragment containing a mathematical text that had been catalogued by Pat Easterling. Nigel found it easy to read and he recognized it as Archimedes based on a technical term used in the text. It came from *Sphere and Cylinder* and it fits between folios 2 and 3 of the Palimpsest.

The fragment was in Cambridge University Library, and it had the number Add. 1879.23. The University Library logs its acquisitions and this was one of forty-four fragments that were sold to the library on Wednesday, February 23, 1876 by the executors of an estate. The estate had belonged to the German scholar Constantin Tischendorf.

Twenty years earlier, Constantin Tischendorf had made the greatest manuscript discovery of all time. This was not the Archimedes Palimpsest. It was the earliest surviving complete copy of the New Testament, together with substantial portions of the Old Testament in Greek. It is now known as the Codex Sinaiticus. It was written between about 330 and 350 AD, and it may be one of the original fifty copies of the scriptures commissioned by the Roman Emperor Constantine after his conversion to Christianity. It was written in the same type of majuscule script in which Isidore of Miletus would have written. Tischendorf found it in the ancient and secluded monastery of St. Catherine's in the Sinai Desert. Tischendorf negotiated with the monks to borrow the codex and conveyed it to the Russian Tsar Alexander. In return, the Tsar gave Tischendorf the title "Von" before his surname, thereby making the son of a German physician a Russian nobleman, and paid the monks 9,000 rubles for the codex. Good deal.

Tischendorf was, among other things, a very great biblical scholar. He had no difficulty recognizing the importance of the Codex Sinaiticus. But why was he in possession of a folio from the Palimpsest, and how on earth did he get a hold of it? Actually, he nearly tells us himself. In 1846, he published a book titled *Travels in the East*. In it he recounts a visit to the Metochion of the Holy Sepulcher in Constantinople where he found nothing of particular interest except for a palimpsest containing mathematics. In 1899, we know that the Palimpsest was at precisely this location because Papadopoulos-Kerameus then catalogued it there. Clearly it was already in the Metochion in the 1840s and clearly Tischendorf had come away from his visit with a folio torn from it.

Of course we do not know how the manuscript moved from St. Sabas back to Constantinople. When John Dean and I had tried to visit the Metochion of the Holy Sepulcher there was no one to ask. It was Easter and all the monks had gone to Jerusalem to their mother institution—the patriarchal Monastery of the Holy Sepulcher in Jerusalem. The manuscripts of St. Sabas had been incorporated into the library of the Greek patriarchate early in the nineteenth century. It is not hard to imagine, therefore, the circumstances in which a useful prayer book ended up back in the city in which it had been made seven hundred years earlier.

Back from the Dead

The front page of the *New York Times* on Tuesday, July 16, 1907 records a sensational discovery: Professor Heiberg, from Copenhagen, had discovered a new Archimedes manuscript in Constantinople. A certain Professor Schone had brought to Heiberg's attention the description of a codex in the 1899 catalogue by Papadopoulos-Kerameus. Papadopoulos-Kerameus didn't have tenure and was paid by the page for his work. Perhaps this is why when he catalogued manuscript number 355, he not only described the contents of the prayer book in detail but he also transcribed a section of an erased text that had been written over. Heiberg recognized the transcribed erased text as the work of Archimedes. He first tried, through diplomatic channels, to have the manuscript sent to Copenhagen, but this failed. So, during his 1906 summer vacation, he traveled to Constantinople and met the librarian, Mr. Tsoukaladakis, of the Metochion who allowed him to study the manuscript. This is when he discovered the staggering truth: Heiberg had found a sleeper, containing the unread greatest thoughts of a mathematician of genius.

Heiberg published Archimedes' letter to Eratosthenes, the *Method*, in an academic journal called *Hermes*. Between 1910 and 1915, Heiberg completely re-edited the works of Archimedes to incorporate his readings from the Palimpsest. His edition is ultimately based on three codices: Codex A (now lost), which was number 612 in the Pope's library in 1311; Codex B (now lost), which was number 608, and Codex C (now found), which is the Archimedes Palimpsest.

Heiberg's publications are the work of an extraordinary scholar, but they are also the work of a man limited by a number of factors. First, the physical constraints of the bound prayer book. As we have seen, the scribes of the prayer book constructed their manuscript in such a way that two or three lines in the middle of every folio of the original Archimedes manuscript were hidden from view in the gutter. In such places, Heiberg simply had to guess what was written. Secondly, he had to work with the technology of his day; he did not even use ultraviolet light, which is now a standard procedure for people reading faint texts. Thirdly, the intellectual framework within which he operated limited him. Heiberg was a philologist. A philologist is a lover of language, not of drawings. He paid no attention to the diagrams in the codex. For his *Hermes* publication he had a mathematical colleague named Zeuthen reconstruct the diagrams from the Archimedes text. But as Reviel jumped up and down to tell me, ancient mathematicians didn't think in text; they thought in diagrams. The Palimpsest was the unique source for the diagrams that Archimedes drew in the sand in the third century BC and they had never been studied. Finally, Heiberg was only really interested in Archimedes. He did mention that there were other works in the Palimpsest. He read just a few words of one of them, but he was only excited by the palimpsested pages that originally belonged to Codex C. Despite the work of the great Johan Ludwig Heiberg, there was still a great deal to be learned from the Archimedes Palimpsest.

So there was a lot of work that still needed to be done on the Palimpsest and scholars throughout the twentieth century knew it. However, they couldn't go and see it. The Archimedes Palimpsest had disappeared.

Lost in Paris

By 1938, the Metochion's manuscripts had been moved to the National Library of Greece in Athens. It was done under the noses of the Turkish authorities who had specifically forbidden such exports. Certainly this was safer than to have the books stay at the Metochion, because life there had become very unpleasant.

At the end of World War I, an English and French military presence in Constantinople supported the Sultan of a crippled Ottoman Empire. Mustafa Kemal—later Ataturk—left the capital and rallied Turkish nationalists to found the modern state of Turkey. In 1923, the Allies and the Sultan were ousted from Constantinople. In the process, Ataturk defeated the Greeks who had rashly invaded Turkey in 1921. In an early example of ethnic cleansing, hundreds of thousands of Greeks living in Turkey were forcibly transferred to Greece. In 1925, Ataturk abolished religious orders and hanged the Greek Patriarch of Constantinople.

It was in this atmosphere that the books in the Metochion were surreptitiously moved to Athens. There are no records of how it was done, but it was done very quietly. And the veil of silence that surrounded the Metochion manuscripts in the twenties and thirties must have been just too tempting for someone, because the Palimpsest was one of a number of spectacular manuscripts that never made it to Athens.

The Metochion's manuscripts that did not make it to Greece are now in various institutions, including the University of Chicago; the Cleveland Museum of Art; the Bibliothèque Nationale in France; Duke University; and the Walters Art Museum. Henry Walters bought one—a beautiful Gospel book, now Manuscript W.529. The Palimpsest was not nearly as beautiful as these books, but someone had done something about that. In one very striking respect the book looks very different from the one that Heiberg saw. The four painted pages that I thought were charming when I first looked at the book were not there when Heiberg studied it. The catalogue says:

> Four leaves, all now detached, are illuminated with full-page portraits, presumably intended to represent the Evangelists. Some of the colors look strangely modern . . . Neither Heiberg nor Papadopoulos-Kerameus in his description refers to them, so they must be relatively recent, presumably a misguided attempt at the Metochion to embellish the manuscript and enhance its value in the eyes of a prospective purchaser. The pictures have been painted over both upper and lower scripts. All four leaves are listed by Heiberg as containing text by Archimedes . . .

In other words, the pictures were forgeries. Gold, lead, copper, barium, zinc, and a whole host of other elements had been plastered over the flesh and iron that encoded the unique text of the letter that Archimedes had sent to Eratosthenes! As if the scribe of the prayer book had not done enough to obliterate Archimedes, his greedy successors had poured insult on to injury and painted over his corpse.

The auction catalogue merely says that the book left the Metochion and ended up in a private collection in France. However, the court case over the rightful ownership of the manuscript meant that further explanation had to be given. The result was a number of documents that Mr. B sent to me after the Palimpsest was left in my care. The most revealing of them is the sworn affidavit from someone named Robert Guersan. Robert Guersan, was the son of Anne Guersan, who had owned the manuscript before the sale. He believed that his grandfather, Marie Louis Sirieix, had acquired the Palimpsest in the 1920s and had kept it in his home in Paris.

Sirieix had served in Greece during World War I and had traveled in Greece and Turkey in the early 1920s. This was presumably when he acquired the manuscript. He had lived in Paris, served with distinction in the French Resistance during World War II, and left for the South of France in 1947. That is when he left the Palimpsest in the care of his daughter, who had moved into his apartment. He died in 1956.

In the 1960s, Anne Guersan began investigating the book she inherited. She sought the advice of Professor Bollack, a neighbor in Paris, and Professor Wasserstein from Leicester. In 1970, she left a few detached leaves of the codex with Father Joseph Paramelle at the Institut du Recherche et d'Histoire des Textes of the Center Nationale de la Recherche Scientifique in Paris. At that point, she knew what she had. In 1971, she took the book to the Etablissement Mallet "to remove fungus stains from a few of its pages and otherwise to preserve its condition." Then she tried selling it. In the 1970s, a short brochure was produced and it was discreetly offered for private sale to a number of individuals and institutions. All of them declined. Anne Guersan finally turned to Felix de Marez Oyens of the Manuscripts Department at Christie's.

The Palimpsest arrived on my desk on January 19, 1999 even before the legal issues, raised at the time of its sale, were resolved. While John Dean and I were on our jaunt around the Mediterranean, Christie's and the patriarchate were still thrashing things out in court. We had more fun than they did. They did not disagree over the facts. Instead, the case turned on the interpretation of the law, and Judge Kimba Wood ruled in favor of Christie's. According to French law, which she judged applied in this case, if Anne Guersan had owned the codex publicly, peacefully, continuously, and unambiguously for thirty years, she had the right to sell it. The burden of proof rested with the patriarchate's lawyer to demonstrate that she had not owned it in these circumstances and the patriarchate's lawyer did not come up with this evidence. Judge Wood also noted that, should New York law be deemed to apply, she would still rule in favor of Christie's, but on a different principle—the principle of laches. Generally, the principle of laches is applied when it is clear that a plaintiff unreasonably delayed in initiating an action and a defendant was unfairly prejudiced by the delay. Judge Wood must have thought that bringing an action the night before the auction was an unreasonable delay. The case was finally dismissed on Wednesday, August 18, 1999 by which time the exhibition was already open at the Walters.

I had learned a lot in five months. Sure, there were plenty of holes in the Palimpsest story, though I knew enough to think that it was tragic. I did not know the name of the scribe who had obliterated the Archimedes text, and I did not know when, why, or where he did it. But John had enough to make a movie, and I had enough for an exhibition. I could give it a happy ending by promising to reveal the erased texts despite all that had happened to the manuscript. "Eureka: The Archimedes Palimpsest" opened on Sunday, June 20, 1999 and traveled to the Field Museum in Chicago in the fall. The Palimpsest was opened to a folio on which visitors could just barely make out the diagram that accompanied proposition 1 of Archimedes' letter to Eratosthenes.

The exhibition started with John Dean's movie. The movie tells a strange story—ideas originate in the head of a man living on a triangle in the middle of the Mediterranean in the third century BC. These ideas are uniquely preserved today on a manuscript written in Constantinople twelve hundred years later. They survive the rise and fall of empires, the sacking of cities, and numerous changes in writing technology. And even though these ideas are scraped off and written over, they are still there. It is an astonishing journey. The letter beginning "Archimedes to Eratosthenes, Greetings," starts right at the top of folio 46r column 2 of Codex C and there alone. Delightfully, you can see the beginning of the letter and the name

"Archimedes" quite clearly before the column gets swallowed up by the text of the prayer book.

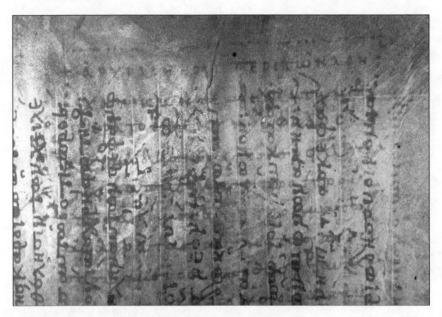

FIGURE 5.2 *The beginning of the* Method

6

Archimedes' *Method,* 1999
or The Making of Science

I was there in June 1999. What a sensation it was to see the Palimpsest opened to the first diagram of the *Method*! I had always dreamed of seeing this diagram. That it was partially hidden from sight, disappearing into the gutter, only added to its mystery. I saw all the visitors coming into the museum to gape at this modest-looking page, and I knew that they were looking at the only surviving evidence of Archimedes' greatest achievement.

The *Method* survives in the Palimpsest alone. There is no trace of it elsewhere—no other Greek manuscript, no Arabic version, no Latin translation. The Palimpsest is the only physical object in the universe to bear witness to this achievement of Archimedes. The *Method* is unique not only among the Archimedean works but also among all other mathematics produced prior to the sixteenth century. Back in June 1999, we already knew—thanks to Heiberg's transcription—that here Archimedes came closest to the modern calculus. We also knew that Archimedes came closest to revealing his method by which physics and mathematics can be brought together. These are the two keys to the science of Archimedes: the calculus, which is the mathematics of infinity, and the application of mathematics to physics. Mathematics, infinity, and physics: this triple combination is all present in the *Method*. We can see how by following two great mathematical proofs.

The first proof, an example of the application of mathematics to the physical world, is Archimedes' discovery of the center of gravity of a triangle. It is a result found outside the *Method*, but it is crucial for the understanding of how the *Method* works. The second proof is an example of the triple combination: mathematics, physics, and infinity. It is the first proposition of the *Method*, in which Archimedes finds the area of a parabolic segment. This brings us to the very height of Archimedes' achievement—collecting along the way the tool kit required for the making of modern science.

The Center of Gravity

The first tool we need for modern science is the minuscule size of a point, and it is of vast significance. Science cannot be made without it. It is the center of gravity.

Let us put ourselves in the place of a physicist—say, in Newton's place. We wish to consider the motions of heavenly bodies under the influence of gravity. There is a fundamental problem: stars and moons are large bodies; they possess *structure*. Let us apply this to the following example: the dark side of the Moon is further away from the Earth during a full moon than the bright side of the Moon. And so, the Earth's gravity acts less powerfully on the dark side, because it is further away, than on the bright side. If we wish to be precise, we can say that each point of the Moon has a slightly different gravity acting on it. There are an infinite amount of points on the Earth each exercising gravity differently on an infinite amount of points on the Moon. How many combinations of gravities are there? The answer: infinity times infinity. The problem has the complexity of infinity multiplied by infinity!

Yet, Newton was capable of calculating his gravities. He dealt with the motions of heavenly bodies based on the assumption that each of them acts *as a single point*. In Newtonian physics, for most purposes, the Earth is a single point and the Moon is a single point. There is only one point—the Earth—exercising gravity on only one point—the Moon. Such points are the *centers of gravity*. That is, we look for the point that is the "average" of the weight or gravity of the Earth and the point that is the "average" of the weight or gravity of the

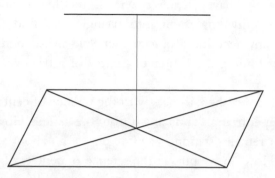

FIGURE 6.1 *Hanging a parallelogram*

Moon. We then treat the Earth and the Moon as if they are all concentrated on those single points. It can be proven mathematically
that, for most calculations, once we find the center of gravity, we can
calculate with a single point instead of an entire object. Physics
cannot exist without the center of gravity. And it is, once again, an
invention of Archimedes.

The idea of "center of gravity" is best understood with a planar,
two-dimensional object. For instance, let's use a circle. Our objective
is to balance the circle and hang it from the ceiling so that it remains
stationary. So, where do we tie the string? This is the easiest case: we
tie the string to *the center of the circle*. Tied anywhere else, the circle will
collapse. To keep it stationary, the circle must hang precisely from its
geometrical center. In this easiest case, then, the geometrical center
and the center of gravity coincide.

A square also hangs stationary when the string is tied to its exact
center. The same is true for all parallelograms, as we will demonstrate.
Simply find the point where the two diagonals meet, and you will
find the center of gravity of a parallelogram (see fig. 6.1). But the
question begins to become truly difficult when we approach more
complex objects. The key to all of them is the triangle. The triangle
has no obvious center in the way that a circle, a square, or even a parallelogram does. But once we find the center of gravity of a triangle,
we will be able to find the centers of gravity of all other rectilinear

objects. As we have already seen, all rectilinear objects can be measured by dividing them into triangles. To find the center of gravity of any rectilinear object, then, we need to first crack the problem of finding the center of gravity of a triangle. The rest will easily follow.

The following, then, is the key to the science of centers of gravity: we cut a paper triangle and hang it from the ceiling. How do we hang it so that it remains stationary? How do we go about answering this question? How do we pursue the science of centers of gravity?

You might wish perhaps, at this point, to conduct an experiment. You might want to take several paper triangles and hang them from the ceiling from various points, in this way finding out where the center of gravity happens to be. This approach makes sense. After all, you can't tell how the world behaves without checking it out for yourself. Your mind cannot dictate to the world how it should behave and so, purely through thought, you are not going to find out how objects hung from the ceiling are going to behave. Science is about hard evidence, not about pure speculation.

Not quite. Much of the time science *is* about pure speculation. Archimedes invented the concept of the center of gravity and found the center without ever conducting an experiment—doing it all *in his head!*

Let us look at the process of finding the center of gravity of a triangle. It is worth our while to follow this in detail. We shall see Archimedes' mind in action. What follows is the already advanced, thirteenth proposition of Archimedes' book *On Balancing Planes.*

PROOF ONE: HOW TO BALANCE A TRIANGLE,
OR MIND OVER MATTER

As you may recall, the language Archimedes uses for his science is beautifully spare. For this reason, it is also a very difficult language to read, whether in the original Greek or in translation. Let me explain it in my own words—closely adhering to Archimedes' own line of thought—how Archimedes balances a triangle. As usual, this involves some twists and turns.

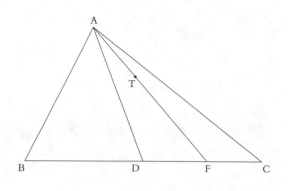

FIGURE 6.2-1

In figure 6.2-1, we find the triangle ABC, which we will ultimately balance. We will find its center of gravity—the point from which we will attach a string that will keep the triangle stationary. The line BC is divided into two at D (so that, BD = DC). The resulting line AD is what is called a median in the triangle. Archimedes is going to prove that THE CENTER OF GRAVITY OF A TRIANGLE MUST FALL SOMEWHERE ON A MEDIAN LINE. This is not finding the exact point; it is merely finding the line on which the point lies. But, bear with Archimedes. In geometry, one needs patience.

First of all, a piece of logical ingenuity: we are going to assume the opposite of what we want to prove. We are going to assume that the center of gravity does *not* fall on the line AD. In other words, we are going to assume that the center of gravity falls on some other line, such as AF. Let us assume, then, that the center of gravity is the point T falling on the line AF. This assumption will lead to an absurdity and, therefore, we will know that we were wrong. We will know that the center does, after all, fall on the median line. As we have seen already, this is a logical technique greatly beloved by Archimedes, known as "indirect proof."

So, initially, we assume that the center of gravity does not fall on the line AD but on some other point, T.

Now, we need to introduce another complex piece of geometrical ingenuity (see fig. 6.2–2). We add the points E and Z to the triangle. E divides the line AB in two (so that, AE = EB) and Z divides the

143

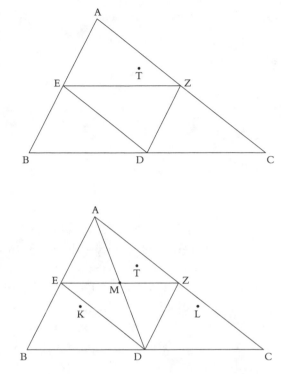

FIGURE 6.2-2

FIGURE 6.2-3

line AC in two (so that, AZ = ZC). We then connect the three points: D, E, Z. Now, inside the big triangle ABC, we have four smaller triangles. If you were a Greek mathematician, it would not be difficult for you to prove the following fact: ALL FOUR SMALL TRIANGLES ARE SIMILAR TO THE BIG TRIANGLE, AND THEY ARE EQUAL TO EACH OTHER. Similar triangles are identical to each other in every way except size. Remember that we have assumed that T is the center of gravity in the big triangle. So, the centers of gravity of the smaller triangles will have to be similarly situated. Let us trace the centers of gravity in two of the smaller triangles (see fig. 6.2–3).

The centers of gravity of the smaller triangles are to be the points L and K. L is the center of gravity for the bottom-right triangle and K is the center of gravity for the bottom-left triangle. What about the

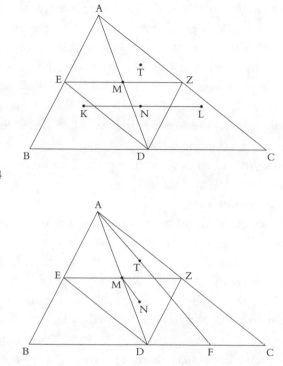

FIGURE 6.2-4

FIGURE 6.2-5

two remaining small triangles? They, in fact, taken together, constitute a parallelogram, and so a simple consideration of symmetry shows that their combined center of gravity must lie at the point where the two diagonals of the parallelogram meet—the point M.

Now, let us create the line KL (see fig. 6.2–4). If we consider the two smaller triangles—the one at the bottom right and the one at the bottom left—as a single geometrical object, it is clear where their combined center of gravity must lie. It must lie on the line connecting their respective centers of gravity at its exact middle. That is, the center of gravity of the two small triangles must lie at the exact middle of the line KL. Let us call this middle point N.

We are now ready to conclude our proof (see fig. 6.2–5). We need to create the lines AT and MN. Now, M is the center of gravity of

145

two of the triangles, and N is the center of gravity of the remaining two. The combined center of gravity of all four triangles, then—that is, the center of gravity of the big triangle—must therefore fall exactly in the middle of the line MN. In this diagram we can clearly see that this is not where point T lies. This is actually a bad argument to follow and a classic example of why one should not rely on diagrams too much. The question is this: how do we know that the point T can never lie on the line MN?

This is how. In any triangle, for the point T to lie on the line MN, the two lines MN, AF must intersect at some point. Indeed, they must intersect at the point T.

And, they can't. It would be an easy task for Archimedes to show that *the lines AT, MN must always be parallel*. Therefore, *they can never intersect*. We have asked the point T to lie on the line MN and by doing this *we have required two parallel lines to cut each other!* This must be wrong. No matter where we place the initial point T, as long as it is on a line such as AF and not on the median line AD, we will always derive the same absurdity of two parallel lines being required to cut each other. So, we know that the true position of the center of gravity of any triangle is on its median line.

In any triangle there are, of course, not one but three median lines. It is proved that when we draw all three median lines of a triangle— any triangle—they meet at exactly one point. In figure 6.2-6, we see this in the triangle ABC. Its sides are bisected by the median lines AD, BZ, CE. All three lines, AD, BZ, CE, meet each other at the point X. The point X lies at an exactly defined position: it is one-third the way along the median line. DX is one third of AD; ZX is one third of BZ; and EX is one third of EC. This is where the center of gravity must lie.

So, Archimedes could have suggested the following experiment. Create a paper triangle. Draw a median line. Find the point one-third of the way along the median line. Attach a string to this point and hang it from the ceiling. The triangle will remain fixed and stationary. How does Archimedes know this? Oh, that's easy; Archimedes

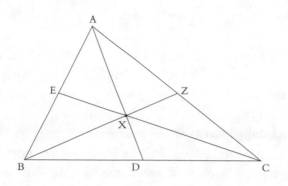

FIGURE 6.2-6

explains. It is because lines, divided in two, give rise to four equal and similar triangles. It is because a certain line happens to be parallel to another. It is because of geometry. Follow logic and you see for yourself. We turn away, in disbelief. But, Archimedes is right.

The products of pure thought, which at first glance have nothing at all to do with each other or the physical world, are brought together. Before you know it, pure speculation binds the physical universe and forces it to behave in a particular fashion. No experiments were necessary to find this out. Mind rules over matter because, ultimately, even brute matter must follow logic.

This is rather like the magician telling us—without even looking—about the contents of our wallets. Archimedes has told us—without even looking—how the world must behave, where a triangle must balance.

Follow this a bit further. We start at Syracuse in the third century BC when all we can do is hang a triangle from the ceiling. But, we follow the line of thought long enough and we are able by the twentieth century to launch a rocket to the Moon and to explode an atomic bomb. All the way, following the same principle, we apply the power of reasoning to the universe, and the universe follows logic. This is the principle discovered by Archimedes. This is science in action.

The Law of the Balance

There is another complementary act of magic. Following the magic of mind-over-matter—pure mathematics discovering a physical fact—comes another act of magic no less spectacular. It is matter-over-mind—physics discovering a mathematical fact. This is done in the *Method*. Most historians of mathematics consider this the most amazing act performed by Archimedes. Besides being a piece of physics-over-mathematics, it also introduces infinity in a puzzling, strange way. In the next few pages, we will follow this.

We need tools for this act. The first we have already: the center of gravity of a triangle. The other is another physical fact, proved mathematically by Archimedes in the treatise *On Balancing Planes*. It is called the Law of the Balance, which we have already mentioned. It may also be called the Law of the Lever. While the two machines may do different things, they work by exactly the same mathematical rule. Archimedes relies on a balance for his measurements in the *Method*. However, he was equally familiar with the lever and the law was most famously and succinctly expressed by him as follows: "Give me a place to stand and I shall move the Earth." That is: "Give me a lever long enough, and I can move any object whatsoever." Why is that? It is because of a principle of proportion. Let me now explain this, first with a balance.

We can take any two objects and put them on a balance. One arm of the balance has Object One, whose weight is, say, 10 pounds. The other arm of the balance has Object Two, whose weight is, say, 2 pounds. The balances are of the moveable type, so that we can make each object nearer or further away from the fulcrum. The question: at which distances will the objects balance? The answer is as follows: the ratio of the weights is 5:1, and therefore the ratio of the distances should be reciprocal—that is 1:5. The distance of the lighter object should be five times the distance of the heavier object, and then they will balance. The rule: weights balance when they are reciprocal to their distances.

The Archimedes Palimpsest, as it arrived at the Walters Art Museum on January 19, 1999.

The Palimpsest open. The right–hand page contains the unique text of Archimedes' *Method*, proposition 14. All you can see is the prayer book text. The indent to the page on the bottom right is the armpit of the goat from which the page was made.

The Euryalus fortress overlooks the city of Syracuse, Sicily. Its ramparts remain imposing more than 2,200 years after the city was stormed by the Romans, and Archimedes killed, in 212 BC.

Built in AD 537, Hagia Sophia dominates the skyline of Constantinople. It was designed in part by Isidore of Miletus, who was responsible for an edition of Archimedes' works in the sixth century.

(Facing page) A medieval scribe. This picture of St. Luke was painted in the Byzantine Empire in the thirteenth century. St. Luke writes on a piece of parchment with a reed pen. On a lectern in front of him is the book he is copying from, written in majuscules. Resting on the table are further implements of his trade, and in the cupboard a vessel containing ink.

Constantinople, present-day Istanbul, as viewed from the Galata Tower, with the Golden Horn in the foreground, and Hagia Sophia on the skyline. It was this view that faced the crusaders in April 1204, when they sacked the city.

The Monastery of St. Sabas in the Holy Land. This was the resting place for the Archimedes manuscript from at least the sixteenth century until the early nineteenth.

This leaf was taken from the Archimedes Palimpsest by Constantine Tischendorf in the early 1840s when the book was at the Metochion of the Holy Sepulchre in Constantinople. Identified by Nigel Wilson in 1968, it fits between folios 2 and 3 of the Palimpsest. It is now in Cambridge University Library.

Abigail Quandt, Senior Conservator of Manuscripts and Rare Books at the Walters Art Museum. The conservation of the Palimpsest rested almost entirely on her shoulders.

Abigail performs brain surgery. Here she mends a damaged leaf of the Archimedes Palimpsest.

It took four years to disbind the Archimedes Palimpsest. This is a rare action shot.

Heiberg's photograph of folio 57r of the Archimedes Palimpsest, which contains part of the introduction to Archimedes' *Method*.

An illustration in H. Omont's 1929 publication of Greek manuscripts in the Bibliothèque Nationale.

Folio 57r of the Archimedes Palimpsest as it is now. The text is covered with a forgery, painted after 1938. The image of the scribe was traced on a one-to-one scale from the picture in the Omont publication.

An X-ray fluorescence image of folio 57r, taken at SLAC, to reveal the texts beneath the forgery.

A detail of the Archimedes Palimpsest before it was disbound. Note how the lower half of the picture contains a very faint diagram that disappears into the gutter.

(Left) The Palimpsest in normal light. It is very difficult to discern any undertext.
(Right) An early experiment, this is a highly processed image of the same area.
It seems to show diagrams and Archimedes text. Despite appearances,
it did not help the scholars very much.

Abigail has set up a leaf of the Palimpsest to be imaged. Bill Christens-Barry of Equipoise Imaging LLC examines it by flashlight. He can look, but he can't touch . . .

Roger Easton, Professor of Imaging Science at the Rochester Institute of Technology inspects the optical imaging system.

Bill Christens-Barry demonstrates the narrow band imaging system that he designed.

Keith Knox, Chief Scientist at the Boeing Corporation, Maui. He invented the algorithm by which so much of the text was revealed. Here he is acting in his capacity as "lights."

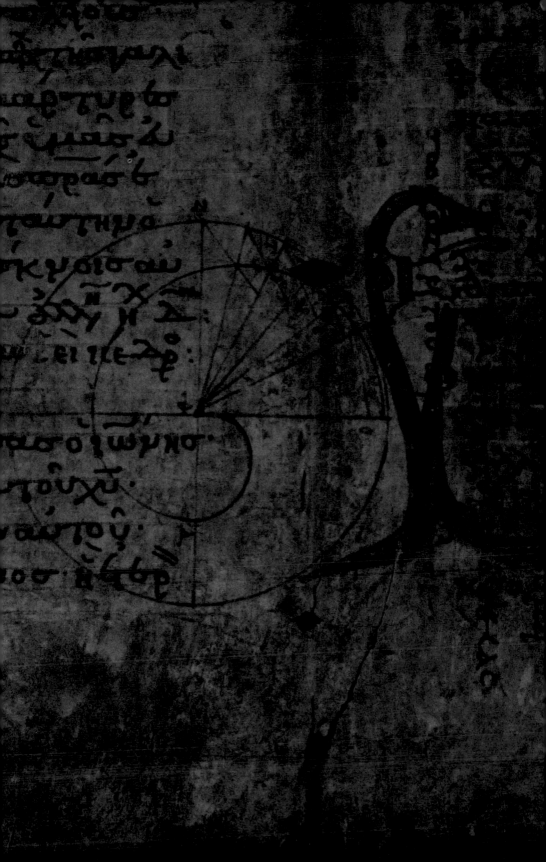

A detail of the Palimpsest in normal light. The Archimedes text is difficult to see.

The same page in the pseudocolor process that Keith Knox developed by combining an image taken in natural light with an image taken in ultraviolet light.

(Previous page) The gorgeous luminous quality of ultraviolet fluorescent light can make the Archimedes Palimpsest look beautiful. Here is the diagram to Archimedes' Spiral Lines, proposition 21 (see Chapter 4). It is obscured by the text and decoration of the prayer book. The hand drawn in the initial letter to one of the prayers seems to use the straight lines of the diagram as a sleeve.

Reviel Netz has annotated this ultraviolet image identifying some characters and guessing at others. The note in the margin is Reviel asking Abigail Quandt whether the small hole in the centre of the parchment was an original blemish in the skin, or made later.

Nigel Wilson works from printed reproductions of the images, mainly in the summer months, when the light is good.

Will Noel and Reviel Netz study a leaf of the Archimedes Palimpsest in the conservation laboratory at the Walters.

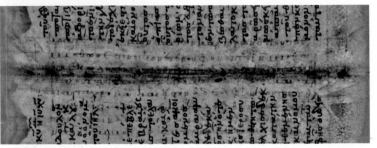

(Left) A pseudocolor image of the Hyperides text in the Palimpsest. Note that the Hyperides text is written out in one column, while the Archimedes text is written out in two.

(Middle left) A detail of the third unique text in the manuscript, a philosophical commentary, in natural light.

(Lower left) A pseudocolor image of the same detail as above, with the word "Aristotle" circled.

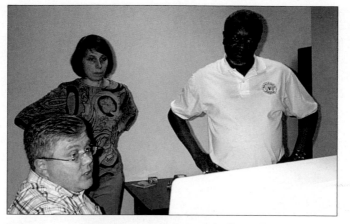

Bob Morton, Abigail Quandt, and Gene Hall watch as an EDAX X-ray image of a forged page emerges, agonizingly slowly, on the computer screen.

After 15 hours of imaging at EDAX a scan was made that had read through gold.

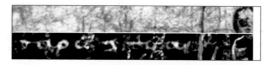

Outside Beamline 6-2 at the Stanford Linear Accelerator Center: Uwe Bergmann, Abigail Quandt, Keith Knox, Mike Toth, Reviel Netz, Will Noel.

A leaf of the Archimedes Palimpsest in the beam at SLAC. The leaf moves on a stage in front of the X-ray beam, which is a hair's width in diameter. The detector, wrapped in silver foil, is on the left, at 90 degrees to the beam.

Uwe Bergmann is delighted as Reviel Netz announces to Will Noel that he can improve upon Heiberg's reading of the manuscript with an image scanned at SLAC.

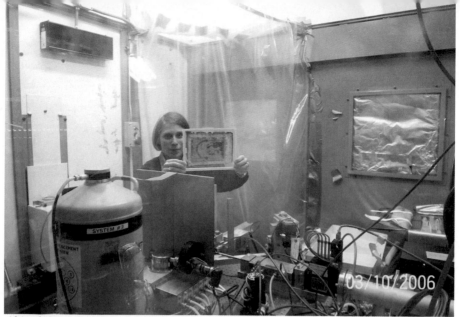

Abigail Quandt inserts one of the forgeries into the beam at SLAC.

(Left) A regular image of one half of a forged page.
(Right) An "iron map" of the same page, taken at SLAC, revealing the text underneath.

03/13/2006

March 13, 2006, was the day that the new *On Floating Bodies* text appeared at SLAC. Reviel rushed up to the Beamline to play with the images. Everybody helped. From left to right: Uwe Bergmann, Abigail Quandt, Keith Knox, Reviel Netz, Roger Easton.

A detail of folio 1v of the Palimpsest, taken in normal light.

An "iron map" revealing the colophon of the scribe of the prayer book: + [This] was written by the hand of presbyter Ioannes Myronas on the 14th day of the month of April, a Saturday, of the year 6737, indiction 2.

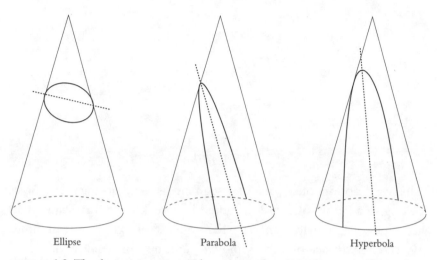

Ellipse   Parabola   Hyperbola

FIGURE 6.3 *The three conic sections. Take a cone and cut it in three ways. If you cut from both sides you create an ellipse; if you cut it parallel to one side you create a parabola; and if you cut it moving away from one side you create a hyperbola.*

If, instead of a balance, we use a lever, the same principle still holds. The object that is five times more distant is capable of balancing an object exactly five times heavier. Make it even more distant and the lighter object will even move the heavier object. All of this Archimedes proved in *On Balancing Planes*, of course by pure thought. By standing in the realm of pure thought, Archimedes moved the Earth.

So I repeat: first, the center of gravity of a triangle is one third along on the median line and second, objects balance each other when their distances are reciprocal to their weights. These are two facts about the physical world. With their aid, we will measure the area of a segment of a parabola. That is, once again, we will find how a curved figure is equal to a rectilinear one. We have already seen Archimedes obtain this result in one way. In the *Method*, he obtains this in another, much more spectacular way, which in itself is quite a surprise. Who would think that triangles and balances would have anything to do with parabolas?

149

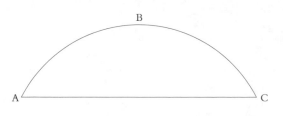

FIGURE 6.4–1

The Parabola

The very notion of a parabolic segment is very abstract. Parabolas belong to a family of curves invented by Greek mathematicians as an act of pure geometrical fancy, having no physical significance in mind. We take the surface of a cone, and we cut it by a plane. Depending on how we produce this cut, we derive one of three sections: hyperbolas, parabolas, or ellipses (see fig. 6.3). Circles, squares, and triangles make sense: we more or less meet them in daily life. This is not so with hyperbolas, parabolas, and ellipses. Their interest is mainly in the fact that—as it turns out—there are all sorts of nice geometrical proportions that arise with the combination of conic sections.

Conic sections are best considered as toys invented by geometers to aid in their geometrical play. I keep returning to the irony of mathematics-over-physics, of how pure thought turns out to rule the physical universe. This is one of the most remarkable ironies: the conic sections, which were invented as geometrical toys, turned out to be the curves defining motion in space. Electrons orbiting around the nucleus of an atom, a rocket launched to the Moon, a rock thrown by a catapult— all such motions obey the curves of conic sections. So that this study is, in fact, one of the major routes leading to modern science.

PROOF TWO: THE AREA OF A PARABOLIC SEGMENT,
OR MATTER OVER MIND

We follow on this route, concentrating on the area of the parabolic segment (see fig. 6.4–1). By a "parabolic segment," we mean the area

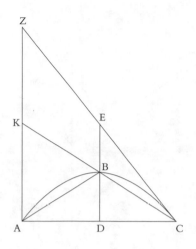

FIGURE 6.4-2

intercepted between a parabola and a straight line crossing through it, such as ABC. (ABC is the parabola; AC is the straight line). You will notice, of course, that a parabolic segment is a curvilinear object. This is the great mystery that constantly exercised Archimedes' mind: how to measure curvilinear objects; how to reduce them to rectilinear objects. Soon we will see.

We move to the next figure and note certain facts (see fig. 6.4–2). First, each parabola possesses an axis of symmetry. In this case, it is the line BD, around which the parabola is "the same," to the left and to the right.

To explain the following facts, I need to add a few bits to the construction. We need to draw a tangent to the parabolic segment at the point C, namely the line CZ. We also need to draw a line parallel to the axis, passing through the point A, namely the line AZ. The tangent and the parallel meet at the point Z. We have enclosed the parabolic segment within a triangle: the segment ABC is enclosed within the triangle AZC. We also need to extend the line DB to reach the point E, and the line CB to reach the point K.

An interesting series of geometrical relations now depends on the fact that the axis cuts exactly through the middle of the

151

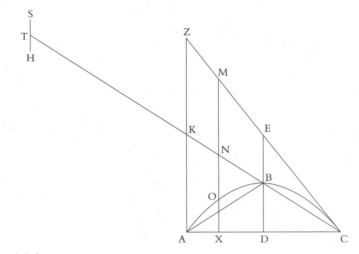

FIGURE 6.4-3

parabola, as well as on some other properties of the parabola. They are as follows:

- The point K is exactly at the middle of the line AZ.
- The point B is exactly at the middle of the line DE.
- The triangle AKC is exactly half the area of the triangle AZC.
- The point B is exactly at the middle of the line KC.
- The triangle ABC is exactly half the area of the triangle AKC.

Taken together, all of the above means, among other things, that:

- The bigger triangle AZC is four times the area of the smaller triangle ABC.

This is rather like the division of one triangle into smaller triangles that we saw with the previous proof, and it will be used by Archimedes later on.

Now I need to mention one of the funny facts about parabolas. We draw a line parallel to the axis of the parabola BD (see fig. 6.4–3). There are infinitely many such parallels, and we take one at random, say the line MX. So, MX is parallel to BD. Here comes the funny fact, which, as is typical, takes the form of a proportion:

- The line MX is to its smaller section OX as the base of the
  diameter AC is to its smaller section AX.

To the algebraically inclined, this can be expressed symbolically as
follows: (MX:OX::AC:AX).

So we return to the line chosen at random, MX. We add a few
more details to the diagram. First we extend the line from C, through
B, onward. It cuts the line MX at the point N, and it cuts the line ZA
at the point K. We further extend it to the point T, so that KT
becomes equal to KC, and the point K is exactly in the middle of the
line TC.

We then do something very unorthodox. It will take us some time
to see why we do this. But what we do is take the segment OX and,
in our minds, transport it to a new position SH. Its middle point is
now T, lying at the end of the line KC, extended. This is a thought
experiment then. We imagine a piece of geometrical line transposed.
This is already sensational, because Archimedes has just moved a geometrical object and treated it as if it were physical—a piece of wood
that one can carry about.

I now note a few consequences. First of all, I recall in the original
proportion, the funny result for parabolas:

- As MX is to OX, so is AC to AX.

Second, because the lines MX and ZA are parallel (this is how we
constructed the line MX), the ratio is preserved:

- As AC is to AX, so KC is to KN.

These are "the same" ratios, simply sliding along parallel lines.
Combine the two above, and you can immediately see (eliminating
the middle term, as it were) that:

- As MX is to OX, so KC is to KN.

The parallel line taken at random, MX, is to its smaller section, OX,
just as the base AC is to its smaller section AX and also as KC is to
KN.

Further, remember that K is the exact middle point of TC (TK = KC). So whatever is true of KC, will also be true of TK. Therefore, it must also be true that:

- As MX is to OX, so TK is to KN.

The parallel line taken at random, MX, is to its smaller section, OX, as TK is to KN.

Notice what Archimedes has achieved. His ratios until now have all been "packed in," with a line relating to its own segment. This final ratio of TK to KN, however, unwraps the package and transforms the relation to one between two independent line segments touching at one point only. This will become useful later on.

Finally, we may bring in another consideration. Whatever is true of OX must also be true of SH. This, after all, was our original thought experiment: to transpose OX so that it becomes SH. The two are identical. We noted above that the parallel line taken at random, MX, is to its smaller section, OX, as TK is to KN.

Now if I exchange SH for OX—since the two are identical—we can say the following:

- As MX is to SH, so TK is to KN.

The parallel line taken at random, MX, is to its smaller section—now SH—the same as TK is to KN.

This last proportion is the one we have been looking for. The magician is about to perform a trick. We have already engaged in one thought experiment—imagining the line OX as a physical line and transporting it to occupy the position SH. We now need to engage in another much more radical thought experiment. No one said anything remotely similar to this prior to Archimedes.

What we imagine now is that the lines MX and SH are lying on the arms of a balance with its fulcrum at K. We treat them as physical objects possessing weights, which are a reflection of their lengths. The

two lines possess centers of gravity, obviously at their exact centers—
that is, respectively, at N and T.

You see what we just did: we considered geometrical objects as if
they were physical. I repeat: no one ever did this prior to Archimedes.
Just as he invented the mathematical treatment of physics, he has also
invented the physical treatment of pure mathematics.

Remember the previous result: "MX is to SH as TK is to KN." So
what is the ratio of weight between MX and SH? It is the ratio of
their lengths; the ratio of the line MX to the line SH. This, we have
seen, is the same as the ratio of the line TK to the line KN. Therefore,
the ratio of the lines is reciprocally the same as the ratio of their distances from the fulcrum.

Apply the Law of the Balance and derive the beautiful observation
made by Archimedes: the two lines MX, SH will balance with K as
their fulcrum.

Dizzying? Hold your breath. We now move onto another thought
experiment, even more dizzying. Fresh from this trick, the magician
now prepares yet another one.

The random line MX exactly balances its smaller section OX,
around the fulcrum K, when the smaller segment is transposed so that
its center becomes T. But we chose the line MX randomly. No matter
which other parallel line we choose, the same will hold true. The
ratios will change, but they will remain respectively proportional.

In other words,

> Each parallel line inside the triangle AZC balances its
> respective section from the parabolic segment ABC (posi-
> tioned at T), around the fulcrum K.

If you agree to that, you must agree to the following:

> All parallel lines, inside the triangle AZC, taken together,
> balance all their sections from the parabolic segment (posi-
> tioned at T), taken together, around the fulcrum K.

Or, better still:

The triangle AZC balances the parabolic segment ABC (positioned at T), around the fulcrum K.

How can it be otherwise? We slice the triangle and the parabolic segment, parallel line by parallel line, and each time we do the slicing, we find the same balance at the same fulcrum. So, when we take the entire triangle and the entire parabolic segment, they must obey the same law of the balance: the entire triangle and the entire parabolic segment must balance each other at exactly the same fulcrum.

So I repeat: the triangle as a whole balances the parabola as a whole, with K as the fulcrum.

We know where the center of gravity of the transposed parabolic segment is: it is at the point T. This, after all, is our thought experiment. Parallel line by parallel line, we have transposed the parabolic segment so that the center of gravity of each line is T. If each line taken separately has its center of gravity at T, then taken altogether they will also have a center at T.

We can then say that the triangle, set at the position of the diagram, balances the parabolic segment, with the center of gravity of the parabolic segment at T and the fulcrum at K.

What about the center of gravity of the triangle? Well, we previously worked very hard on this question. The center of gravity of the triangle is at the point one-third the way along the median line—that is, at the point one third of KC.

However, one third of KC is also one third of KT. That is, the distance of the center of gravity of a triangle from the fulcrum K is one third the distance of the center of weight of the parabolic segment.

The parabolic segment is three times as far from the fulcrum as is the triangle. Therefore, the triangle must be three times the weight of the parabolic segment, and the area of the triangle must be three times the area of the parabolic segment.

We can make this result even more elegant. Consider the triangle ABC, which, as we recall, is exactly one-fourth the triangle AZC. In other words, the parabolic segment ABC is four-thirds the triangle ABC.

Put simply: a parabolic segment is four-thirds the triangle it encloses.

This was a moment of magic. Consider that each treatise by Archimedes contains at least one such moment of magic and you can begin to see the measure of the man. In the *Method*, each proposition is just as magical. No wonder Heiberg was so excited in 1906.

Note the complex route leading to this magic. We had the thought experiment—considering geometrical objects as physical ones. And then, something even further. We had a result for *pairs of slices*—pairs of random lines taken of the triangle and the parabolic segment. We then moved to *the triangle itself* and *the parabolic segment itself*, each taken as a whole.

In other words, we took a proportion involving four lines and turned it into a proportion involving infinitely many lines—all the infinitely many parallel lines constituting the triangle or the parabola.

Are we allowed to do that? This question, from then on—from Archimedes' time to our own—became the central question of mathematics. The *Method*, by bringing together mathematics, physics, and infinity, raised the most fundamental questions of science. It anticipated Newton's calculus, but it also anticipated the conceptual difficulties of that calculus.

How much did Archimedes know about infinity? In June 1999, we did not know. The question on everyone's lips: what are we going to find, further, in the *Method*—if anything? We needed to look inside the Palimpsest and be able finally to read it. But in June 1999, Abigail had not yet unwrapped the book. The brain was still caged inside its box, as I waited, impatiently, for it to be freed.

7

The Critical Path

~

Conservators don't like being the center of attention, but that's just where I had put Abigail Quandt—in the public eye and subject to its scrutiny. If you work on Leonardo's *Last Supper,* Michelangelo's *David,* or the unique witness to the thoughts of Archimedes, you'd better not slip up. Everyone tells you what you should be doing, but only you can do it. And no one had any idea about the problems that Abigail faced. They do now, but they didn't then. Hers was not only the critical path, as program manager Mike Toth characterized it; it was also the most important and the most onerous. Like Reviel, you are going to have to wait until you get more of the *Method.* This is Abigail's story.

Abigail is not your normal book conservator. Most book conservators work with paper books, very few work on parchment manuscripts. There are good reasons for this. First of all, there are many more paper books in the world than there are parchment ones. Second, in general, paper books need conservation treatment much more often than parchment ones. This is particularly true if they are printed on bad paper with a high acidity level. As I write, such books are literally self-destructing in libraries across the globe. Many are the paper conservators who fight this battle. Parchment does not have this acidity problem, and it is much tougher than paper. One essential difference between parchment and paper, is that parchment is much more sensitive to changes in temperature and humidity—it is skin, after all. If you lay a sheet of parchment over your sweaty hand it will quickly curl. Actually, it will curl into the shape it had on the back of the animal from which it came. With finely illuminated manuscripts, such as those at the Walters, this can have serious repercussions. The pigments in the illuminations do not change shape with the parchment as humidity changes and after a while the pigments flake off. Abigail had been working on parchment with this kind of problem for more than twenty years. She is a parchment expert, and very few people have her skills. This was why she was uniquely qualified to work on the Palimpsest.

Normally, the best thing to do with a historic object is absolutely nothing, which is what conservators do most of the time. Don't touch it; secure and monitor its environment. After all, a codex that has survived a thousand years is unlikely to degenerate much further if it is not handled and if it is not subject to pollutants or extremes of climate. In the past, even well intentioned treatments resulted in permanent damage and the loss of important historical evidence. In the nineteenth and early twentieth centuries many palimpsests were wrecked by the treatment they received. Scholars routinely read palimpsests by applying chemicals to them. In 1919, English novelist and manuscript scholar M. R. James wrote that erased text could be

> revived by the dabbing (not painting) upon it of ammonium bisulphide, which, unlike the old-fashioned galls, does not stain the page. Dabbed on the surface with a soft paint-brush, and dried off at once with clean blotting paper, it makes the old record leap to light, sometimes with astonishing clearness, sometimes slowly, so that the letters cannot be read till next day. It is not always successful; it is of no use to apply it to writing in red, and its smell is overpowering, but it is the elixir of paleographers.

There were other elixirs, too. The most powerful was Gioberti's tincture—successively applied coats of hydrochloric acid and potassium cyanide. I'll just repeat that—successively applied coats of hydrochloric acid and potassium cyanide. Needless to say, ammonium bisulphide, too, has a severely detrimental effect on parchment. Working in the twenty-first century, Abigail couldn't apply chemicals to reveal text in

FIGURE 7.1 *The spine of the Palimpsest*

Mr. B's book. There was little that Abigail could do to make the erased text appear. This would be a challenge for the imagers.

However, it was not an option for Abigail to do simply nothing with the Palimpsest. Despite all the lessons of history, Mr. B gave the go-ahead for her to perform radical surgery on the manuscript. It was a brave decision, and we hope that history will say that it was the right one. The reasons for it certainly sounded excellent at the time. The only way that scholars would be able to read the Archimedes text now hidden in the book's binding and the only way that imagers would be able to take the scientific images that were needed, was for Abigail to take the entire manuscript apart.

The Path Is Blocked

On Monday, April 3, 2000, Mr. B, Reviel, Natalie, and Mike gathered at the Walters. It was a historic day. Abigail was going to disbind the Palimpsest. All went smoothly at the start. Just before the sale, in order to make the book presentable, Scott Husby from Princeton had carefully put a temporary binding on the codex that was designed to be easily taken apart. Abigail quickly took this binding off, leaving the parchment text block naked, without its covers. It was a pitiful sight, though it took Abigail some time to make clear that it was also a tragic one. And here begins the worst part of the story of Mr. B's book. If, to Reviel Netz, the Palimpsest was the unique source for the diagrams that Archimedes drew in the sand, to Abigail Quandt it was a conservation disaster zone.

The spine of the book was covered in glue. This was a post-medieval practice, which helped to secure the structure of the codex but which obviously presented problems for Abigail in taking it apart. If you look carefully (see fig. 7.1), you can see that the spine seems to have two separate colors. The darker color is hide glue, made from animal skin, and Abigail could remove it with reasonable ease. This section forms the second half of the codex from folio 97 onward. The real problem was the light glue from folios 1 to 96. According to Abigail, "The other half of the text block has been coated with a transparent adhesive, probably a type of poly(vinyl) acetate (PVAC) emulsion. While PVAC will swell in contact with water and/or alcohol, there is no way to dissolve it once it has formed a dried film on the surface of an object. Attempts to remove this adhesive from the spine folds of the Palimpsest have proved to be extremely risky, since the glue is stronger than the parchment." In other words, this is stock-in-trade wood glue. Precisely those lines that Heiberg could not read, because they were hidden in the spine of the bound codex, were now coated and stuck together with commercial glue.

This was not the worst problem. Let's look at the unique surviving folio of Archimedes' *Stomachion* (see fig. 7.2). Think of it as a cross section of the brain of a great man. It is, quite literally, in pieces and large parts of it are simply missing. The rest of it is covered in an awful purple color. Now, up until this point, I have insisted that parchment is tough. Its basic constituent, after all, is the stuff that makes up your shoes. There are only two ways in which you cannot only wear out your shoes, but destroy them. One is to burn them. But, the Palimpsest had survived a fire at St. Sabas. Another is to throw them into a bucket of water and then expose them to air. Pretty soon they will get moldy. And that is, more or less, what happened to this folio

FIGURE 7.2 *Archimedes' Stomachion!*

and in varying degrees to the entire Palimpsest. If you immediately take care of your wet shoes, then you can clean them up reasonably well. But that's not what happened to the Palimpsest—far from it. The Palimpsest was left to stew and the mold was left to grow. And mold grows by eating what it is growing on. The mold actually

163

digested the parchment. All the folios of the Palimpsest suffered in some degree from the mold. Normally, the side of the parchment that was on the inside of the animal is in a poorer state than the side that the animal presented to the outside world. This is because the skin has evolved—or been intelligently designed—to resist microbe attacks from the environment. But in the face of the mold attack that the Palimpsest was subjected to even the hair side was often heavily damaged. Sometimes it didn't look so bad, and the folios seemed strong enough. But Abigail showed them to me backlit over a light box and the light shone through like stars in the night sky.

So, the leaves were stuck together, and they were extremely fragile. And then, of course, four of them were painted over with forged portraits of the Evangelists. Worse, the forger did not just scrape off the prayer-book text and paint on top of it. He also "distressed" the folio. For example, he made incisions into folio 57r and took nicks out of it to make the picture look older after he had finished it. It is often tempting to display pictures in manuscripts independently of the codex itself. Perhaps this is why there was a nice curved rust stain at the top of the folio. Abigail believes it was made by a paper clip. Not formal enough for you? Maybe. Then why not take a piece of Blu-tack (a blue putty-like substance) and stick it to its backing that way. There's plenty of Blu-tack on the back of this folio—just try reading through it. What a way to treat a book—any book. What a tragedy that it was this book.

The disbinding of the book, upon which everything depended, came to a virtual standstill. The Archimedes Project took what can best be described as a duck dive. Reviel went back to Stanford, Natalie to Cambridge. The lights went out in the studio that had been especially prepared to image the book, and Mr. B went home. Abigail spent days just looking at the book, thinking, and documenting. The days turned into weeks and the weeks into months. I dodged press inquiries with breezy comments about the importance of the book and some small conservation issues. Abigail and I stopped talking—always a bad sign. Then she asked for what seemed to me to be an extravagant amount of money to employ her colleagues at the Canadian Conservation Institute to begin a whole battery of tests. To my surprise, Mr. B wrote the check. Mike Toth sent me dark emails warning of slippage in the schedule early in the project and the dangers of pure research taking us away from our well-defined and limited objective. There was nothing I could do about it. At the Walters, as in many American museums, curators cannot tell conservators what to do. This is ultimately a very good thing, but occasionally also an incredibly frustrating one. It just didn't seem that much of a problem to me, and yet it brought my whole system to a standstill. Never mind about me. Picture, if you will, Assistant Professor Netz, newly installed in the Department of Classics at Stanford, trying to get tenure. The one manuscript that he needed had almost miraculously appeared. He had seen it; he had even touched it; he knew better than anyone the secrets that it contained. But now, he was reduced to begging for glimpses of only parts of it. Noel was out of leaves; Netz was out of luck.

The world was watching, the scholars were poised to read, and the scientists were ready to image. But everybody was waiting for Abigail—not all of them patiently.

The Heiberg Photographs

Reviel made himself busy, stirring every bush he could about the Palimpsest and digging into its history. He studied Heiberg's work over and over again. He read it cover to cover. And then, in the introduction, he noticed that Heiberg had said that he took photographs of the manuscript when he was in Constantinople. Since the manuscript itself had disappeared into private hands for most of the twentieth century, the photographs would have proved extremely useful to anyone who could find them. The trouble was that no one had. There is a large archive of Heiberg material in the Royal Library of Denmark, but repeated searches in the archive had not revealed the photographs. Reviel, however, thought he would give it another shot, so he wrote an email to a colleague of his, a Danish historian of ancient science, Karin Tybjerg. Karin prevailed upon the Keeper of Manuscripts at the Royal Library, Erik Petersen, to have another look, and Erik had an idea. The Heiberg archive had been deposited at the Royal Library after Heiberg had died. But what if Heiberg had given the photographs to the library *before* he had died? Heiberg would have understood the importance of the photographs and, as a good humanist, might well have wanted to make them publicly accessible. If so, where would they be? In among the photography collection, of course. And Erik found them. They were Ms. Phot 38 in the Royal Library. In June of 2000, Reviel and I visited Copenhagen to see the photographs. Erik warmly welcomed us and we were handed a plain album full of photographs of a manuscript. There were sixty-five in all, and they were the smoking gun.

The photographs give a clear picture of what the manuscript looked like in 1906. If you compare the leaf containing Archimedes' *Stomachion* now, with its condition then, you can see that they are barely recognizable as the same folio. The *Stomachion* page was whole in 1906. It is a moldy fragment now. Of course, some folios in the Palimpsest are worse than others. The tragedy is that their condition is almost in an inverse relationship to the importance of the texts that they contain. Archimedes has been extremely unlucky: the folios containing the *Method* and the *Stomachion* are in the worst condition of all. When I tell you that Abigail marked the *Stomachion* folio as "very poor," you will understand that she is a master of the under-statement. That's not my style. I tell you: the body of Archimedes may have died by the sword at the hands of a Roman soldier in the third century BC, but the genius of Archimedes was eaten by mold over two thousand years later.

There is, of course, no sign of the forgeries in Heiberg's photo-graphs. On the photograph of folio 57r Heiberg had written "M16"—it was the sixteenth folio of the *Method*. Now, a picture was on this page. A balding man with a white beard, wearing a green robe, sits in a chair with a high, curved back with his feet resting on a blue stool. In his right hand he holds a pen and in his left a scroll upon which he is writing. In front of him is a desk with the instruments of his trade and before him at eye level upon a lectern is the book from which he is copying. He is set within an archway, and the whole picture is framed with a border. The background is gold. There is hardly even the faintest trace of the prayer-book text, let alone the writings of Archimedes.

The Heiberg photographs are dramatic and unequivocal evidence that most of the damage to the book occurred in the twentieth century, after it had been revealed as the unique source of treatises by Archimedes. Abigail was stuck with an old book, but one that had only recently sustained such serious damage. Who was responsible for it?

The Forged Miniatures

In early March of 1999, I stopped in to see John Lowden in his rather cramped office on the top floor of the Courtauld Institute, where he is the Professor of Medieval Art. I showed him a picture of one of the forgeries. To my astonishment, he immediately cried out "Snap," and pulled out a publication that he had written on a manuscript in Duke University Library, North Carolina. The codex at Duke contained four Evangelist portraits very similar to the ones in the Palimpsest, and John had demonstrated conclusively that they were modern forgeries.

He told me to go downstairs into the library and pull out a publication by Henri Omont, published in 1929, of Greek manuscripts in the Bibliothèque Nationale in Paris. I quickly found what he knew I would. The figures of the Evangelists in the Palimpsest, like those from the Duke manuscript, were copied from illustrations in that book. They were not exact copies; their backgrounds were much simpler than the backgrounds of the pictures in Omont's publication. But the figures of the Evangelists themselves, their chairs and their writing desks were the same. Abigail established that the drawings were actually traced on a scale of 1:1 from the publication.

Following the Christie's catalogue, I had been cursing the scribe of the prayer book and the greedy and careless monks at the Metochion for the appalling state of the book. The Duke codex, too, had belonged to the Metochion. Since both books had paintings by the same forger, I was more sure than ever who was to blame for the books' condition.

But I was wrong. In May 2001, Abigail received back a monumental work of research and scholarship. The Canadian Conservation Institute delivered their report on the Archimedes Palimpsest. It's an impressive but depressing read. It is also full of useful information about the appalling condition of the book. Among a whole range of pigments that they chemically identified in the forgeries, one was particularly revealing—phthalocyanine green. This color only became commercially available in Germany in 1938. As we have seen, by 1938 there were no manuscripts at the Metochion. In fact, the forgeries were made at least fifteen years after Marie Louis Sirieix was supposed to have acquired the codex.

The realization that I had entirely misunderstood the story of the Palimpsest made me angry, and I wanted to set the record straight. I wanted to know who was responsible for the catastrophic treatment of the book after it left the Metochion. Now it seemed likely that Marie Louis Sirieix was to blame. But the story told by Robert Guersan was short on particulars. Perhaps Sirieix had not even known that the book contained the unique letters of Archimedes; Anne Guersan seems to have recovered this information. Without further documentation, it would be impossible to be sure.

The Willoughby Letter

In May 2006, I walked into work and found placed upon my desk, without ceremony, a copy of a letter. It had been left there as an early-morning gift by my good friend Georgi Parpulov, a Bulgarian scholar of Greek manuscripts with a wry smile and an extraordinary ability to uncover the deeply buried. Georgi had dug this letter out of an archive of photographs, the Harold R. Willoughby Corpus of New Testament Iconography at the University of Chicago. The letterhead made it clear that it was from an antiquities dealer living in Paris. It read: Salomon Guerson, Rare Carpets, Antique Tapestries, 169 Boulevard Haussmann, Paris, and it was addressed to Professor Harold R. Willoughby at the University of Chicago, Illinois:

February 10, 1934

Dear Professor Willoughby
    Pursuant to our correspondence of 1932 with regard to a manuscript that I had shown to you and a folio which was identified through your mediation by the curator of the Huntington library as being the manuscript of Archimedes described by J. L. Heiberg in *Hermes* vol. 42, page 248, I would like to let you know that I wish to sell this manuscript.
    I have shown it to M. Omont of the Bibliothèque Nationale as well as to the Bodleian Library and both have made me offers that I found insufficient. You would greatly oblige me if you would let me know whether this manuscript interests you or at any rate if you would write to me to whom I could offer it with a chance of selling it. I am asking $6,000.
    In expectation of receiving news from you, I ask you, dear professor, to be assured of my highest respect for you.

    S. Guerson

The evidence of this one letter meant that the twentieth-century history of the Palimpsest needed to be rewritten. Not only were the forgeries painted after the manuscript left the Metochion, but the manuscript was identified in 1932 as the Palimpsest and Sirieix had not owned the manuscript until after 1934. How had the manuscript gotten from Constantinople to Paris, and who was responsible for the forgeries?

A New History

The person who first recognized the Archimedes Palimpsest for what it was after it left the Metochion was the curator of the Huntington Library in Los Angeles in 1932. I wrote to my colleague Mary Robertson, curator of manuscripts at the Huntington Library, and although she could not come up with definite proof, she thought it most likely that the curator in question had been Captain Reginald Berti Haselden. Between 1931 and 1937 Haselden had been in correspondence with Professor Edgar Goodspeed of the Department of New Testament Studies in Chicago over some palimpsested material. He was particularly interested in ultraviolet photography and wrote a book in 1935 entitled *Scientific Aids for the Study of Manuscripts*. This was exactly his cup of tea.

It seems that Haselden only had the opportunity to identify one folio of the manuscript, not the entire codex, and that this one folio had been transcribed by Heiberg on page 248 of his article in *Hermes*. This is folio 57. How it was that Haselden identified this folio alone is something of a mystery. Maybe he saw a photograph of just this one page. Just possibly it had already been separated from the manuscript—as it is now—and Haselden merely studied this single leaf. Be that as it may, it is further proof that the forgeries were added after Salomon Guerson wrote his letter, and therefore after the book had been identified as Heiberg's Codex C. Folio 57 is now covered with a forgery. Not even Haselden, with his interest in scientific aids, could have identified the Archimedes text through the forgery. The forgeries were indeed done after 1932, and after Salomon Guerson had acquired the manuscript.

Even before Georgi had unearthed the Willoughby letter, John Lowden had already suspected that the Guerson business was involved in the history of the Palimpsest. He had his own very good reason for suspecting that they were indeed responsible for the forgeries. He discovered that the Guersons owned a leaf from a Byzantine manuscript that was exhibited in a famous exhibition of Byzantine art in Paris in 1931. The unusual way in which the figures in the Palimpsest forgeries were framed was exactly like the leaf that the Guersons owned and exhibited in the 1931 exhibition. The Willoughby letter was an extraordinary confirmation of John's insight. It demonstrated that not only did the Guersons own the manuscript, but that they also had known Henri Omont, from whose publication the Evangelists in the forgeries had been traced.

John had also made substantial progress in determining how the Palimpsest might have traveled from the Metochion to Paris. Salomon Guerson certainly knew one of the most famous dealers of the twentieth century, Dikran Kelekian. And it might well have been through Kelekian that they had acquired some of their manuscripts. In 1931, Kelekian owned two miniatures taken from the same book as the miniature that the Guerson business had displayed in Paris in the same year. The manuscript from which they all came is known to have been perfectly intact in a convent in Constantinople as late as 1922. By 1931, Kelekian had inserted his two miniatures into yet another manuscript, which came from—guess where—the Metochion. The Guersons had good access to manuscripts from the Metochion. The circumstantial evidence that the Guerson business was responsible for the forgeries in the Duke manuscript, as well as the Archimedes Palimpsest, is compelling.

But one small thing doesn't add up. The Guerson business was a respectable and successful one on Boulevard Haussmann. The Willoughby letter shows that Salomon Guerson knew what he had, and he knew it was worth a lot of money. Conservatively, $6,000 is $70,000 today, which was a lot of money for a medieval manuscript in those days. Salomon Guerson thought the book was valuable precisely because he knew it contained the writings of Archimedes. The Canadians, for their part, had demonstrated in their report that the forgeries could not have been done until after 1938. So we are left with the situation that the Guersons hung on to the book for at least seven years, waiting patiently for someone to pay the appropriate price for it, before suddenly making forgeries out of the mathematician's letter to Eratosthenes after 1938. Something doesn't add up. Salomon Guerson may have been a little unscrupulous in his treatment of Byzantine manuscripts, but he didn't have sufficient motive for this particular crime. We needed to find one.

The Casablanca Hypothesis

On Friday, June 14, 1940, the Germans entered Paris. They wore gray; the Norwegian Ilse Lund wore blue. Czech resistance hero Victor László was sick in a freight car on the outskirts of Paris. American freedom fighter Rick Blaine stood on a station platform in the rain with a comical look on his face because he'd been stood up by a girl. Rick got on the train and left Paris, along with three and a half million others. He eventually made it to Casablanca, where he made a handsome profit at his Café Américain, which was mainly populated by once-wealthy Europeans, most of whom were selling family treasures for a song in order to bribe their way to safety. This is the plot of a movie starring Humphrey Bogart and Ingrid Bergman. Reviel and I have a similar plot to account for what happened to Archimedes. It is just as short on hard facts as the movie and should be similarly understood as fiction. It has a much darker plot than *Casablanca*. Here is the summary:

On Friday, June 14, 1940, the Germans entered Paris. Salomon Guerson and Archimedes do not leave town, at least not on the same day as Rick Blaine. Salomon thinks that he can stick it out in Paris. Forty-eight hours later he isn't so sure: all Jews are ordered to register at a police station. But he is still there on Wednesday the twenty-sixth when Hitler arrives. Salomon is thankful that Hitler heads down the Champs-Elysées from the Arc de Triomphe rather than up the Boulevard Haussmann, but he can hear the noise down the street from his shop, which he has closed for the day. Salomon never reopens his shop. Its contents are plundered by the Nazis. They take any artwork of value to the Jeu de Paume to be sorted and then ship it back to the motherland. Salomon goes into hiding, with just a few of his possessions. One of them is the Palimpsest. It is small, portable, inconspicuous, and, he thinks, valuable.

Two years later, Salomon gets increasingly desperate. On Wednesday, July 16, 1942, the Vichy police begin deporting Parisian Jews, rounding them up at the Winter Velodrome. Their more permanent deportation camp is at Drancy, from which, in the next two years, 70,000 people, including many of his friends are shipped to Auschwitz and disappear. Salomon is struggling to stay alive. He looks at his remaining assets; he is reluctant to part with the Palimpsest, but eventually he must. He cannot sell it himself, of course; if he tries, the book will simply be confiscated. He decides to give it to a friend to sell on his behalf. But Salomon finds himself short of friends and the friends he does have find the book a hard sell, at any price. Finally Salomon turns to Marie Louis Sirieix. He is hopeful of a good reception. Sirieix is a Resistance hero and his daughter, Anne, is married to someone with an extraordinarily similar surname— Guersan. Sirieix is sympathetic, and he even believes Salomon when Salomon tells him that it is the unique key to the mind of Archimedes. But Sirieix also says that no German will believe that it is Archimedes, and anyway, the Nazis are not interested in ugly books. They are interested in art. The Germans have been systematically looting art from Jews in Paris for months. Sirieix is a freedom fighter, not an intellectual, and he takes the pragmatic approach that if only the book had pictures in it, then it would have real currency. Indeed, it would be more valuable than gold.

Salomon Guerson leaves with a seed planted. The screen goes black for a moment and resumes with Salomon, a few days later, returning to Sirieix. He says that he hadn't noticed before, but there are several pictures in his book. Sirieix is suspicious but generous. He is much more impressed with Salomon, and he agrees to buy the book. Archimedes' parchment letter to Eratosthenes becomes Salomon's letter of transit, and it is now covered in pictures. Salomon successfully escapes Paris; Sirieix returns to fighting the Germans, confident of an eventual victory. He has never been particularly interested in the Palimpsest and hides it in his damp basement. The credits roll over a backdrop of the Palimpsest slowly gathering dust and being devoured by a purple mold.

A Plea to the Reader

Abigail now had the data she needed to start work. She had all the documentation from the Canadian Conservation Institute, she had undertaken her own research, and others had helped too. It was clear that once Anne Guersan paid attention to the book that she had inherited, she took steps to have it restored. But she may have only contributed further to Abigail's problems. The PVAC glue that locked the Palimpsest pages together was widely used for the spines of manuscripts in the sixties and seventies. Perhaps this is another example of someone trying to do their best for a book and making the problem worse. Someone also seems to have paid particular attention to the forgeries, keeping them separately and mounting them with Blu-tack, which only came on the market in 1970.

There were, however, several leaves that Abigail could not do any work on. These were the three that I had noticed were missing when Mr. B first left the book with me. They were present when Heiberg looked at the codex, and he even took a photograph of one of them. Abigail had found traces of pigment transferred on to the facing folios of these now-lost leaves. It was safe to assume that the forger had painted these folios as well. Some forgeries made from the book might have been successfully sold and they might be decorating the walls of an apartment in Paris, in Germany or, perhaps more likely, in the United States. Look out for them. If you see them, turn them over. If they have two texts on the back, one much fainter than the other, then please let me know. They are very valuable and not because they have paintings on them. Remember: value translates into cash. You can contact me through http://www.archimedespalimpsest.org.

Intensive Care

If caring for Mr. B's book sounds like a daunting job, then I have succeeded only in hinting at the true magnitude of the task facing Abigail and her colleagues in the book and paper conservation lab at the Walters. Every aspect of the material characteristics of the codex has been investigated. The Canadian Conservation Institute took a microscopic core sample from a folio containing the Archimedes text. Analysis of the sample only reinforced the fact that the collagen was breaking down and that the surviving palimpsested text was extremely thin—a mere stain engrained in the parchment. Before any work was done on a folio, a color-coded map was made recording its condition—the tears, the drops of wax, the mold stains, the rust, and the Blu-tack. The manuscript was also comprehensively photographed. Each bifolio of the prayer book had its own written condition report, its own treatment proposal, and its own treatment log. If the treatment proposals had been for patients in hospital, then those patients would have been in the intensive-care unit. And intensive care is exactly what they were given. As she worked, Abigail saved everything. To this day there is a box of carefully bagged fragments of the Palimpsest. Each bag is labeled, telling us which bits of thread, glue, wax, pigments, and paper came from which folio of the prayer book. The myriad tears in the parchment were given tiny mends, so that more bits did not fall off when they were imaged.

It was not until Saturday, November 8, 2003, that Abigail started to treat the beginning of Archimedes' letter to Eratosthenes. I have edited her treatment log, which might not be a great read but which does demonstrate the intensity with which she worked on the only surviving copy of the letter.

175

On that Saturday, Abigail separated it from the bifolio that was wrapped around it. It took all day to do this, because the two bifolios had been stuck together with PVAC. She removed loose debris from the gutter. The next day, Sunday, Abigail relaxed the parchment at the spine by lightly brushing it with a mixture of isopropanol and water. Then she made a tracing of both sides of the bifolio, showing the damaged areas and those that had been obscured by glue and paint. This took two hours. Among other things that Abigail documented on her tracing was a paper reinforcement that had been attached to the spine-fold with PVAC and which obscured Archimedes' text. Abigail also plotted on her tracing several small fragments of parchment and a small deposit of purple paint. She concluded that one of the forgeries had once been stuck in the book next to this leaf. Abigail then comprehensively photographed the bifolio. Then she applied more isopropanol and water to the paper reinforcement. After 15 minutes she began to take it off. By the end of the day, she had removed it completely. Monday was a day of recuperation, not for Abigail, but for the bifolio. On Tuesday, November 11, Veterans' Day, Abigail looked at the other side. Around the spine-fold, there were large gritty deposits, colored fibers, white fibers, black accretions that might have been hide glue, and white crystalline particles that she thought might have been silica gel, put there possibly in 1971 by the Etablissement Mallet when they were trying to stop the mold. She also noted further blobs of PVAC on the bifolio. She began cleaning the residual adhesive and accretions from the spine-fold. The fold itself was very cockled and creased; Abigail tried to flatten out these creases. All the residues and accretions that she removed that day were saved. She did not return to the bifolio again until Sunday, November 16. In the spine-fold, around the fourth sewing station, Archimedes' text was obscured because the parchment was torn and crushed and a loose flap of it was

FIGURE 7.3 *A section of the Palimpsest, before treatment, after treatment, and in ultraviolet light. Note Netz's circled "kuklos"*

embedded with the PVC and white paper fibers. Repeated applications of ethanol and water freed the flap, which was realigned. The area was then dried under pressure. The next day Abigail started work on several flaps of parchment that were curled up in a severely degraded and perforated area of the bifolio. She applied tiny amounts of ethanol, the flaps gradually relaxed, and Abigail secured them back in place. The area was then dried under pressure. On that day Abigail also worked on areas of parchment that were folded over around the edge of the leaf and these she reinforced with Japanese paper. Abigail never attempted to remove wax droplets on this leaf, because it was simply too fragile. When she had fully prepared the leaf for imaging, she sent a sample of the PVAC for analysis at the Canadian Conservation Institute.

All the other folios of the manuscript got this same level of care. I show you one untypically spectacular example. Abigail mended the gutter of one of the Archimedes folios. Here, a flap of parchment had been scrunched up and broken and it had to be unfolded so that the text could be read. Abigail performed brain surgery that morning. Later in the day, we took an ultraviolet photograph of the folio and sent it as a jpeg attachment to Reviel Netz. This is the email I got by return:

From: Reviel Netz
Sent: Sun 4/15/2001 10:14 AM
To: "William Noel"

Dear Will,
The attached is your recent AQ picture, fantastic. Circled is the self-obvious symbol for the Greek word Kuklos, meaning "circle." First time I've seen this symbol in the Archimedean manuscript tradition, and this has consequences for working out the relationship between the branches of the tradition, as well as of course for the history of mathematical symbolism. Kudos to AQ.

In his enthusiasm, Reviel was actually wrong; Heiberg had noticed the kuklos. Luckily Reviel only told me this a lot later—thank goodness. It was one day when our spirits rose and those days were rare and precious, because, basically, preparing the Archimedes leaves for imaging was a time-consuming nightmare.

Most of Abigail's work occurred under the microscope and most of it is now not apparent to the naked eye. The flash of a camera and a clever algorithm, as we shall see, can transform a page. A brilliant scholarly insight can transform our understanding of Archimedes. But Abigail and her colleagues always knew that this was not what their work was about. Except to the very careful observer, other than the fact that they are disbound, the folios of the Palimpsest look little different after Abigail's treatment from how they looked before she started work.

I had originally hoped to see a dramatic change in the forgery pages. In fact, I wanted Abigail to scrape the forgeries off. But other people had very different views. John Lowden, for example, considered that they were an important part of the history of the codex. What was for me merely incidental graffiti that obscured the writings of a genius was to John a record of twentieth-century attitudes toward the Byzantine past. This was a view that Abigail shared. And she brought two more observations to the table. First, if she tried to take off the images, she might destroy the Archimedes text underneath. Second, even if we did not have the technology to read through the forgeries now, the technology might exist in the future. We could always wait. After all, Heiberg waited. He had not taken the codex apart, and he had not painted it with Gioberti's tincture. He must have been sorely tempted, but, for the good of the codex, he didn't. Eventually I saw Abigail's point. More importantly, so did Mr. B.

Yet it was here, truly in the emergency room, that the tide of the project almost imperceptibly changed. It was upon Abigail's patient work that the later triumphs of the project were built. For, by hook or by crook, she did do it. She took the thing apart. The disbinding started on April 3, 2000. The final folios were disassembled on Thursday, November 4, 2004. On average, one palimpsested folio was liberated from the prayer book every fifteen days. After she had prepared them as best she could, the folios were mounted in specially prepared mats so that the scientists could image them.

Discoveries

Of course, the scholars did not wait until the scientists had taken their images of these folios. Their view was that, if they were in good enough shape for the scientists to image, they were in good enough shape for them to try to read. Once Abigail had started to disbind the leaves, Natalie, Reviel, and John Lowden came and studied them.

The first scholarly discovery came quickly, on April 3, 2000. On the very day that Abigail took the book apart, Reviel and Natalie were scrutinizing parts of the Palimpsest with ultraviolet lamps. They sat next to each other conferring. Understandably, the first folio came under their gaze quickly. I have explained already that this page is in very bad condition. But as Reviel stared at it under UV, he thought he saw underwriting, and he thought it was underwriting by the Archimedes scribe. He discussed it with Natalie. Natalie, too, studied the leaf. "Yes," she said. They had just discovered a new page of Codex C. The very first page of the codex contained *Floating Bodies* text in Greek that Heiberg simply hadn't noticed. On the first day of disbinding, on the first day of reading, and on the first page of the codex we had discovered a whole new page of *Floating Bodies* in Greek. It was a major triumph for the project.

It was slowly becoming apparent that Heiberg had not known the manuscript quite as well as people thought. This became even clearer when Reviel and I went to see the Heiberg photographs. There were sixty-five photographs in all, and they were marked up with notes by Heiberg, who identified folios of the Archimedes text as he went along. Naturally, all the photos were of folios that contained Archimedes text. We could see the way he worked. He labeled those folios containing the *Method* "M," *Stomachion* "St," and the rest he labeled by reference to his own previous edition, which he had published in 1880. However, there were only sixty-five photographs. Of these, thirty-eight were openings, the rest were single folios. Heiberg had photographs of only 103 rectos and versos of folios out of a codex that contained, in his time, 354. One photograph in particular caught Reviel's eye. It was of the right-hand side of an opening. But I noticed that Reviel was not looking at this folio; rather he was looking at the little bit of the preceding folio, on the left-hand side of the original opening, which was by chance included in the photograph. It contained only three lines of Archimedes text. Reviel looked, and looked again. "This is *Floating Bodies*," he said. Reviel knew instantly that he was reading a section of *Floating Bodies* in Greek and for the very first time. Heiberg had overlooked the folio on the left. He had not taken a photo of it, and he had not transcribed it. Looking at the photographs now, one can only admire Heiberg's skill. It is extraordinarily difficult to read the Archimedes text from the photographs, and he had read them. Nonetheless, there were whole sections of *Method* and *Floating Bodies* for which he hadn't taken photographs, and which he had left largely unread.

The best day for Abigail and me in this challenging period was Saturday, April 13, 2002. John Lowden was in Baltimore to look at the Palimpsest. I knew that he had to fly to London at 3 p.m., so I went down to the conservation laboratory at about midday to see how he was doing. He popped his head out of a black curtain to tell me that the Palimpsest had been presented to a church 773 years ago . . . exactly. With the help of an ultraviolet lamp John had looked at the very first folio of the Palimpsest. The first folio of any codex is normally in worse shape than those that follow, but the first folio of the Palimpsest is a wreck. Bookworms don't actually like parchment folios, they like the wooden covers in which the folios are bound. But they don't have a very good sense of direction. The first folio of the Palimpsest is covered in wormholes. Also, the outside two inches of the folio are stained very dark by the oils in the leather of an old binding. John gave it another look. In the bottom margin, right in the stained area, he discovered an inscription, technically called a colophon. He could not decipher it completely, but it was clear that the prayer book had been given to a church by the scribe on April 14, 6737. But this is in Greek Orthodox time. In the thirteenth century, time was not calculated from the birth of Christ, but from the origin of the world. As we all know, the world was formed on September 1, 5509 BC. To get the modern date for April 14, 6737 one must therefore subtract 5,508. The answer is April 14, 1229. Seven hundred and seventy-three years later, we knew when the Palimpsest was made.

Reflections

As this story unfolded, a picture of the history of the Archimedes Palimpsest was emerging in my mind, which is at odds with the one I have previously recounted. The roles of those who had played their part in the history of the book now seemed extraordinarily different. I began to question my hasty condemnation of the scribe who had erased the Archimedes text, to rethink my description of St. Sabas as a tomb for Archimedes, and to feel shame for my mistrust of the monks of the Metochion. It was because the monks of the Metochion had their manuscripts documented that the Archimedes texts were redis- covered; St. Sabas is better characterized as a safe house for Archimedes than as a tomb. If the price for that safety was the Christian disguise that the scribe of the prayer book provided, it was a price well worth paying. And if it was love of mathematics that had ensured the survival of Archimedes' letter to Eratosthenes for the first thousand years, it was love of God that ensured its survival to the twentieth century.

The scribe was the unwitting savior of Archimedes and not his nemesis. The Palimpsest was the creation of religion, not its victim. It was the victim, rather, of two world wars and the art market. It was the damage sustained in the twentieth century that had led most to believe that the Palimpsest was now a battered relic of little research interest. Reviel was convinced that this was a false assumption and the breakthroughs that we made only increased his insistence that he be allowed to see the book. Once a few leaves were disbound he arranged a trip to Baltimore together with his friend Ken Saito. They were going to come the first weekend in January 2001, the sixth and the seventh. This was the moment of truth. Could Reviel and Ken really get more Archimedes text out of the book than Heiberg? Every time I spoke to the press I said, "Yes"; every time I looked at the wrecked folios of the book I thought, "No." In the end, it didn't matter what I said or what I thought. It merely mattered that the book now had its chance and that Reviel was flying in from California to pass judgment.

8

Archimedes' *Method,* 2001
or Infinity Unveiled

⌐∽⌐

It was nearing the end of 2000. The Palimpsest had been available for research for almost two years, and yet, there was very little to show for it. I was driven back to the traditional routines of library work: visiting the manuscript; holding a magnifying glass in one hand and a UV lamp in the other; and looking at the manuscript intently, one character after another. I envisaged myself doing just this—slowly and painfully going through the manuscript. To be honest, though, I wasn't sure I would be able to read much more this way than Heiberg did. Would it all be just a waste of time?

Will insisted that we had to make priorities. Only a few pages could be made available for my next trip in January 2001, so which ones would I really would like to have? Only a handful of the potential folios were from the *Method* and of those only one had a substantial gap left by Heiberg's own transcription.

I therefore asked for the bifolio 105–110 to be ready for our visit. I wouldn't be alone: I had a guest with me, a tourist or, more precisely a pilgrim. For now, while the Palimpsest was there, this was how historians of mathematics would think of a trip to Baltimore— as a pilgrimage. I knew Ken would value the experience and, besides, I like talking to him. Who knows? We might even get to find out something about Archimedes.

Professor Ken Saito teaches at the University of Osaka, and he is one of the best historians of mathematics at work today. I have always admired his early study of the way in which Euclid's results were used in the theory of conic sections. He is a master of the logic of Greek mathematics: when he reads a text, he sees precisely where it comes from and where it leads to. If anyone could work with me on the Palimpsest, I knew this was the man.

Saito first came to visit me at Stanford. It was his first time in America, and I thought he would like to visit my advanced Greek class. I had my students translate Euclid and Archimedes (most of the Greek language students at Stanford can easily handle the mathematics), and I enjoyed showing my students off. We also spent a day in San Francisco, which Ken enjoyed a lot, although I think he just couldn't wait to travel, at long last, to Baltimore.

We had a long flight ahead of us—enough time to prepare for our visit. As we were flying to Baltimore, Ken and I discussed some of the perennial questions of the history of mathematics. To what extent did Archimedes anticipate the calculus? How much did he know about its conceptual difficulties?

Here, in outline, is the history of mathematics as it was known, back then, in January 2001. The Greeks invented mathematics as a precise, rigorous science. They avoided paradox and mistakes. In doing so, they also avoided the pitfall of infinity. Their science was based on numbers that can be as big as you wish, or as small as you wish, but never *infinitely* big or small. Numbers that are as big or small as you wish are known as "potentially infinite," instead of actually infinite. The Greeks did not use actual infinity.

In the scientific revolution of the sixteenth and seventeenth centuries, scientists such as Galileo and Newton incorporated new techniques into mathematics by employing actual infinity. They utilized magnitudes that were in fact infinitely small or infinitely big. This allowed many important breakthroughs, but there was a price to pay: infinity introduced the paradoxes and errors that follow upon it. Mathematics became more powerful but less precise.

In the nineteenth century, mathematicians created new techniques for dealing with infinity. Gradually, a new mathematics evolved where infinity was introduced and tamed, so to speak. One could deal with infinity, without any paradoxes or errors. The precision of Greek mathematics was regained, on a new level with infinity being used as a precise mathematical tool. This allowed the great explosion of mathematical discoveries—and therefore of scientific discoveries—in the nineteenth and twentieth centuries.

In a nutshell, the Greeks had precision without infinity. The scientific revolution had infinity without precision. Modern science, since the nineteenth century, has had both precision *and* infinity.

What was the potential infinity used by Archimedes? Recall the imaginary dialogue. Archimedes packs a curved object so that a certain area has been left out, an area greater than the size of a grain of sand. A critic comes along and says: "There is still a difference greater than the size of a grain of sand." "Is that right?" exclaims Archimedes. "All right then, I shall apply my mechanism successively several more times," and then the area left out is smaller than the grain of sand. "Wait a minute," says the critic, "the area left out is still greater than a hair's width." Archimedes goes on, and so on, and on and on it goes. The difference always becomes smaller than any given magnitude mentioned by the critic. This dialogue goes on *indefinitely*. This is *potential infinity*.

Let us take another example. First consider the collection of whole numbers using only the principle of potential infinity. Then say that, for each whole number, no matter how large, we can think of another one bigger than it. This is another imaginary dialogue, a kind of auction. You say a million, I say two million; you say a billion, I say a trillion. This bidding sale has no end. But no one is allowed to say infinity itself; there is no such number allowed.

But then, the guidelines are altered, and we can use actual infinity. Suppose someone enters the auction and says, "I have a number, which is even bigger than all the numbers you have mentioned. This is the number of all whole numbers. It says how many whole numbers there are." The auction ends with a bang: actual infinity has brought it to an end.

There are clearly more whole numbers than a million, a billion, or a trillion. The number of all whole numbers is infinity. And it gives rise to all the paradoxes of infinity.

Suppose, for instance, you wish to compare the number of whole numbers to the number of even numbers. We may put them side by side in two rows.

1	2	3	4	5	...
2	4	6	8	10	...

For each number in the top row there is a number in the bottom row (its double). The bottom row does not get exhausted, ever. For each whole number there is an even number and vice versa. The number of whole numbers is the same as the number of even numbers. In the case of whole and even numbers, we find that they are the same size even though there are clearly, in some sense, twice as many whole numbers than there are even ones. In infinity, "normal" concepts collapse: a collection may be equal to its half. And so we cannot count on ordinary rules of addition and summation. Infinity gives rise to too many paradoxes. This is why it is such a difficult tool to handle.

In the nineteenth century, mathematicians found the techniques to calculate with infinity. (The main insight came from Archimedes' imaginary dialogues.) The Greeks never made this step (it is a big one). They had collections that were "as big as you wish," but never collections that were actually infinite.

Even in the *Method*—so we thought, back in January 2001— Archimedes did not break this rule. He played, dangerously, with infinity. But he did not speak of "the collection of all the parallel lines in the triangle." All he said was that, since each parallel line balanced its paired section with a certain fulcrum, so would the entire triangle. Whether this was true or not depended on techniques of summing up infinitely many objects. But Archimedes never explained what he was relying upon for his summation. Even in his most radical experiment actual infinity was avoided. It was left for Galileo and Newton to uncover it.

So went our conversation. During breaks, Ken Saito would return to the book he had brought with him: a copy of Heiberg's edition of

Archimedes' *Method*. True to form, Saito was immersing himself in the ancient text. We were about to read a hitherto unknown piece of the text. For some reason—we didn't know why—Heiberg had a gap in his edition. What could Archimedes have written there? To make sure that we got to the bottom of it, Saito wanted to know everything about the context.

This, then is the overall structure of the *Method*. Archimedes begins with an introduction addressed to Eratosthenes. It is a very flattering introduction: "You are such a mathematician that you are capable of passing a real judgment on my method." As we were talking, I suggested to Saito one of my hobby horses. Wouldn't it be like Archimedes, I said, to be *ironical* in this introduction? That is, did Archimedes not intend, perhaps, to unmask Eratosthenes? I suggested that we think of the *Method* as a puzzle sent to Eratosthenes and intended to defeat him. It is, after all, a very puzzling text—could it be intentionally so?

Perhaps, nodded Saito, and he returned to the text.

The *Method* is indeed a puzzle. We have followed the first proposition with its remarkable combination of physics, mathematics, and infinity. Proposition 1 has two striking properties: the application of physics to mathematics and the summation of infinitely many lines. The same combination is repeated throughout the first thirteen propositions of the *Method*.

Archimedes promises in his introduction that, at the end of the treatise, he will repeat the proofs for some of the results, deriving them now in an "orthodox," standard way. Most of this disappeared either when the palimpsester discarded parts of the original manuscript, in the year 1229, or at some later time, when a few of the prayers for reasons we do not understand got cut out of the prayer book. Either way, much of the end of the *Method* was lost. But proposition 15 survives in part, and it is indeed an orthodox, standard proof based on the imaginary dialogue of: "I shall find you an even smaller magnitude."

Proposition 14 is different. It is neither an orthodox proof, nor is it like the first thirteen propositions of the *Method*. It does not rely on the combination of the application of physics to mathematics and infinite summation. Instead, it is based on infinite summation alone. Not that people have paid much attention to it throughout the twentieth century. Propositions such as proposition 1 appear to be puzzling enough. Why bother with this one as well? Especially since this proposition survives in fragmentary form only. Heiberg could read its beginning and its end, but not its middle. The writing was too faint. Could it be read now?

This was precisely why Saito was preparing himself. We were going to look at the middle of proposition 14, the part that Heiberg had not read. Abigail had just unwrapped it, and the scientists were about to produce a digital image.

This would be the first major trial for the project. Either we make readings where Heiberg had failed or we give up, content with Heiberg's edition. Perhaps he had done as much as could be done. This would be a pity in terms of the Greek edition, where every word counted. But I doubted how much interesting material could be revealed for the history of mathematics. In truth, I thought I could use the Palimpsest to further the understanding of the cognitive history of mathematics—looking at such questions as the nature of diagrams and abbreviations. In terms of the traditional concerns of the history of mathematics, I doubted that the Palimpsest could teach us much that was new. Perhaps we would be able to read something, perhaps not. But it would not be of much consequence to the history of mathematics.

After all, the general outlines of Archimedes' principles of summation were clear enough from the first thirteen propositions of the *Method*. Heiberg had not read the middle of proposition 14, but he had read enough of other propositions to develop a clear enough guess of how Archimedes would proceed here. The object of the proof was clear, from its beginning and end. Archimedes was measuring the volume of a cylindrical cut. That is, we take a cube (see fig. 8.1). We enclose a cylinder in it. We cut the cylinder (and the cube) by an oblique plane passing through the middle of the base of the cube and an edge of its top. What is the volume of the cylinder that

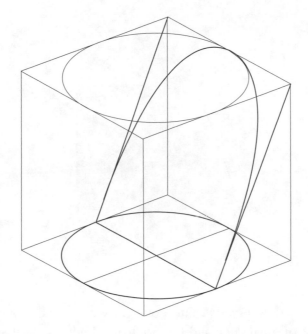

FIGURE 8.1

has been sliced off by this cut—the fingernail-like shape that is shaded in figure 8.2? This is a very strange figure, framed by a combination of a semi-circle, a semi-ellipse, and the contours of a cylindrical surface. This is the entire point for Archimedes. A very strange and unwieldy figure is going to be measured, very precisely, in terms of a rectilinear figure. Let us see how Heiberg understood this measurement. (For the more geometrically inclined readers, please note now that I am treating the enclosing figure as a cube. Archimedes himself approaches the problem in the more general terms of any parallelepiped, but we gain a lot in simplicity by considering the case of the cube alone, which is then very easy to transfer to the general case treated by Archimedes.)

Once again, then, we witness the measurement of a curvilinear object. And once again—as everywhere else in the *Method*—Archimedes uses some kind of slicing by parallels. Heiberg was capable of reading that a random plane is drawn, parallel to the vertical edge

FIGURE 8.2

of the cube (see fig. 8.3). This results in various cuts being sliced off from the original cube and the original cylinder, as well as from the bases of those figures. Archimedes considers certain planes and lines and derives certain proportions (we will look at these in more detail). Heiberg followed all of this. And then—the gap in the argument. Heiberg could read no further for a long stretch and then, when he picked up the text again, he was already near the end of the proposition. There Heiberg found Archimedes' conclusion, which was that the cylindrical cut was exactly one sixth of the entire enclosing cube.

How had Archimedes got there? Had he actually proved his result? Heiberg couldn't read the relevant passage. Everyone since Heiberg has assumed that it involved the same kind of implicit summation used in proposition 1. That is, having obtained a proportion for the randomly chosen slice, Archimedes implicitly transferred that result to the entire cylindrical cut—the way Archimedes moved in proposition 1 from the randomly chosen parallel line to the triangle and parabola taken as a whole. This was everyone's guess; and my guess, too—nothing new would come out of this proposition. Saito, meanwhile, was immersing himself in his text: perhaps we were wrong after all?

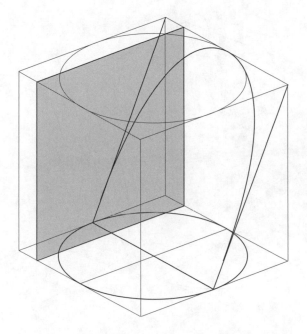

FIGURE 8.3

The Volume of a Cylindrical Cut

Saito and I finally sat there, in front of the bifolio 105–110. We turned quickly to the area that Heiberg had left as white lines, remarking in a footnote: "*quid in tanta lacuna fuerit dictum, non exputo*" or "I shall not speculate as to what could have been written in such a large gap."

In order to follow the mathematical argument in more detail, let us concentrate on just the object that interests us. In figure 8.4, we "slide out," as it were, a section of the cube—the triangular prism cut off by the inclined plane. From now on we will concentrate just on this triangular prism. We now draw three further diagrams, reconstructing the text as far as the lacuna. These diagrams (see fig. 8.5–7) are simply three different views of this triangular prism. It is so difficult to perceive that one needs to view it from certain angles, simultaneously, to gain a sense of it. (Archimedes, however, visualized the object clearly enough on the basis of figure 8.7 alone!)

191

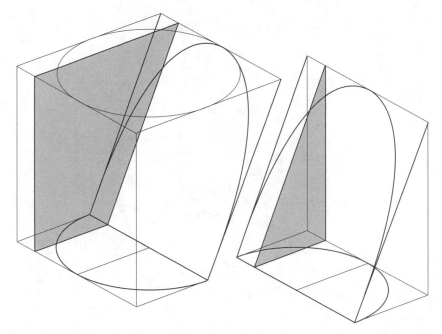

FIGURE 8.4

In figure 8.5, we see the entire complicated triangular prism with a randomly chosen plane running parallel to the upright edge of the cube.

Figure 8.6 shows the randomly chosen plane *from the side.* The randomly chosen plane cuts off a triangle from the original triangular prism. It also cuts off a smaller triangle from the original cylinder. Thus, figure 8.6 shows two triangles, one enclosed within the other—the bigger triangle, from the triangular prism, and the smaller triangle, from the cylinder. The smaller triangle is especially important, because the strange figure that we are about to measure— the fingernail-like figure cut off the cylinder—is made up of the collection of all such triangles cut off from the cylinder. (These triangles get bigger and bigger as the randomly chosen plane gets removed further away from the edges of the cube.)

Figure 8.7, finally, offers a bottom view. The randomly chosen plane creates not only triangles from the triangular prism and the

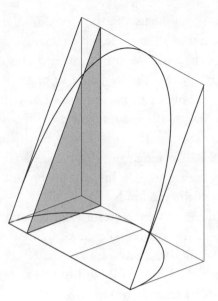

FIGURE 8.5

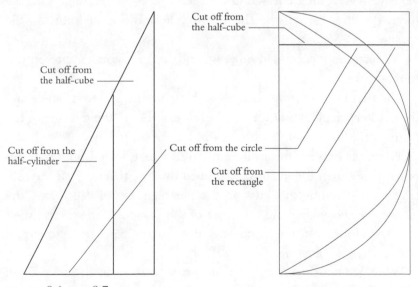

Cut off from
the half-cube

Cut off from
the half-cube

Cut off from the
half-cylinder

Cut off from the circle

Cut off from
the rectangle

FIGURE 8.6 AND 8.7

cylinder but also line segments on the bottom of the cube. The bottom of the half-cube is a rectangle. This rectangle is the footprint of the entire triangular prism. Within this rectangle we also find a semi-circle. This semi-circle is the footprint of half the cylinder—the half whose slice we are about to measure. To really spice things up, Archimedes then drew another curve inside this rectangle, and— what do you know—this figure happened to be a parabola! And so we have, in figure 8.7, a rectangle, inside it a semi-circle, and inside that a parabola. And then, a straight line passes through them all. The line is the footprint of the randomly chosen plane.

The randomly chosen plane creates a line through the rectangle. This line is the base of the greater triangle of figure 8.6, the one that is cut off from the triangular prism. The randomly chosen plane also creates a line through the semi-circle within the rectangle. This line is the base of the smaller triangle of figure 8.6, the one that is cut off from the cylinder. It also creates a line through the parabola. This time, the line has no three-dimensional meaning in terms of figure 8.6 and functions in the context of figure 8.7 only. Once again, then, we have several lines encased inside each other—one that cuts off the rectangle, one that cuts off the semi-circle, and one that cuts off the parabola.

We have now presented our cast, and we may concentrate on just four actors.

The first two are from figure 8.6: these are the greater triangle and the smaller triangle of figure 8.6. Let us call them "the triangle of the prism" and "the triangle of the cylinder," respectively.

The next two are from figure 8.7. We actually need only two out of the three mentioned above. We need the line that cuts off the rectangle, and the line that cuts off the parabola. Let us call them "the line of the rectangle" and "the line of the parabola," respectively.

These four cast members will now participate in a four-part arrangement of *proportion*.

What Heiberg managed to read, prior to the gap in his reading, was already a magnificent result. Archimedes, through tremendous geometrical ingenuity, had succeeded in proving that in such an arrangement:

- The area of the triangle of the prism is to the triangle of the cylinder as the line of the rectangle is to the line of the parabola.

A triangle is to a triangle, as a line is to a line: two dimensions as one dimension.

Here came the long gap in the text. The text picked up again with Heiberg reading the following:

- The volume of the triangular prism is to the volume of the cylindrical cut as the area of the entire rectangle is to the area of the entire parabolic segment.

The triangular prism is to the cylinder as the rectangle is to the parabolic segment: three-dimensional figures are to each other as two-dimensional figures are to each other.

Archimedes' geometrical discovery was that the triangles in figure 8.6 related to each other as certain lines do in figures 8.7. This, in other words, is a statement about a random slice, exactly the same type of statement that we saw in the first proposition of the *Method*. It appears, therefore, that Archimedes was once again making the move, implicitly, from a statement about random slices to a statement about the entire objects from which the slices were taken. The first triangle is a random slice of the triangular prism, the second triangle is a random slice of the cylinder; the first line is a random slice of the rectangle, the second line is a random slice of the parabola. And since, in each random slice, the first triangle is to the second triangle as the first line is to the second line, so, with the entire objects, the triangular prism will be to the cylinder as the rectangle is to the parabola.

So the text states, with Archimedes appearing to make an implicit move. But the thing is, there was, after all a gap—a space for Archimedes to make his argument explicit.

What could that explicit argument have been?

We could see why Heiberg had not made much progress. The page was largely illegible. Once again, we found ourselves admiring Heiberg for what he had been able to read. Even with the UV light the gap seemed hopeless, and we turned instead to the passages Heiberg had read already, trying to verify them. But even those we could hardly read. How had Heiberg ever made it?

We looked again at the conclusion to the proposition. Having shown that the half-cube was to the cylindrical cut as the rectangle was to the parabola, Archimedes went on with a quick calculation. We remember from the first proposition of the *Method* that a parabolic segment is four-thirds the triangle it encloses. Everyone knows that the rectangle is twice the triangle it encloses. So how much is the rectangle to the parabolic segment? It is as "two" is to "four-thirds" which (to simplify a bit) is as "six-thirds" is to "four-thirds." It is as six to four or as three to two. The rectangle is therefore to the parabolic segment as three to two or, more comfortably put, the parabolic segment is two-thirds the enclosing rectangle. We've got it! The cylindrical cut is two-thirds the triangular prism that encloses it or, better put for our purposes, it is four-sixths of the triangular prism that encloses it. It will take a while to show the following result: the triangular prism enclosing the cylindrical cut is exactly *one-fourth* the original cube as a whole. The cylindrical cut is *four*-sixths the triangular prism; so it is *one*-sixth of the original cube as a whole. The strange, fingernail-like object is exactly one-sixth the cube. We've got it! Yet another curvilinear object successfully measured using a rectilinear object.

Another elegant result by Archimedes and no application of physics, it appears this time. The triangles and lines are not put on an imaginary balance. They are simply summed up: infinitely many proportions being summed up into a single proportion. How does Archimedes do this? Does he simply ignore the paradoxes, the errors of infinity?

We would not give up. We went back to the gap in the text. We swapped positions, first Ken looking at the page, then me. I was more trained and quickly it became clear that I should be doing the looking and Ken should be writing down what I saw.

Will left the room, counting on our good behavior. After many minutes of frustration, I did something I shouldn't have done. I slipped the bifolio out of its plastic encasing. Unprotected by the plastic, the reflection from the ultraviolet lamp was clearer. I stared hard into the area on the page—those white lines left by Heiberg— trying to find some traces of Greek characters.

I thought I did see something. At first I discarded it, because it did not make sense in the context. There was no reason for Archimedes to be using such a word. But I did think I saw the three characters in sequence—epsilon–gamma–epsilon, or ege.

"I think I see 'ege,'" I finally told Ken. "Probably something to do with *megethos*, the Greek word for 'magnitude.' This does not make much sense."

Because, you see, Archimedes was talking about certain concrete geometrical objects—a cylinder, a triangle, and a parabola. In such a context, a Greek mathematician would not make the transition into speaking about magnitudes in general terms. The word "magnitude," with its generality, is appropriate not in a concrete, geometrical context, but in a more abstract context such as in a study on the theory of proportions or of magnitudes. It was as if, in the middle of a calculation with concrete numbers, the text moved to a discussion of the principles of calculation as such.

"Oh, that's very interesting," said Ken. I should explain that Ken is a well-behaved Japanese scholar. That was an expression of extraordinary agitation. I know he wanted to ask me whether I was sure, but he probably thought such a question would be impolite.

"I am quite sure," I said, looking at it again. Indeed there was less and less doubt the more I looked at it. In fact, I began to see the traces of a theta, immediately following the epsilon–gamma–epsilon. It was epsilon–gamma–epsilon–theta. There was no doubt that Archimedes was talking about a *megethos*. He was talking about abstract magnitudes.

This process of gradual certainty is so typical in the reading of the Palimpsest. By getting acquainted with the page, you gradually learn how to discard the noise; you learn to concentrate on the signal. It's a little bit like tuning through the airwaves. The radio signal is at first noisy, but then you settle on it and it begins to transmit. I now actually saw this "magnitude." I stared at it, dumbstruck.

"Archimedes must be applying result 11," said Ken. At first I didn't quite hear, looking as I was, so closely at the page. And then I began to be even a bit annoyed. How could Ken be telling me what was happening through the lacuna, based on a single word? I was still looking for more words. Ken went on.

"In the introduction to the *Method*, Archimedes mentions that he will use certain basic results. One of these results is proved elsewhere, in the treatise on *Conoids and Spheroids*. It deals with general magnitudes. I always thought Archimedes meant this result to be used only in the later parts of the *Method*, where he uses orthodox, geometrical methods. But apparently he uses it in proposition 14 as well."

Now this got me interested. I put the page back into its plastic casing and picked up the copy of Heiberg's edition that Ken had been reading the whole time. By God, what he said did make sense!

We were now both feverishly going through the possible argument—drawing figures, sketching proportions, seeing for ourselves how this result could be used for bridging the gap from the random slices to the entire objects. The result had to do with the summation of proportions. It did make sense. Archimedes could have been summing up proportions. So it was not an implicit move after all. Archimedes must have had an argument.

"But wait, Ken; there's a problem." I stopped, tearing myself away from the figure we had just drawn. "If this is right, then Archimedes must be summing up a collection made of infinitely many magnitudes. This does not sum up. It becomes infinite; you can no longer calculate with it."

Ken agreed. Something was still missing. The basic result used by Archimedes was based on a proposition proven in *Conoids and*

Spheroids. In this work, it was clear that it could be proven only for sums involving a finite number of magnitudes, because otherwise you would have to speak about an object made up of infinitely many magnitudes, which made no sense. That was actual infinity. How would Archimedes even go about talking about it?

"If one thing is clear, it is that the Greeks did not use actual infinity. There is something wrong here. Or else, something very new."

This was clear, indeed. It was January 2001, and we knew that we had hit on a major discovery for the history of mathematics. Just what, though?

Could we simply be mistaken? I trusted Ken's insight into Greek mathematics. It all made sense. And I was sure I did see that word, those four letters epsilon–gamma–epsilon–theta. Well, at least the first three were certain. . . . But could we base a new interpretation of Greek mathematics (a new twist to the entire trajectory of Western mathematics) on this evidence alone?

That evening Ken and I explained to Will that we really, really wanted to see digital images of this page. An entire chapter in the history of science was waiting to be written based on those images.

The Method, March 2001

I kept going in and out of my office, checking my mailbox. When would it come? It took the imagers just over a month and then, early in March, the CD-ROM arrived. I knew this CD-ROM contained high-resolution, sharp digital images, made with UV, of a single piece of the Palimpsest. It was a small piece of the Palimpsest, no more. But this piece included one side of the bifolio 105–110. The side I truly needed to read.

For the rest of the day, I put all my other work aside. I was looking at a jungle of digital traces, enlarging them so that the pixels blew up and then reducing them again to see the entire picture. I was getting my mind tuned off the noise and tuned in to the signal.

199

I could easily pick up the εγε again. It was clear as daylight in the digital image. Indeed the theta was very clear as well, and, looking for it, I could quickly pick up several other appearances of the word "magnitude." Undoubtedly this was what Archimedes was talking about. A few additional words became visible as well, referring to certain geometrical objects—a cylinder here, a rectangle there. Archimedes was probably applying the general principles of summation of proportion to the concrete, geometrical terms of the figure at hand. And there was no doubt: the digital images made a world of difference.

After making those first inroads, the reading stalled. This was once again a typical part of the cycle of reading. Once you gained your first, easy conquests, there would come a pause. There were no longer any "easy" words to read, even with the digital images. We needed to do some work. Looking and thinking: what could those traces mean?

I looked in this manner for a couple of hours, making little further progress. I needed to clear my head a little, so I went out for a walk, after which I took another look. Just out of curiosity, I stared not at the line of writing itself but a little bit above it. Something there arrested my attention. It was not just a smudge of digital noise; it had the texture and consistency of real ink. Blowing up the pixels, I saw it—the kind of trace that I would normally skip as being too inconsequential but one that, in such a fragmentary text, could be meaningful. It was an accent mark, an acute sign above the line, like this: ´. And because of my acquaintance with the scribe, I knew it was the type of acute sign the scribe used on top of an iota. It is rather like reading the dot of an "i" and identifying the "i" on that basis.

More than this, I knew which "i" it was. It was an iota with an acute accent, and it could belong only to a handful of words where an iota is stressed this way. One likely candidate, in a mathematical context, would be the word *ísos*. Archimedes could have been speaking about this being equal to that, right? And I could indeed see a sigma, now that I was looking for it.

What kind of "equal" then? Looking ahead, I thought I saw another one of those general words of proportion theory. However, this time it wasn't "magnitude" but "multitude." The couple of words fell into place: "equal in multitude." *Isos plethei.* This was good mathematical Greek. This was "equal in multitude" to that. I looked further and further. The text was peppered with "equal in multitude." It appeared that this was what Archimedes was doing throughout this passage. He was showing how the result pointed out by Ken applied to the case at hand. He was showing how this was equal in multitude to that. It was all about such-and-such magnitudes being equal in multitude to other magnitudes.

How I wished Ken was with me then! It was just too good to be true. The expression "equal in multitude" is used in Greek mathematics when discussing the numbers of objects in two separate sets. Suppose I have a set of three triangles and a separate set of three lines. A Greek mathematician would say that the two sets are "equal in multitude," meaning that they are each made up of three objects.

This is what Archimedes was doing. He was saying that, with the infinitely many slices produced in the cube, after all the random slices were made and the cube was entirely cut, the triangles, produced in the cube by all the possible random cuts, were "equal in multitude" to the lines in the rectangle. You see? In each random slice there was a triangle in the cube, standing on top of a line in the rectangle. And Archimedes pointed out that the number of triangles of which the prism was made was the same as the number of lines of which the rectangle was made. Surely he meant this to be verified by the fact that there was a one-to-one relationship. Each triangle stood on an individually separate line and each line was at the bottom of an individually separate triangle.

Archimedes repeated this type of statement three times: he went through the various configurations produced by the slices, showing which set was equal in multitude to which set. And once those equalities of multitude were secured, the result pointed out by Ken

201

applied. This was typical of Archimedes. He did not actually refer, explicitly, to his result; he did not even quote it. He set up the conditions under which the result could apply; and this he did by showing, in detail, which equalities of number applied in the configuration at hand.

Only, of course, those equalities of number were like nothing else we ever knew from Greek mathematics. The objects Archimedes counted—the sets of triangles and lines—were all infinite. Archimedes was explicitly calculating with infinitely great numbers.

More than this, Archimedes was making his calculations based on a sound principle. He apparently was stating that this infinite set was equal to that infinite set, because there was a one-to-one relationship between the two sets. He did not say so in so many words, but Archimedes was never an explicit author. He always left much of the work for the reader.

Note the following fact. Archimedes could have assumed, in principle, that just because the two sets were infinite, they were also equal. This would have been a very natural assumption to make. But the very fact that Archimedes found it necessary to state that particular sets of infinitely many objects are equal, shows that he avoided this naive assumption. Instead, he must have assumed that infinite sets could be said to be equal only when a special argument could be made for their equality. And this leaves only one possible argument for this equality—the argument of one-to-one correspondence.

It so happens that the tool of one-to-one correspondence is the one by which the concept of infinity was finally structured in the late nineteenth century. It is no less than the cornerstone for modern Set Theory. And so we can sum up the lessons learned from pages 105–110 of the *Method*.

First, we find that Archimedes did not merely make an "implicit" move from a random slice to the object made up of those random slices. He relied instead on certain principles of summation. This means that he was already making a step toward the modern calculus and was not merely anticipating it in some naive way.

Second, we find that Archimedes calculated with actual infinities in direct opposition to everything historians of mathematics have always believed about their discipline. Actual infinities were known already to the ancient Greeks.

Third, we see that with this concept of infinity—as with so many others—the genius of Archimedes pointed the way toward the achievements of modern science itself. Back in the third century BC, at Syracuse, Archimedes foresaw a glimpse of Set Theory, the product of the mature mathematics of the late nineteenth century.

Mathematics, Physics, Infinity—and Beyond

It appears that there is some kind of complementary structure in the *Method*. Thirteen propositions apply both physics and the implicit summation of infinitely many objects. In proposition 14 physics is no longer applied. The summation of infinitely many objects is not implicit, but explicit, based on a rule of infinite summations. It therefore appears that, for Archimedes, the application of physics could act as some sort of short cut. When this short cut was not available, one needed instead an explicit, mathematical rule for infinity. It is as if Archimedes thought that, in the physical world, the summation of infinitely many objects was not such a problem. After all, physical objects *are* made up of infinitely many parts. But when one moved to abstract, mathematical objects, there was a need for a special, mathematical principle for doing such a summation.

Archimedes, after all, did not produce the science of the physical world that Galileo and Newton would later produce. This is even though he had assembled—as we have just seen—the tool kit for the making of such science. I think I understand why. The reason was that, for Archimedes, the combination of physics and mathematics was important not for the sake of physics but for the sake of mathematics itself. Archimedes' great desire was not to find out about the motions of planets but to measure curvilinear objects. It so happens that, in our universe, mathematics, physics, and infinity are so closely tied together that, looking to advance pure mathematics, Archimedes also laid the foundation for modern science.

Whichever interpretation we choose, it is clear that our understanding of the historical relationship between mathematics, physics, and infinity will now have to be drastically revised in light of proposition 14. But more than this. We will need to revise our understanding of the Greek treatment of infinity. I like to sum this up with the phrase: "it's not that they couldn't." They could very well envisage actual infinity; they could even operate with it. For various reasons, in most contexts, they preferred to avoid it. But this avoidance was a conscious decision, not some kind of reflection of a shortcoming on the Greeks' part. They were ahead of the infinity game. And so the same goes, in my view, of science. I think Archimedes was capable of producing the kind of science of physics that Galileo and Newton produced. He made the decision not to—other things occupied his mind.

So much for the broad picture of the history of science and mathematics. Another thing became clear now—of great interest to everyone involved with the Archimedes Project. The work *mattered*. There were important passages to still be read. Already, with 105–110, my reading managed to move substantially beyond Heiberg's. Other pages appeared to be even more difficult, but now it became even more crucial to make them visible. The pressure was now on the imagers to produce a completely new kind of product—an image to make the invisible come to light. Would it be possible?

9

The Digital Palimpsest

Abigail had disbound the Palimpsest, and Reviel and Ken Saito had rewarded her work with an insight that blew apart the boundaries of Greek mathematical thought. But it was clear from the start that Abigail's work was merely a step on the way toward a more radical transformation of Mr. B's book. As she was taking the prayer book apart, I was asking the scientists to put all the palimpsested codices that it contained back together again just as they had been before the year 1229.

I did not want the scientists to reproduce the Palimpsest; I wanted them to replace it. I wanted them to make something that was so much better than the codex that scholars would no longer need to make the pilgrimage to Baltimore. I asked them to make the invisible visible, to make it available on desktop computers around the world, and to make it appear in its correct order. Archimedes first, of course, but then the palimpsested texts from the other codices. This was a utopian fantasy. After all, we didn't even know how many other codices there were, let alone what was in them! Yet the result in 2005 exceeded everyone's expectations. Today, scholars can read texts that they literally had not dreamed of reading in 1998. They had been unable to read the texts directly from the manuscript, but now they can read them on a computer. This success was hard won, and it was a long time coming.

It was clear from the beginning that both imaging teams—the one from Johns Hopkins headed by Bill Christens-Barry and the one from the Rochester Institute of Technology headed by Roger Easton and Keith Knox—would be putting most of their efforts and most of their faith into a technique called "multi-spectral imaging." I needed to understand what "multi-spectral imaging" involved, and my guide was the only teacher among them, Roger Easton, Professor of Imaging Science at RIT. I thought of images as shapes produced by artists. Roger thought of images as numbers produced by light. Not surprisingly, it took him a little time to explain his view of things to me.

Light

Light, Roger told me, be it from the sun or from light bulbs, comes in waves of electromagnetism, which themselves consist of tiny energy bundles called photons. The photons can be characterized by the distance between their peaks—their wavelength. Some photons come in long wavelengths, such as radio waves, microwaves, and infrared waves. Some come in much shorter wavelengths, such as ultraviolet waves, X-rays, and gamma rays. Visible light forms a very small part of the entire electromagnetic spectrum, between infrared and ultraviolet. The shorter the wavelength of a photon, the greater its energy. But all photons travel at exactly the same speed in a vacuum: the well-known speed of light—186,282 miles per second.

Photons interact with matter, which is made up of atoms. More specifically, they interact with electrons that take their places at various distances from an atom's nucleus. Not all photons interact with all electrons. Crucially, the interaction depends upon their respective energies; they have to resonate with each other. If they do, a photon will change the energy state of an electron and in response the electron will itself emit a photon. The photon emitted by any given electron will have a precise wavelength and a precise energy; its wavelength will depend upon the energy an electron needs to shed, which in turn depends upon an electron's place in the composition of an atom.

The human eye uses photons to make all the colors of the rainbow. This is how it does it. With its lens, the eye focuses photons emitted by the electrons on to the photosensitive cells of the retina. The photons induce chemical changes in these receptor cells. The changes in the cells depend upon the wavelengths of the received photons. When your cells receive photons with a wavelength of about 400 nanometers, they will change in such a way that they generate an electric current that will travel via the optic nerve to the visual center of the brain, which will interpret the current as a color: blue. When your cells receive photons with a wavelength of about 700 nanometers, the same process will occur, but the chemical change will be slightly different as will the resulting current and the color. In this case, you will see red. We read by recognizing patterns of intensity and color generated in the visual center of our brain as letters. The problem is that many of the letters in the undertext of the Palimpsest cannot be read, even in bright sunlight.

"What could be a better light source than the Sun?" I asked Roger, "and what could be a better receptor than the eye?" The trouble with the Sun as a light source is that it gives off photons at all sorts of different wavelengths. The image that your eye sees under sunlight is the sum of images created at all of the visible wavelengths. If you can create a source that emits light over a relatively narrow band of the spectrum, then the resulting image will just carry the information from that one wavelength, which will not be over-whelmed by light at the others.

Consider, for example, images created using ultraviolet lamps. Although photons from these lamps have wavelengths shorter than those that the eye can detect, they have a remarkable effect on the parchment that they hit. They energize the atoms and molecules in the parchment, which absorb some of the energy and re-emit the rest as photons with a wavelength that happens to be in the blue section of the spectrum visible to humans. While the parchment re-emits visible photons, the ink on the parchment obscures them. As a result, the ink is effectively "backlit" by the soft blue light from this "fluo-rescence," the contrast of the faint undertext increases and thus the text becomes more readable. Ultraviolet fluorescent light has long been used by scholars reading palimpsests and with great success. Reviel and Ken used it to read *Method* proposition 14. But you cannot use an ultraviolet lamp effectively except in a dark room; photons at other frequencies completely obscure what they do.

The eye itself is such an amazing piece of machinery that it is hard to imagine how a manmade version can be better. But the eye has plenty of limitations that we normally do not notice because it has evolved to suit our everyday needs. Its limitations become more apparent when you try to do something extraordinary, though. Looking at planets is difficult, explained Roger, because the size of the image on the retina is so small that it covers only a few of the eye's sensors. Since each sensor "sees" a large part of the planet, the eye cannot see ("resolve") the fine detail. Here, telescopes come in handy. Or try another problem: I find it difficult to see my cat Gracie after dark because the cells of the human retina do not respond to the waves emitted by warm-blooded animals; these infrared waves have much longer length than the light we can see. The human eye is responsive to only a tiny part of the electromagnetic spectrum. But modern cameras can detect infrared waves and can find warm-blooded animals in the dark. This is the basic reason why we use cameras rather than our eyes to read the Palimpsest. Unlike the human eye, modern cameras are sensitive to light outside the visible spectrum, and thus can "see" information to which our eye is "blind."

In short, you can get very different results using narrowband illumination captured by a camera from those you get when you look at an object under the Sun. The successes of imagers around the world in revealing hidden text by using cameras under different narrowband lighting conditions are remarkable. For example, a team at Brigham Young University has attained extraordinary results by imaging the carbonized rolls of a library that was buried in Herculaneum under the volcanic ash of Vesuvius in the early afternoon of Tuesday, August 24, 79 AD. When viewed in normal light, you cannot see any text written on many of these rolls at all. But when imaged at a specific wavelength, the text "pops out" in the most remarkable way. We did not think that imaging Archimedes would produce such clear-cut results, primarily because the Palimpsest is, physically and chemically speaking, a much more complicated object. The text in the Herculaneum rolls had not been scraped off, it had not been over-written, and its support hadn't suffered the mold damage that the Palimpsest had. The rolls had been subject to just one catastrophic incident that had changed the chemical composition of the rolls themselves and the text on them. We were right, too; there is no one wavelength at which the Archimedes text pops out. But this is where multi-spectral imaging comes into its own.

Numbers

Roger told me that multi-spectral imaging was a relatively new technique that had become widely available only since the arrival of computers and digital-imaging technology. Computers turn all the information they receive into numerical values—digits. Actually just two "binary digits" ("bits") are used—0 and 1—but they are combined in a great variety of ways. For example, your laptop computer converts your taps on the keyboard into different combinations of 0 and 1, which it can store and use as instructions to make certain patterns on your screen. When you digitally record music on your computer, the loudness of sound at each time interval is again interpreted as a number. When you take a picture with a digital camera, the light that hits the camera sensor is turned into numerical values. Each "piece" of the image, each so-called "picture element" or "pixel," is given a number made out of 1s and 0s. Many images are "8-bit" images, and the numbers attached to these pixels are made out of eight-figure combinations of 1s and 0s. So, for example, the number 10101010 actually has a value of 170. The number 11111111 has a value of 255. This is the highest value that an 8-bit number can have because, including 00000000, there are only 256 ways in which 0s and 1s can be combined in an eight-figure series. To extract this numerical information you need a software package—a series of instructions to your processor that sorts the numbers and presents the information in useful ways. And you had better have the appropriate software package. Beethoven's Ninth would not make a pretty picture, and the Archimedes Palimpsest is unlikely to sound any better than it looks.

One of the great advantages of digital technology is that it is possible to combine the numbers from images in different ways. You can instruct the computer to adjust the numerical values in the image—to suppress numbers that are too high or too low and to amplify small differences if you decide that they are important. This is how computers get rid of the red-eye caused by the flash out of your family photos. But another advantage of digital technology is that you can overlay one set of numbers with another. You can, for example, add a backbeat behind the voice of a rock star. More importantly for our purposes, you can combine an image taken at one wavelength of light with an image taken at another one to make some feature in that scene more visible. If you take images at many different wavelengths and stack these different images in order of wavelength, one upon another in a computer, you produce a "data-cube" of digital information in which each is seen in different wavelengths of light. Do not imagine this data-cube as a hologram; imagine it as a sea of numbers containing patterns—or curves—that reflect the characteristics of the area imaged. By writing computer algorithms (recipes for retrieving data in a certain way), scientists can carve up the data-cube to manipulate the values of the numbers, accentuate certain curves, and extract the information they want. Much more information can be extracted from a digital data-cube created using narrow bands of light than can be retrieved from the Palimpsest under any single lighting condition.

The most basic procedure to extract information from a data-cube, Roger explained, was "principal components analysis." You ask the computer to make a set of pictures from weighted combinations of the numerical values of images taken at each wavelength. The images in this new set are based on the amount of difference between numerical values of pixels that are close to each other. As a result they do not show patterns of color, but patterns of contrast. The first image in the new set highlights those areas where contrast between different features is greatest; the second image shows the next greatest contrast, the third image the next, and so on. By this process, you start out with a set of images of the same area in different wavelengths of light and end up with a set of images that combine the wavelengths of light to show the different objects of the image. Obviously, in the Palimpsest the first principal component shows the image feature with the most contrast, which is the prayer-book text with its nice dark ink outlined against the light-brown parchment around it. But the second principal component is indeed, in large part, the Archimedes undertext. Yet another principal component image might show the mold. Once you have separated out the components, you can make them as bright or as dark as you like by manipulating the numbers.

Modern science has turned light into numbers, and modern scientists can change the numbers. But the skill is in how you change the numbers and this is as much an art as it is a science.

Digital Cooking

The two teams of imagers started their competition in June 2000, and they worked with five leaves that were already detached from the binding of the codex when it arrived at the Walters.

Bill Christens-Barry took his images with a Kodak digital camera. This is a standard type of camera used by professional journalists the world over. It couldn't make a very big data-cube, but it could create images with a high spatial resolution. Bill and his colleague Joanna Bernstein imaged at 600 dots per inch. Bill called his best shot at manipulating his data his "cookie-cutter" technique. He chose a set of images from the ultraviolet range of the spectrum in which he could see both the prayer-book text and the Archimedes text reasonably well. Then he separated out the principal components of the images he took in normal light and selected one that just showed the prayer-book text. He then played with these two pictures in the computer; he subtracted the image of the prayer-book text from the ultraviolet images that showed both texts well and was left with just the Archimedes text.

Keith and Roger's camera made Bill's look like Fred Flintstone's. To select their wavelengths of light they didn't use glass filters placed in front of the lens; they used the latest technology, a "liquid-crystal tunable filter" (LCTF), by which they could select the wavelength of the incoming photons by turning an electronic knob. The camera even had a tiny electrical refrigerator to keep its sensor cool. With this camera Keith and Roger built data-cubes at thirty-five different wavelengths across the spectrum—a much bigger data-cube than Bill's camera could make. The only disadvantage was that this camera could only image at 200 dots per inch. It had much greater spectral resolution, but less spatial resolution than Bill's camera.

Keith and Roger processed very differently from Bill. They examined each folio that they were looking at and determined pixels that belonged to three different classes of object: pixels that were definitely parchment, those that were definitely prayer book, and yet another class—the important one—pixels that were definitely Archimedes. They then located the corresponding pixels in the images that they took—all thirty-five of them—and made a computer evaluate the vital statistics for each of the pixels. Then, the computer calculated the degree of likelihood that any given pixel was a prayer-book pixel, an Archimedes pixel, or a parchment pixel. If the computer was sure that a pixel was Archimedes, it would be very bright; if it was less sure, it would be dimmer. The computer then combined the results from the different wavelengths. This technique is called "matched spectral filtering."

It looked as if Bill had come to a gunfight with a knife, or at least with a point-and-shoot camera. But, actually, I looked at the images from both teams and thought that they were marvelous: Bill's images were just as good, in my eyes, as Roger and Keith's. In the image showing the Archimedes text, I could see diagrams where previously I had seen nothing. I could see Archimedes text appear from nowhere. And I couldn't see the prayer-book text. It had all but disappeared into the parchment background. I thought that we had cracked it already. I held out the hope that with these pictures we could recreate the Archimedes manuscript as it had been even before it was palimpsested. This would be the Jurassic Park of medieval manuscript studies, and the resurrection of Archimedes. If you looked at one of these pictures, you would understand my excitement. I thought that both teams of imagers had done the job that we had asked and that the only real problem we had was how to choose between them.

On Friday, October 20, 2000, a segment on the Palimpsest was broadcast on ABC's news program *World News Tonight* with the late Peter Jennings. It detailed the remarkable efforts of imaging scientists to uncover the erased texts of Archimedes in an ancient manuscript in Baltimore. Suddenly the imagers were stars. Three days later, on the Monday, they were to present their results to Natalie and Reviel. We were all in for a shock.

Bad Recipes

Reviel could not make the review meeting; he had pneumonia. Natalie Tchernetska, however, voiced complaints for both of them. In her words, the photographs of both teams, but particularly Keith and Roger's, were "out of focus." They had all sorts of unexplained white spots on them. They were not of sufficient resolution. Getting rid of the prayer-book text had not helped at all in reading the Archimedes text. Plain old high-resolution photographs and photographs just taken in ultraviolet light were much better, she said, than these processed images. What had gone wrong? As it turns out, it is not easy for imaging scientists and medieval paleographers to understand each other. So let us, like the imagers, take each of Natalie's complaints in turn.

Her first complaint was that the images were out of focus. Actually they were not out of focus. The problem was one that all multi-spectral imagers face. To get images of different wavelengths of light they had had to change the filters on their camera. Because the light going through different filters refracted at slightly different angles, the resulting images were of slightly different sizes. Since they had taken images at many different wavelengths, and these images had not "registered" properly, the result was that the processed images looked blurred. Now, this doesn't matter much when you are imaging large tracts of ground from space, trying to find a coca field in the Amazon rainforest, which is normally how this technique is used. But it does matter—very much—when you are trying to read the niceties of tiny Greek script from the tenth century. Clearly, Roger, Keith, and Bill were going to have to use fewer wavelengths or find another way to get around this "registration" problem.

Her second complaint was that the images had lots of white spots on them, which looked as if they were supposed to be Archimedes text but were not. Imaging scientists call these spots "artifacts." The imagers had in fact found imaging Mr. B's book to be extremely difficult. As a result, they had had to write very complicated algorithms to extract the Archimedes text. Now, every time you manipulate an image you are playing with data. You might be bringing out the text that you want, but you are also, inevitably, adding noise just by stirring the ingredients. Again, in most applications of multi-spectral imagery this doesn't matter, at least not very much. But in trying to read the Archimedes text, it does matter, very much. The scientists had to come up with simpler algorithms.

Roger and Keith took images at 200 dots per inch—about 8 pixels per millimeter. This was a perfectly sensible thing to do. It is, more or less, the resolution of the rods and cones of the eye if the page is viewed at normal viewing distances. It allowed a complete single folio of the Palimpsest to be imaged in two sections with the available digital camera. They did not make enlarged images of the folios, which would have required a much higher resolution. We simply did not know that Reviel and Natalie wanted to read magnified images to see all of the critical features in the text. If possible, they would have wanted a single Archimedes character to fill up the entire computer screen and still not appear pixilated; Natalie would have loved to see the image as though through a microscope. In reading palimpsest texts, size matters after all. This was another lesson that the scientists had to learn and another way in which the camera could potentially improve upon the eye.

But the most revealing and unexpected complaint that Natalie had was that the imagers had taken away the prayer-book text. They wanted it back again. What on earth had we been doing and why? The scientists had actually succeeded in separating the Archimedes text from the prayer-book text and then in eliminating the prayer-book text. Now the scholars were saying that this didn't help. The reason that it didn't help is actually quite straightforward. The scientists had made the prayer-book text disappear by making it exactly the same color as the parchment. The trouble was that now, when the Archimedes characters disappeared beneath a bit of prayer-book text, the scholars didn't know why. It was no longer clear to them whether the Archimedes letters were invisible because they in fact did not exist or because they were actually hiding underneath the letters of the prayer book. The scientists had created images with characteristics that the scholars simply did not value, however impressive I thought them to be.

The whole day was a litany of complaint. I was as confident in the afternoon that the results were useless as I had been in the morning that they were a triumph. Mike Toth, Abigail, and I met in a closed session at the end of the day. And then, to my amazement, Mike insisted that nothing at all had gone wrong. In fact, he explained, this was how experimental imaging projects worked.

If you ask scientists to come up with a solution to a difficult problem, you will make errors in defining that problem and they, more likely than not, will fail to get the best solution the first time. Really difficult problems, said Mike, get resolved in incremental steps. These steps begin with criticism and end with under- standing. Mike said that it was quite normal in such imaging projects for scientists to produce a misconceived product. We were just at the beginning of a long process by which the imagers come to understand fully what the scholars need and through which they could refine their techniques. Furthermore, Mike insisted, the imagers had done well. They had succeeded in separating the Archimedes text from the rest of the manuscript and there were signs that they were pulling out Archimedes text that could not be seen at all under normal light conditions. Actually, he went on, instead of firing the imagers, we should make them join forces and hire them all. In other words, Mike thought that Mr. B should pay for all three of them to work on the project; we could combine Bill Christen-Barry's experimental approach with the processing skills of Keith and Roger.

I didn't actually think that Mike was nuts, because I knew that he had a vast amount of experience in judging the results of technical projects. But I could not see the way forward, and I dreaded to think what the reaction of the "source selection authority" would be when I emailed him. His reply was, typically, far briefer than my wordy missive. His verdict: "OK."

The First Words

Throughout the taxing period up to March 2001, Reviel and Natalie had been trying to transcribe the Archimedes texts from the scientists' images. I was copied on emails that reveal like nothing else the difficulty of their task. Here is a typical one from Reviel to Natalie:

Natalie, I'm making progress!

Take a look at 48v col. 1 line 6, after the easily readable word perile/psomen. Heiberg is surely wrong to get the rho immediately after without a gap—there is surely a one character gap; furthermore his undotted eta is a very bad eta. This scribe tends to have a small foot of the eta flexed inside a little bit, like a knee reacting in a knee-jerk, but this foot is very smooth, a continuous parabolic curve; in fact, this is more like the scribe's kappa than like his eta. Now, the character just preceding the rho is faint, but does suggest an alpha. Heiberg's concluding to/s seems likely, and so we may have ark[2-3 characters]to/s. How about arkounto/s? Then the immediate couple of words is perile/psomen arkounto/s—"we shall include," "sufficiently." The entire passage could be made to read, e.g., kai allo/n pleiono/n (homoio/n touotois) theo/roumeno/n ta (pleista) ou perile/psomen, arkounto/s gar ho tropos hupodedeiktai dia to/n proeire/meno/n. I bracket words that are truly speculative, though there is some trace of a lambda for pleista, and the famous "moi" at the beginning of line 5.

This transcription was one that Reviel made from one of the trial images. The transcription might have been helpful to Natalie, but it was of absolutely no use to the imagers. Reviel found his own way to show what text he could decipher and what still needed work. He drew pictures.

Working mainly from the ultraviolet images, Reviel would write in green what he could read and in red what he could only guess. There are alarming amounts of red in these pictures. Sometimes he would send images with questions on them. One particularly important passage seemed to be on folio 105. Reviel writes in what he sees but frankly admits to total guesses on the folio. It seems like an extraordinary struggle. And indeed it was. It was worth it, of course, because eventually we would discover that Archimedes knew about "actual" infinity. But we couldn't go on like this indefinitely.

Making Light Work

Roger, Bill, and Keith had a lot to prove. But they not only learned from the criticism of their efforts; they came up with a new concept for the imaging of the Palimpsest based on their early results. They would address the resolution problem and image not at 200 dpi but at 600. To address the registration problem, they were not going to filter the light at all. Instead, the images would be collected under three different lighting conditions, with low-wattage tungsten lights (which give off a very "reddish" light), with Xenon strobe lights (which give off short flashes of bright, white light), and with "long-wave" ultraviolet lamps that emit most of their light at 365 nanometers, which is just barely shorter than the short-wavelength limit of the human eye. They would also take the images with a professional color digital camera, the type now used by every professional photojournalist in the country. There is no point in using the latest technology if the latest technology doesn't help you. Although Bill's Kodak camera didn't have the spectral precision of Roger and Keith's, it could get the spatial resolution that the scholars wanted; it meant that the registration problems would be less severe; and Bill had demonstrated in his experiments that more processing was not needed to separate the prayer-book text from the Archimedes text. So, the knife won out over the gun after all. The Proof of Concept imaging took place in early 2001. I had to wait several months for the imagers to come up with a processed product.

Success was achieved by trial and through error, but this time the imagers had good data and a much better idea of what the scholars wanted. The imagers were, of course, playing with numbers. But in what follows I explain their solution visually, in terms of colors. It is, quite literally, easier to visualize this way.

Up until this point, the scholars had found the UV images to be the most useful. The scientists therefore looked at what it was that the scholars didn't like about the UV images. They had two serious deficiencies. Firstly, they were rather "soft"; they seemed to lack definition. Secondly, they were essentially monochromatic. They were shades of blue: the parchment was bright blue and the ink was dark blue. Although the texts stood out better than they did in natural light, it was harder than ever to distinguish between the prayer-book text and the Archimedes text. Keith took the UV images as his starting point. He wanted to make it clear which text was Archimedes and which text was from the prayer book with a minimum of image processing. He also had to restore the sharpness that the UV image lacked.

In the Proof of Concept imaging, the imagers noticed that there was a big difference in the appearance of the manuscript when it was imaged using white strobe lights from when normal tungsten lights were used. Low-wattage tungsten light is, as I mentioned, very red compared to strobe light and in tungsten light the Archimedes text was much fainter. The image consisted of red, green, and blue "channels," and they saw that in the red channel the Archimedes text almost disappeared completely. To me this was a bad thing, but not to the imagers. They had two simple, unprocessed images of a page and these images were completely different. By combining them they could come up with a different, synthetic image.

So Keith made a new picture altogether. He started with a blank "digital canvas." On to this canvas he could insert his images. He had three digital channels in which to do this—red, green, and blue. In the red channel, he put the tungsten-red image. In the blue channel, he put the ultraviolet-blue image. And in the green channel, he simply put the ultraviolet-blue image again. The important point for Keith was not that the Archimedes text disappeared in the tungsten-red image; the important point was that both the parchment and the Archimedes text were red. So in the red channel of his picture, he had bright Archimedes, bright parchment, and dark prayers. In the blue and green channels, he had dark Archimedes, bright parchment, and dark prayers. By combining these elements into one picture, he got bright parchment, dark prayers, and dark Archimedes with a red tint.

This was a very elegant solution. It involved far less processing than the images produced in the initial trials. It clearly differentiated the prayers from the Archimedes text by color, and it gave the Archimedes text a greater clarity than the UV image. The images were really just what Reviel wanted. They had a resolution of more than 600 dpi; they made a clear color difference between the parchment, the Archimedes text, and the prayer-book text; they had few artifacts; and they were not blurry. The process had another great advantage: it worked well over relatively large areas of the palimpsested texts and little local processing was necessary. In fact, the processing could be automated. An entire day's worth of images could be processed overnight on Keith's laptop computer as it ran on the desk in his hotel room. We called them "pseudocolor images," the method that produced them "pushbutton processing," and Keith's package of software code for making them "Archie 1.1." By September 2001, we had the key to unlock the secrets of the Palimpsest.

A New Box for the Brain

Writing books in the Middle Ages was a laborious business. A scribe named Raoul working in the Monastery of St. Aignan in France, wrote: "You do not know what it is to write. It is excessive drudgery; it crooks your back, dims your sight, twists your stomach and sides. Pray, then, my brother, you who read this book, pray for poor Raoul, God's servant, who has copied it entirely with his own hand in the cloister of St. Aignan."

Roger, Keith, and Bill became twenty-first-century Raouls, and we should spare a thought for them. They created text just as surely as Raoul did, and although their procedures were very different, they had exactly the same feelings about the process. From 2001 onward, they would visit the Walters every six months or so and, for ten days at a stretch, image the fifteen folios of Mr. B's book that Abigail and her team had most recently liberated. And while Abigail liberated the leaves, I placed the scientists in their very own cell—a bare white-painted cinder-block room with no windows that cannot have been much bigger than the average medieval monk's living quarters. And I had to lock them in it. Frequently they were working after hours in a museum containing thousands of priceless treasures, and they would have to call me to let them out if they so much as wanted to use the restroom.

Each time they came, the imagers filled their cell chock-a-block with equipment, which Roger drove down from Rochester. Roger had made a special gantry for the imaging of the codex: the cameras were mounted above a motorized X-Y stage, upon which each bifolio was placed and imaged. The imagers to this day have not touched the Palimpsest. A conservator wheeled in each folio from the conservation studio about fifty feet away. Each folio was mounted in its own bespoke mat. A conservator would place it carefully on the X-Y stage. Once it was on the stage, a computer moved everything. To turn the leaf, the imagers had to make a phone call to the conservation studio and someone would turn the leaf for them.

Roger was in the driver's seat, literally. He drove the X-Y stage, and he took the pictures with a click of the mouse. Each side of each leaf was photographed thirty times. To get a resolution of 600 dpi, ten separate pictures of each folio had to be taken and in three different lighting conditions. Keith was "the lights." He flicked the switch that turned on and off the strobe lights, the tungsten lights, and the ultraviolet lights. Bill recorded every move on spreadsheets. We now have over 15,000 records. For each image we recorded the following: the folio; the side of the folio; the position on that side of that folio; the date that the image was created; the camera make; the camera serial number; the lens brand; the lens serial number; the lens size; the wavelength of the illumination and whether it is fluorescent or reflective; the make, serial number, and wattage of the illumination source; the size of the aperture on the camera; the shutter speed; the resolution; the pixel X count; the pixel Y count; the camera incident

221

angle; and the distance of the camera from the folio. There are more columns than this, and some of them, even today, I do not understand. But the scientists needed to document everything thoroughly, not just for their own records, but for posterity. There is always the possibility that someone might use this data to make better images with more effective processing algorithms in the future.

If you think this is boring, you are not alone. Ten days sitting in a cell-like room, taking pictures in the bright light, and then in total darkness. Bill called it "trained-monkey work." It was unbelievably boring. It was also frustrating. Things broke and they had to be fixed; there were long pauses when leaves needed to be delivered; and the worst thing was the "whirr" of the X-Y stage as it moved from one section to the next. They couldn't oil the cogs. And for Keith it didn't stop. Each night he would take the data collected back to his hotel room and make his marvelous creations—new images using the ultraviolet and low-wattage-tungsten images as ingredients. This is an important conceptual point. These are not images of the Palimpsest; they are synthetic creations made from images of the Palimpsest. They are works of art. Well, they work, anyway. And that's the point.

Still, at this stage, we had no product. All the images had to be assembled so that scholars could access them. First, the ten individual shots of each folio had to be "stitched" together and this had to be done for the strobe, ultraviolet, and pseudocolor images. Roger Easton and his graduate students at RIT performed 5,520 stitching operations. They then had to devise a way that the scholars could access the images easily. The browser that Roger and his students designed is the mechanism by which the scholars access the texts in the Palimpsest. It is infinitely more flexible than the Palimpsest itself. If they want they can read the prayer book with the leaves falling in the right order. At the click of a mouse, however, the images magically reorder themselves so that they appear in their Archimedes order just as they were before they were palimpsested. The scholars can also choose whether they want to see the pages in normal light, ultraviolet light, or in synthetic pseudocolor. They can see the Archimedes pages in more detail than the eye can see the original. they can zoom in on a section of a page and "blow it up" without losing any resolution.

New Text

Of course, the imagers did not understand the text they were creating. It was up to Nigel Wilson and Reviel to read the Archimedes text. Nigel and Reviel are now working on completely new editions of *Method, Stomachion,* and *Floating Bodies.* Theirs is, in many ways, an ideal collaboration. Nigel has greater familiarity with the transcription and decipherment of tenth-century Greek cursive than Reviel. On the other hand, Reviel understands Archimedes' mathematics so well that he can guess words that are no longer visible in the codex. When you make a scholarly transcription of a text, you need to note what it is that you can see and what it is that you can guess. For a word to be really solid in our transcription, therefore, both Nigel and Reviel have to see it. They work independently of each other—Reviel in Stanford, California and Nigel in Oxford, England. They confer when they have completed a passage and compare notes. Here is a typical example, from folio 105v, which contains *Method*, proposition 14. Nigel writes:

> Dear Reviel,
> In col.2 line 4 I think the reading PhANERON hWS EIRHTAI does not fit the spaces as exactly as we should like, and my suggestion, based on staring a long time at the image, is that we read PhANEROI TO SKhHMA. This introduces a verb which A. does not use much if at all elsewhere, but it is good enough as Greek. Have another look and see what you think.

To which Reviel replies:

> I definitely see now your Chi, which makes SKhHMA a very attractive reading. Looking at it further, I wonder whether I

do not see a nu after all at the end of PhANERON. How about TOUTO GAR PhANERON TWi SKhHMATI, with the scribe substituting, as he does so often, omicron for omega, and then, following upon those two neuter accusatives, he can find no fault in SKhHMA? I am not sure TOUTO GAR PhANERON TWi SKhHMATI is very good Greek, but it is less radically deviant than TOUTO GAR PhANEROI TO SKhHMA (which, if correct, would be rather exciting). Perhaps, if we ask for a super-high-resolution X-ray of this particular point, this may serve to clarify the possible value of the technology.

Occasionally Reviel writes to me when he is excited. The first folio of Archimedes' letter to Eratosthenes was imaged on Thursday, November 20, 2003, four days after Abigail had finished preparing it; but it wasn't until Wednesday, October 12, 2005, that Reviel transcribed it. He left the most difficult pages to the end, because by then, he could read faint traces of script with much more fluency:

> I'm making some progress here. Was a funny sensation to transcribe the introduction to the *Method*, rather like a Shakespeare scholar transcribing the manuscript text for "To be or not to be." Surprisingly many subtle changes, of some significance (e.g. Eudoxus was the first not to "discover" a result, but to "publish" it, etc.). It will help morale to notify everyone that reading of the forgery pages 57–64 is absolutely crucial. And I so want this border paper to be removed by Abigail. Talk to you—Reviel.

I already own two printed results of the digital Archimedes. The first is a beautiful book, printed by Nigel. Like Archimedes' letters this book is private for Nigel's friends. It exists in only fifty copies. It is his transcription, made from the pseudocolor images of *On Floating Bodies* propositions 1 and 2, including the diagrams. It also includes a transcription of folio 81v, which Heiberg overlooked and which is now on the back of a page containing a forgery, covered in glue. There are no gaps in Nigel's transcription that I can see. However, some of it is in Latin, based on Moerbeke's text, because Nigel printed this book in 2004 and at this stage he didn't have a pseudo-color image of folio 88r.

The second is the monumental first volume of three by Reviel entitled *The Works of Archimedes* and published by Cambridge University Press. This is the first proper translation into English of Archimedes' *Sphere and Cylinder* and Eutocius' commentary on the same. It is peppered with diagrams. These, I have no doubt, more accurately recreate the designs manufactured by Archimedes on the sands of Syracuse than any yet made. That's why Reviel's first words to me were: "Yes, I need to see the diagrams, especially of *Sphere and Cylinder*." Clearly, we gave him what he wanted, and we gave the world a better understanding of the most important scientist who ever lived.

The digital Palimpsest is encased in a silver box—a 300-gigabite external hard disk drive that you can plug into your computer. Scholars no longer read Archimedes by looking at iron marks made with a reed pen on animal skin. Archimedes' treatises are now digitally stored as 1s and 0s in a computer. Archimedes has received his latest IT upgrade. Only Nigel Wilson does not use this computer disk. To the amazement of the imagers, Nigel prefers to use hard-copy prints of the pictures. Nigel is an end-user; he gets what he wants. Even now, he does most of his transcription work from these prints, in the summer months, when the light is good, using a magnifying glass.

A New Voice

A great codex that had already revealed most of its secrets. As you will recall, that's what most of the experts thought when the Palimpsest was auctioned at Christie's. Given the reputation of Heiberg as a philologist of ancient texts, and given the treatment that the Palimpsest had received since Heiberg's time, this skepticism seemed well founded. Even Reviel thought that his work would actually be mainly on the diagrams. The discovery of two unknown folios of *Floating Bodies* and the new reading of *Method* proposition 14, changed Reviel's view of things. It didn't take long for the rest of the world to be convinced of the importance of the Palimpsest. On Wednesday, December 6, 2000, I got a call from Will Peakin. He wanted to write an article on Mr. B's book for the color magazine of the *Sunday Times* of London. The June 17, 2001 cover of the magazine has an image of the Palimpsest and the words "EUREKA: It's just a few lines of scrawled Greek text, but new technology has identified the hand of Archimedes—and the results are rewriting history." But we hadn't seen anything yet. It was just the start.

Up until the summer of 2002, we had all been working for Archimedes. But that was about to change. About thirty folios of the Palimpsest do not contain Archimedes' treatises. They come from other palimpsest texts. It was Natalie Tchernetska's task to look into them. She started with one particular page on which Heiberg had read just a little phrase that no one subsequently had been able to identify. When she received pseudocolor images of this page, she painstakingly transcribed just a few more lines. Then she tried to find a match for these lines in Byzantine texts. One particularly rich source for Byzantine texts is called the Suda. It is a massive tenth-century encyclopedia of authors ancient and modern. Eventually Natalie found a close match: it was a quotation of a lost speech by an ancient author named Hyperides. A few days later, on Saturday, October 19, 2002, Natalie sent me the following email.

> Dear Will, In the course of further exploration of the non-Archimedes folios, I recently deciphered the text of a Greek orator, unknown otherwise. I could identify parts of lost speeches by Hyperides: ff. 135–138 contain a fragment of his lawsuit speech "Against Timandros;" ff. 136–137 a fragment of a political speech, possibly "Against Diondas;" ff. 174–175 possibly a fragment of the same political speech. Kind regards, Natalie

Natalie had never heard of Hyperides; nor had I. He sounded like a character out of Asterix, perhaps a close cousin of Ekonomikrisis, the shrewd Phoenician merchant in *Asterix the Gladiator*. But no. It dawned on us quickly that this was truly a sensational discovery. Hyperides is, in fact, one of the ten canonical orators of antiquity. He was born in 389 BC, five years before Aristotle. Like Aristotle, Hyperides lived in Athens, and he was a politician in the world's most influential democracy.

In the ancient world, seventy-seven speeches were attributed to Hyperides who was celebrated for his style and his wit. His most famous speech is lost. It concerns Phryne, a prostitute famous for her beauty. In fact, legend has it that her body was the model for Praxiteles' famous statue of the goddess Aphrodite at Cnidus. But Phryne was also Hyperides' mistress, and when she was accused of offending the Eleusian mysteries, Hyperides defended her. He wasn't doing very well, so he ripped open her robe and exposed her breasts to the jury. It worked, and she was acquitted. But despite the style and subject matter of Hyperides, his speeches suffered from the transition from roll to codex. In 1998, László Horváth, from Budapest, valiantly searched for a codex that was mentioned as containing Hyperides' speeches in the sixteenth century, but he never found it and its contents were never known. Indeed, until the nineteenth century, Hyperides was only known through quotations from later authors. Then, in 1847, papyri containing his texts were discovered in a tomb in Thebes, Egypt. The last big discovery was in 1891. But, in 2002, Natalie had discovered a new Hyperides text, and what's more she had found it in a codex. If we can read all of these folios, we will have added more than 20 percent to the surviving work of this great figure from the golden age of Athenian history.

Hyperides was outspoken in his support of resistance to the military might of Philip of Macedon and his son Alexander the Great. When Alexander died, in 323 BC, he advocated full-scale rebellion against the Macedonian overlord. The rebellion failed. Hyperides had his tongue cut out to make a mockery of his oratory and then was executed. Plutarch, in his *Lives of the Orators*, writes of Hyperides: "His monument is now altogether unknown and lost, being thrown down with age and long standing." Not so. Natalie found ten folios of the Palimpsest that contain his speeches. But retrieving the literary legacy of this great figure is appallingly difficult. The pages of the Palimpsest containing his speeches are even more difficult to read than the Archimedes pages. As I write, an international team of scholars, including Natalie, Pat Easterling, Eric Handley, Jud Hermann, László Horváth, and Chris Carey are working collaboratively to provide a critical edition of the texts.

One of the speeches that Natalie identified mentions some of the great historical figures from antiquity—Demosthenes, the well-known orator, as well as Philip of Macedon and his son, Alexander the Great. It also mentions a figure far less well known—Diondas. Natalie boldly suggested the circumstances in which this speech might have been delivered. Philip of Macedon's military might had been growing, and Athens needed to react. Demosthenes was particularly hostile to Philip, calling him "the pestilent knave from Macedonia," and he successfully negotiated an alliance with the city state of Thebes. Hyperides was delighted and supported a proposal that Demosthenes receive an honorific crown for his diplomatic triumph. But in 338 BC, despite their alliance, the Athenians and the Thebans lost disastrously to Philip's forces at the Battle of Chaeronea. At this point, Diondas indicted Hyperides, because, he argued, Hyperides' support for Demosthenes was unconstitutional. It seems to have been a blatant and cynical political move to damage both Demosthenes and Hyperides who had spearheaded that anti-Macedonian sentiment in Athens. We know that Hyperides wrote a speech in his own defense and that he was acquitted. This, Natalie deduced, was Hyperides' lost speech. It not only sheds light on Athenian politics in the grim days after Chaeronea, but it also provides new context for one of the greatest speeches of antiquity—Demosthenes' own speech, "On the Crown." These pages will be studied for years, but already great progress is being made. László

Horváth is deciphering one of the most difficult of the Hyperides leaves. He emailed me to tell me that on his page, when Hyperides discusses previous alliances between Athens and other Greek city states, he differs from the great historian Herodotus. The difference is in number of ships that Athens contributed to the Greek fleet at the great Battle of Salamis when the Greeks, led by Themistocles of Athens, triumphed over the Persians who had threatened to overrun them under Xerxes in 480 BC. Hyperides gives the total as 220 ships, while Herodotus says that the Athenians provided 180. Since Herodotus' total for the number of ships provided by all the city states does not tally with the figures that he gives for individual cities, László thinks that Hyperides' speech might be crucial in assessing the details of one of the most important battles of Western civilization.

There seems to be no end to the secrets of the Palimpsest. On Monday, June 11, 2005, I received an email from Nigel Wilson, in which he wrote that he had identified several further leaves of a philosophical text and on one he "read the name Aristotle clearly enough." There are seven folios of this text in the Palimpsest, and this text has yet to be transcribed and identified. I passed this information on to Reviel, who transcribed more words. He could not match them in any search engine for Greek texts. This sounded familiar. Perhaps it is a yet unknown commentary on Aristotle. Since Nigel thinks this manuscript was written in the late ninth century, this would make it a commentary from the ancient world. It is not difficult to come up with suggestions. Perhaps the most convincing so far is a suggestion by Marwan Rashed, a French scholar whom Reviel contacted. He suggests that it might be a text by an early Christian author criticizing various Greek philosophies, including the Pythagoreans, for their failure to take into account the possibility of creation out of nothing. As such, we might have uniquely preserved in the Archimedes Palimpsest the views of an early Christian author on the inadequacies of the pre-Christian worldview.

We now know that Mr. B's book is not really the "Archimedes Palimpsest" at all; the Archimedes codex is only one of the important manuscripts wrapped up in it. Mr. B's prayer book houses a small library of unique ancient texts. In addition to the Archimedes manuscript, it contains five leaves that uniquely preserve speeches by one of Athens' greatest orators and seven leaves that uniquely preserve ancient views on Aristotle. It also contains some Byzantine texts: four leaves from a late tenth-century book of hymns partly in honor of St. John Psichaites, an abbot in Constantinople who rebuilt his monastery after it was destroyed in 813 BC by the Krum, the Bulgarian Khan with the curious wine cup, and two leaves from a saint's life. Seven leaves, from at least two separate manuscripts, have not been identified at the time of writing.

The Palimpsest might not ever reveal all its secrets, but I will make one prediction. I think it is very likely that Reviel and Ken Saito will be the last people to discover new text from the Palimpsest, because since their visit the texts in the Palimpsest have undergone another transformation. In the twenty-first century, if you want to read what Archimedes had to say to Eratosthenes in the third century BC and what Hyperides said to the Athenians in the century before that, you should not make the pilgrimage to the codex in Baltimore. You can't read it there. You need one of Roger Easton's little silver boxes.

Parenti's Twin

We know the scribe of the prayer book used several different codices, but exactly whose library was he recycling? It must have been extraordinary. John Lowden once said to me, in jest, that it was the library of Photius. It could not have been his, of course. With the possible exception of the Aristotle commentary, the palimpsested texts were written long after Photius died. Still, Hyperides was one of the authors mentioned by Photius. No modern scholar believed that Photius had actually read Hyperides, but now it seems that Photius has been telling us the truth for a thousand years. Like Photius' library, these texts must have been collected together in Constantinople. But this does not mean that they stayed in Constantinople. Books traveled with their owners. So where were these texts when they were turned into a prayer book?

Understandably perhaps, in assembling the scholars to work on the book, I had concentrated on those who could help with the palimpsested texts. It was not until the legendary liturgist Robert Taft got in touch with me that I paid much attention to the texts of the prayer book. He suggested that I give photos to an Italian scholar, Stefano Parenti. Stefano noted that the prayer book contained certain very rare texts, including one for the purification of a polluted container and another for the storing of grain. These prayers, and others, Stefano also found in a manuscript that can almost be described as the twin of our prayer book. It is in St. Catherine's monastery in Sinai, the same place where Tischendorf found the Codex Sinaiticus, and it was written by a priest named Auksentios in 1152–3. Some of the prayers are in the very same order. Others, such as a group of prayers at the elevation of the host and a prayer for the consumption of the leftover gifts of the presanctified liturgy, Stefano knew to be specific to Jerusalem in the Middle Ages. Finally, Stefano noted that there were frequent references to prayers "for this city" in our prayer book. It seems unlikely, therefore, that the prayer book was made at St. Sabas, even though it ended up there in the sixteenth century. But it is eminently likely that it was finished in Jerusalem, just fifteen miles away, on April 14, 1229.

We do not yet know how the palimpsested texts made it to the Holy Land and perhaps we never will. The problem is not that it is so unlikely, but rather that there are so many ways that books could travel there from Constantinople in the thirteenth century. The reason for this is that the Holy Land, at this time, was a destination of choice for Christians from Europe both for pilgrimage and for crusade. Jerusalem was a particularly interesting place to be in 1229.

Frederick II, the Holy Roman Emperor as well as the King of Sicily, Cyprus, Jerusalem, and Germany, the wonder of the world for his energy, learning, and religious skepticism had finally fulfilled his vow to go on crusade. On Sunday, February 18, 1229, less than two months before the date in our book, he liberated from Muslim control all of Jerusalem, except the Dome of the Rock, as well as other cities, including Nazareth, where Jesus grew up, and Bethlehem, where Jesus was born. This indeed was something for Christians to celebrate. The scribe of the book had joy in his heart as he wrote his prayers. Now that I knew that we could recover the texts in the Palimpsest, I had nothing but understanding for the scribe and thanks for the fact that he had used such treasures to write his book. Indeed I wanted to thank him personally. The trouble was, I didn't even know his name.

10

The *Stomachion,* 2003
or Archimedes at Play

A Package from Mr. Marasco

It was September 2003; and I was just back from my summer
vacation; and a Mr. Joe Marasco had sent me a present. There was
a funny-looking package waiting for me together with the rest of my
mail. Its sender described himself as a fan of Archimedes, which, to
be honest, was rather worrying. I had fewer nuts calling me than Will
did, but I did get my share of them. (And no, I didn't discover
Rasputin in the Palimpsest either.)

I opened it, cautiously, to find a truly gorgeous toy—large pieces
of red glass cut in all sorts of shapes and fitted together to make a
square. Nice, I thought. A pity, of course, that the pieces were fragile
and sharp, because we were expecting our first child and I was
shopping for toys. But I could keep it at my office and show it off as
an example of the funny things you get when you are an Archimedes
scholar.

I understood Mr. Marasco's point. He was sending me a replica
of the Stomachion. I vaguely remembered that it was an ancient
game in which the objective was to use fourteen pieces to create
some form. But this just about summed up my knowledge of this
strange toy. I knew there was an obscure fragment by Archimedes
dealing with the Stomachion, but no one had really studied it. The
standard view was that Archimedes used the game as a starting point
to motivate a geometrical discussion of some kind. No one had

even guessed the nature of the geometrical discussion. I knew why. Our knowledge rested on a small fragment preserved in a mutilated form.

I also knew that this fragment was right here in my office. The new hard drive from Roger Easton had recently arrived. It contained, among other things, the digitally processed images of folios 172–7. Well, I thought, Mr. Marasco made a nice gesture. The least I could do as recompense was try and see if I could read anything from the *Stomachion*.

This would be tough. Some time in the sixteenth century, or even before, the Euchologion manuscript had lost its final folios, 178–185. They had been replaced by a paper supplement, inserted into the manuscript in the sixteenth century. Folio 177 became the last folio and, therefore, the one least protected from mold and other damage.

I did, of course, ask to look at this folio when I visited Baltimore, but it immediately became clear that nothing could be gained by the naked eye. The parchment was so worn down that in places it literally had disintegrated. There were holes in the parchment—Greek words gone forever. It was not even a well-defined piece of rectangular parchment. It was made up of precarious, unwieldy pieces—an eaten surface that only barely held together.

But this was just part of the problem. Even where the parchment existed, the writing was so faint, so thoroughly covered with mold stains that nothing could be made of it. To the naked eye, it was as if this folio had never been palimpsested. The first thing that struck the eye were large blobs of an ugly, blackish substance—the remains of the mold. Other than this, you could see—with difficulty—the top layer of text, but the underlying text had disappeared completely. I approached the folio gingerly. This was not anything I was going to extract out of the plastic coating, so I lit it with the UV lamp. Not much more came up.

Well, that's it, I thought at the time. We weren't going to make any progress with the *Stomachion*. A pity but, then again, it wasn't such an important treatise. And, even if we were able to read more, would it

help at all? The text was just too fragmentary. We would never understand the *Stomachion*, and it was best for me to invest my time more
profitably elsewhere.

In all of this, I was merely following the traditional response.
Heiberg was only able to read some fragments of the text and he
didn't venture an interpretation of it. Dijksterhuis, a great Archimedes
scholar, wrote a careful commentary on each of Archimedes' treatises,
but he had practically nothing to say about the *Stomachion*. Indeed,
we can see his growing impatience. He began his commentary with
speculation: "[the treatise] may indicate that [Archimedes] studied the
game from a mathematical point of view . . . [he] discussed some of
the properties of the so-called Stomachion." But then he lost his
confidence: "In the Greek fragment, however, we do not find much
about this investigation." Dijksterhuis concluded: "It can no longer
be ascertained whether this result was the object aimed at or whether
it played a part (and if so, what part) in the investigation as originally
announced."

The fundamental point is that this single bifolio of the Palimpsest
is nearly all we had to go by. On this bifolio, Archimedes concluded
his treatise on the *Measurement of the Circle* and began a new treatise
whose title was barely legible but may have been *"Stomachic"* or
"Stomachion." There were some words of introduction, a single
simple proposition, and the beginning of another one. Both, obviously, were mere preludes to the real action of the treatise. None of
the substantial mathematics was left. Essentially, when the maker of
the Palimpsest chose which folios to use out of the original
Archimedes book, he threw away all of the *Stomachion* folios except
for this single bifolio. It is easy to see why. The *Stomachion* was the
final treatise in the original Archimedes book, and as we have already
learned, the important rule of manuscripts is that *the end is always in
the worst shape.* The parchment on which the *Stomachion* was written
was probably already in bad shape in the thirteenth century. Thus the
treatise was simply thrown away—not good enough to serve even as
recycled parchment. The maker of the Palimpsest probably reasoned

that this particular piece of animal skin would not survive another round of scraping.

There were some additional pieces of evidence, without which our position would have been even more precarious. The references were from antiquity to a game called the Stomachion or "Bellyache." The game was supposed to be so difficult that it made your belly turn. (The difficulty of putting the pieces together was a constant theme throughout the history of the *Stomachion*.) It involved fourteen pieces, put together to form a square. So much was implied by the ancient testimony on the game itself. The evidence suggested that Archimedes did not invent the game but that he did make some mathematical reflections upon it. (In the same manner, contemporary mathematicians sometimes use the Rubik's cube to introduce ideas from Group Theory.) These mathematical reflections became so well known that some people called the game "Archimedes' Box." However very few people ever read Archimedes' actual treatise. The only surviving Greek manuscript containing the text of the *Stomachion* was in front of us—the original Archimedes book serving as foundation for the Palimpsest. And so, in the year 1229, when the maker of the Palimpsest threw away the bulk of the *Stomachion*, he threw away the only evidence the world had in Greek.

There was one additional piece to the puzzle. Just like the Palimpsest, this evidence was ignored for years. In this case, obscurity was the result not of the ravages of fortune—as with the Palimpsest—but of scholarly neglect. The manuscript in question was in plain sight for all to read, but it remained unread for generations simply because *too few scholars read Arabic*. Only in 1899 did Suter, a German scholar, come across an Arabic manuscript from the seventeenth century that mentions the "Stumashiun of Archimedes."

Indeed, much of the Greek heritage survives only in Arabic. (Much of it is still unpublished, because of the same scholarly neglect; quite possibly, there are more works by Archimedes that remain unnoticed in Arabic manuscripts.) Starting in the ninth century, translations of Greek texts were made in Arabic centers of learning, such as Baghdad. Typically, however, the Arabic versions are far removed from the original. Arabic mathematicians were very good scientists. They added a great deal that was original and not present in Greek science. They would often rewrite the sources, abridge them, rephrase them, and so on. This clearly was the case with the *Stomachion*. The manuscript found by Suter is unfortunately no more than an Arabic abridgement of a small part of the original Archimedean text. The Arabic manuscript is a very brief text indeed—a couple of folios long—and, once again, furnishes us with very little information. But it does one crucial thing: it discusses the construction of the Stomachion as a square divided into fourteen pieces. Based on the Arabic text, we can reconstruct the precise shape of the Stomachion puzzle (see fig. 10.1). This is a famous diagram—everyone who knows anything about the Stomachion is familiar with this figure of a square divided into fourteen pieces, the canonical form of the Stomachion puzzle. This is what Archimedes was playing with. So, Marasco's model was essentially a copy of a diagram contained in a seventeenth-century Arabic manuscript—with a certain proviso—more of which later.

This, then, was the sum of our knowledge. There was a treatise by Archimedes dealing with a certain game, the objective of which was to construct some shapes from fourteen given forms. This was all we knew.

No one had even bothered extending this knowledge any further. When the sale of the Palimpsest was made everyone was excited that we might get new readings of the *Method*. Literally no one suggested that we might get new readings of the *Stomachion*. This treatise was the poor relation, the one everyone kept forgetting. Partly, this was because there was so little left with which to work. More importantly, the thinking was that it was *just a game*. It could not possibly rank with the significance of Archimedes dealing with such major

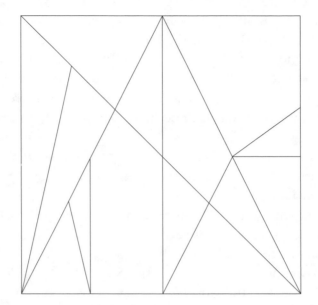

FIGURE 10.1

issues as infinity and the application of mathematics to the physical world. It was Archimedes at play, an Archimedean pastime. It was a pity we knew no more about it, but at the end of the day, we could survive without it.

Such was the feeling—my feeling, too—when the Palimpsest resurfaced. So it was only with reluctance that I turned on my external hard drive to try and see what the pseudocolor images might teach me. It would be hard, grinding work, probably for little gain. But I was going to try nonetheless. At one point or another, I reasoned, I must look at it and if I did it now I would have something interesting to tell Mr. Marasco when I wrote him my thank-you note.

Making Sense of the Stomachion

One would have hoped, in principle, that the remaining text we had would furnish us with enough clues. We had no more than a single Greek bifolio, but after all this was a crucial one. It was the first in the treatise, so it included the *introduction*. Surely the intro-duction would give us a sense of the goal of the work. Yet what Heiberg had managed to read was fragmentary and obscure. He translated, more or less completely, the first paragraph and it read as follows:

> As the so-called Stomachion has a variegated theory of the transposition of the figures from which it is set up, I deemed it necessary: first, to set out in my investigation of the magnitude of the whole figure each of the figures into which it is divided, by which [number] it is measured; and further also, which are the angles, taken by combinations and added together; all of the above said for the sake of finding out of the fitting together of the arising figures, whether the resulting sides in the figures are on a line or whether they are slightly short of that but so as to be unnoticed by sight. For such consideration as these are intel-lectually challenging; and, if it is a little short of being on a line while being unnoticed by vision, the figures that are composed are not for that reason to be rejected.

This paragraph may be obscure, but it does tell us something. Archimedes would look at the measurements of the various pieces that composed the Stomachion. He would look at the angles to see which pieces, put together, would fit in combination to create, for instance, a straight line. So the treatise was some kind of study of the ways in which the pieces of the Stomachion could be made to fit together.

Now, here comes an important consideration. The people who most influenced Heiberg's interpretation of the *Stomachion* were the Roman grammarians of the late Imperial period who wrote many centuries after Archimedes' death. It so happens that this group of authors was fond of a certain cliché: they compared the many expres-sions one can form with just a few words to the many ways in which one can make different figures with just a few basic shapes. Thus, they said, one could take the Stomachion pieces and fit them together so

239

FIGURE 10.2

as to make an elephant, a warrior, or a bird; the possibilities were unlimited (see fig. 10.2).

So, the pieces could fit together in a free game of creativity. What must be stressed is that there is *no limit* to the number of shapes one can make in this way. This is because, to make an elephant or a warrior, one must be allowed to put together pieces in a free manner, not necessarily setting a vertex next to a vertex. In figure 10.3, we see a close-up of the "elephant," and we see how several of the pieces are placed "loosely" next to each other and do not meet exactly vertex to vertex. Now, if this is the rule—that pieces may be placed "loosely" next to each other—then the logic of infinity applies. It means the pieces can be placed *continuously* along any edge. One is

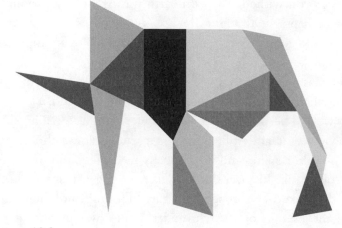

FIGURE 10.3

allowed to attach piece X one-half the way from the end of the edge, or one-third the way from the end, or one-fourth, or one-fifth . . . There are literally endless ways of positioning one piece next to another. The number of different elephants one can make with fourteen pieces is literally infinite. We are reminded, once again, of how ubiquitous infinity is in mathematics.

Heiberg, with his huge learning, was aware of this Roman grammarian cliché. And so, as he turned from the first paragraph to the second, he thought he had an idea of what Archimedes meant. He thought Archimedes was talking about the boundless plurality of the elephants. Now there was very little Heiberg could read at this point—the writing becomes nearly illegible—but he thought he could reconstruct some traces of meaning: "So it is possible . . . many . . . with the same shapes . . . moved around. . . ." So Archimedes was saying, Heiberg thought, that there were both elephants and warriors to be made and many of them too.

What was the point? Heiberg did not know and nor did we, following him. If the point was that there were many elephants to be put together, then there was no interesting mathematical question to ask. How many elephants and warriors? Infinitely many or, better put, as many as you wished. What on earth was Archimedes trying to determine? Perhaps, we thought, he was just making some random comments on the geometry of the fourteen shapes. Not an important treatise, for sure.

So I still reasoned. I was in good spirits, though, studying the images on my hard drive. The pseudocolor worked. Indeed, it worked incredibly well. The manuscript had deteriorated terribly since Heiberg reviewed it and still, with the pseudocolor technology, I could go through the lines and occasionally read them as if they were written in plain ink. In places, it was like waving a magic wand; I looked at the naked-eye image and saw nothing and then, after turning on the pseudocolor, Archimedes' Greek was plain to see. I quickly confirmed Heiberg's readings and made a few additional completions, to make better sense of the first paragraph. Heiberg had not read everything, but he certainly got the drift, and I could prove this based on Archimedes' Greek.

Still, I could not see Archimedes' point. To make some better sense of it, I decided to take a step back and read Heiberg's text again for whatever it was worth. This was a standard move in such research. Before taking a plunge into the deciphering of a text, it was good to try and gain some kind of understanding, however imprecise, to guide the reading. I turned off the computer and picked up Heiberg, reading first through the little he could make of the Greek, and then through Suter's text.

Just to make sure I was following the text, I compared the diagram Heiberg provided—the canonical diagram of the Arabic manu-script—with the model I had from Marasco. Anyway, it would be more fun working with the model than with the diagram!

At this point, I became furious with Marasco. His model did not match the diagram. There was something wrong. Was he, after all, a fraud, someone who couldn't even read a diagram correctly? Or had I misread the diagram? I looked at it again and began to wonder if perhaps something had gone wrong by accident. Perhaps Marasco had prepared the model from the correct diagram and then his shapes had gotten mixed up through some kind of error?

But wait, I wondered: was it possible to fit the pieces together in a square by placing them in some arrangement other than the original diagram? I mean, surely there was no more than one way of fitting all fourteen complex shapes together? It seemed like quite a complicated arrangement. But then again, maybe there was more than one way of fitting the pieces together.

Well, it had to be clarified. I certainly was *curious*. I checked the figure, piece by piece. Marasco's model *was*, indeed, the original diagram with the pieces of the square arranged differently. Of course, I saw it now. There were multiple ways in which the diagram could be rearranged. There was certainly more than one way of fitting the fourteen pieces together into a square.

And then, all of a sudden, my throat went dry.

Could this have been Archimedes' point? Were there many different ways in which *the same square could be fitted together with the same pieces*? This would be too exciting. Let me explain why.

Improbable Combinations

The significance of my new thought was that, finally, we had a meaningful problem. We were no longer dealing with the continuously changing, infinite number of arrangements of elephants and warriors. We were dealing with a certain finite number of ways in which a square could be made from the given pieces. I always imagined the number to be 1. That is, my intuition was that the accepted diagram represented the *only* way that the square could be fitted together. Now, thanks to Marasco, I saw that my intuition was plain wrong. I still had to show that there were *many* ways. If there were only a handful of ways of arranging the square, then it wouldn't have been an interesting problem for Archimedes to solve. I also needed to show that the number could in principle be calculated, and that it did not involve a huge calculation beyond Archimedes' means. And so I needed to study, in pure mathematical terms, the problem of the Stomachion square: how many ways were there to fit the given pieces together to form a square? Also, of course, I needed to go back to the hard drive, read more of the introduction's second paragraph, and see if it fitted into the new hypothesis. There was lots of work to be done. We were going to uncover the prehistory of combinatorics.

Combinatorics is essentially a simple science. As its name suggests, it is the study of combinations. Suppose, for instance, that we need to make a choice: we have three candidates for the presidency. How many combinations do we have? Obviously, the answer is three. Now, we need to make it slightly more difficult: imagine that we are choosing not a president but a Roman-style pair of consuls of equal powers. We need, therefore, to choose two consuls out of three candidates. How many options do we have? This may appear tricky at first sight, but actually the answer, once again, is three. Choosing two out of three is really the same as choosing one out of three, because each time we are choosing a single candidate *to be left out*. To choose A and B is the same as to leave out C; to choose A and C is the same as to leave out B; and to choose B and C is the same as to leave out A. This exhausts, once again, our options.

Now imagine that we are selecting consuls not of equal power but instead a president and a vice-president. How many options do we have? This is somewhat more complicated. Essentially, each of our previous choices bifurcates. Each of them can be turned into two choices—president and vice-president. If we choose A and B then we have two president and vice-president pairs to form out of this selection—A as president and B as deputy or vice versa. In short, for each choice of consuls we have two choices for a president-and-vice-president pair. In other words, the number of options becomes $3 \times 2 = 6$. There are six ways of choosing a president-and-vice-president pair out of three candidates.

This is all suggestive of the nature of combinatorics. In some ways, indeed, it is a simple science. Many of its questions, even the more interesting ones, can be approached without any complicated tools. This is related, however, to the main drawback in combinatorics—there are very few short cuts. There is no surprising theory on the basis of which we can easily solve everything. Rather, it is almost as if for each new problem we need to invent a new, ingenious approach. Combinatorics is a science of endless ingenuity, of endless puzzles and games.

Where did this science come from? This in itself has always been something of a puzzle. Most scholars think it emerged out of games. After all, this was what gave rise to the science of probability. In the seventeenth century, card games were introduced in Europe. Quickly enough, Europeans everywhere were busy playing card games. Everyone was betting: which hand would be dealt next? When you bet fortunes on hands, your mind tends to focus on some very well defined questions. How likely am I to get an ace? How likely am I to get a joker? The answers to these questions essentially involve combinatorics. You need to calculate how many combinations of cards are possible and then how many of them contain an ace. If there are a million possible combinations and a hundred thousand of them contain an ace, it means that the odds are one-in-ten that an ace will be dealt. Its worth betting if the return is over one-to-ten and not worth it otherwise.

Now this is very useful to know. In the long run, the card player who has combinatorics up his sleeve is bound to win. He is no more likely to win each individual bet, but he is certain to place his bets in such a way that, in the long run, he will end up the winner. Which is precisely why casinos in Las Vegas are prosperous. They apply the science of combinatorics against people who fail to apply it. Science wins.

Fermat, known for his Last Theorem, and Pascal, known for his deep theological observations, were among the first to apply this science. They did not make a fortune with their bets. (Historical evidence suggests that mathematicians—unlike Las Vegas casinos—are not very good at following through with their scientific knowledge.)

Instead of making a fortune, they created the science of combinatorics, quickly using it to calculate the probabilities of events not only in card games but in many other domains as well. The calculations of combinations are much more than a trifling game, it turns out—they serve as the foundation for the science of probability.

Probabilities now serve as one of the cornerstones of science. And that's the reason why combinatorics is so important. Indeed, today's physicists believe that the universe is governed by quantum mechanics, which is essentially probabilistic in character. There are no rules saying that this or that must happen; physics merely asserts a certain *probability* of events happening. Einstein, famously, differed. He passionately refused to concede to "God plays with dice." The evidence, so far, seems to suggest that on this Einstein was, for once, wrong.

Ancient Combinatorics?

There is a certain puzzling, intangible quality to combinatorics. It's frequently a very abstract science. There are often no diagrams to be drawn. You just go through the problem in your head, considering the various options and possibilities. It is a fun subject—but, generally speaking, not a visual one.

Now this non-visual character of combinatorics makes a world of difference. We have already seen many diverse problems discussed by Archimedes, but even with all their diversity, the great majority them still dealt with *geometry*. After all, the diagram was the key tool of Greek mathematics. Even though Greek mathematicians made interesting discoveries in, say, number theory (for instance, showing that there are infinitely many prime numbers), their main field was the visual, concrete science of geometry. Calculating how many ways there were to make certain selections and combinations? This would be just too abstract, too non-visual. And for this reason, we didn't think combinatorics was a field that Greek mathematicians were likely to tackle. The standard opinion was that problems of pure calculation were not made an important part of mathematics before the seventeenth century.

This view changed in 2002 during the international meeting of historians of Greek mathematics held in Delphi, Greece. It happened following a presentation by Fabio Acerbi. Fabio studied physics, earning a PhD, but then decided it was not his field after all. He became a high school teacher so that he could concentrate on his love of the ancient world. (He is the graduate of an Italian public high school where students study not only the sciences but also Greek and Latin.) He quickly produced a series of original, inspired studies of ancient mathematics, combining both his mathematical and linguistic gifts. The first to make a real splash was the one he presented to us at Delphi. Its topic was Hipparchus' numbers.

Here, again, was a question that few had paid any attention to at all. Plutarch mentions (in the course of an otherwise unrelated philosophical discussion) an ancient quarrel between a philosopher and a mathematician. The philosopher, the Stoic Chrysippus, said that by the rules of Stoic logic one could combine ten assertions in more than a million ways. The mathematician Hipparchus countered stating that the correct number was either 103,049 or 310,954, depending on how the number was defined but, either way, Chrysippus was wrong. Hipparchus was a great mathematician and astronomer. (Among other things, he was the first to produce a catalogue of all the stars visible to the naked eye—a remarkable achievement by any standard.) But this reads more like some kind of private joke that doesn't need any special attention paid to it. And indeed, historians of mathematics have never tried to make any sense of the numbers.

Let me now move back to the year 1994 when David Hough, a graduate student of mathematics at George Washington University, leafed through a textbook of combinatorics. He came across Hipparchus' numbers, which were mentioned as a kind of curiosity. He also happened to consult a handbook of important mathematical numbers. This handbook contained, among other things, what are known as "Schröder numbers." The tenth Schröder number was 103,049—the same as the smaller Hipparchus number.

Now this is some coincidence, thought Hough. He consulted with the author of the combinatorics textbook, Richard P. Stanley, an MIT professor of mathematics. And in 1997 they published a small notice in the *American Mathematical Monthly* suggesting that Hipparchus could have produced some genuine combinatorics. Lucio Russo, an Italian historian of mathematics, came across this notice and suggested to Fabio Acerbi that he should look into it. In the summer of 2002, Fabio had a theory of how Hipparchus' problem could be defined and how the two numbers—103,049 and 310,954—could be seen as the correct solutions to this problem. In addition, he could show, by means available to an ancient mathematician, how the numbers were obtained.

In essence, one of the possible interpretations of a Schröder number was the number of ways a sequence of characters could be put inside brackets. For example, the four characters, abcd, could be put inside brackets in various ways:

(a(bcd)), (ab(cd)), ((a)(b)(cd)) etc . . . .

The fourth Schröder number was eleven. That is, there are eleven different ways that the four characters, abcd, can be put inside brackets. (This is surprisingly high, as is so often the case with combinatoric problems.) Acerbi showed that, according to Stoic logic, the problem of combining ten assertions was analogous to putting ten characters inside brackets. He then developed a method for solving this problem within Hipparchus' means. He showed that with one extra condition—allowing not only to "assert" claims, but also to "negate" them—the number becomes 310,954, which confirms the second number reported by Plutarch.

At the conference, we were skeptical at first. Everything went against our hard-won intuitions. But the more we looked at Acerbi's evidence, the more we became convinced. The numbers just could not be a coincidence. We were not going to hit upon the tenth Schröder number by sheer accident. The only way Hipparchus could have come up with his numbers was the way Acerbi did—by doing the math. And so, even though the brief mention by Plutarch tells us almost nothing, it is sufficient to prove, beyond a doubt, that ancient combinatorics did exist.

This was a stunning discovery. The study of pure calculation—of counting the number of possible combinations—was invented by the Greeks, and it was brought to a high level of sophistication by the time of Hipparchus.

Hipparchus lived in the second century, which makes him fifty years or more younger than Archimedes. But there was now nothing unlikely in assuming that Archimedes was engaged in combinatorics. It would make him the first person—as far as we can judge—who ever produced a study of combinatorics. Indeed, it would make perfect historical sense. Archimedes would be at the inception of a tradition whose culmination would then be the work of Hipparchus. The pieces fit together. My interpretation of the *Stomachion* could fly. Just to be sure, I sent a quick email to Acerbi—was he familiar with anyone ever suggesting that the *Stomachion* was a study in combinatorics? I then went feverishly back to work on the transcription. Another email went to Nigel Wilson, alerting him to the significance of folios 172–7 and asking him to make as much progress as he could on the reading of those folios. I knew I needed his expertise to confirm my own guesses.

I also sent another email, to my colleague Persi Diaconis in the Mathematics Department at Stanford. Persi is a magician-turned-mathematician. He still likes to perform tricks and one of his favorite pursuits is the application of mathematics to games. He is famous for his proof that one must shuffle a deck of cards *at least seven times* to make it thoroughly remixed. More recently, he studied the flip of a coin showing that it is not truly random after all. About 51 percent of the time coins actually end up landing *on the same side as they started*. He likes all sorts of surprising combinations. I knew he would like my problem, and I also knew that he was a distinguished combinatoricist. Most importantly, he was a friend. He would not laugh at me for asking such a trivial question. And so I put the question to him: how many ways are there of fitting together the Stomachion square?

Fitting the Pieces Together

The first reply I got was from Fabio. He was quite sure that no one had ever considered the possibility that the *Stomachion* was a combinatoric study. He pointed out, quite rightly, that until recently no one had considered the possibility that *any* ancient treatise was dedicated to combinatorics. I replied quickly, sharing with him the few readings that I had and suggesting that he join Nigel Wilson and me in the writing of an article on the *Stomachion*. I liked the spirit of teamwork we had when we wrote the publication concerning infinity and the *Method*, and I relished the prospect of another collaborative effort. However, in this case, the collaboration would be based on email alone. To this day, Fabio has never laid eyes on the physical manuscript bifolio of the *Stomachion*.

The team would expand further. I did not hear back from Persi for quite a while. It turns out that he doesn't use computers. Eventually I left him a note and the next day he showed up at my office telling me that they were working on it. He had given the problem to his students. His wife, Susan Holmes, a distinguished statistician was also hooked on the problem. A number of colleagues, hearing what I was working on, were sending me emails with calculations. Everyone was trying out combinations with the fourteen pieces and a square. And no two solutions were alike. Clearly the precise calculation was much more complicated than it had appeared at first sight. We were all coming to terms with the mathematics of the Stomachion.

The easiest way of visualizing the various possible combinations of the Stomachion puzzle is by thinking of them as the results of substitutions and rotations. Suppose you start with the original arrangement of the Arabic manuscript (see fig. 10.4). You could then take the triangle BZE (composed of the four pieces ZLF, LFEHT, TKH, KHB) and substitute it for the triangle ZDG (composed of the

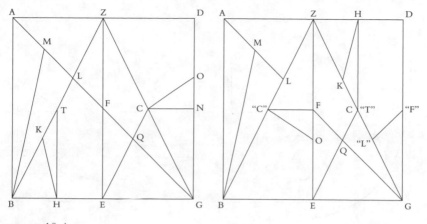

FIGURE 10.4

three pieces ZDOC, ONC, NCG). The result is a new arrangement. This is an example of a substitution. Let's call this substitution S (above right).

Alternatively, take the triangle AGB (composed of the seven pieces AMB, MLB, KHB, TKH, LFEHT, FQE, QEG) and rotate it around an imaginary axis passing through the points F and B. The result is a new arrangement (see fig. 10.5). This is an example of a rotation. Let's call this rotation R.

It would be the easiest if we could just count all the possible substitutions and rotations and then multiply them to get the number of possible arrangements. This was the basic approach everyone was taking at the outset. But it would not do. This is because there are very complex ways in which the various substitutions and rotations interact. For example, when you've applied substitution S, you can no longer apply rotation R. Substitution S destroys the line AG in the triangle ABG. There is no longer a triangle to rotate. Reciprocally, once you've applied rotation R, you can no longer apply substitution S, because rotation R destroys the triangle ZBE. There is no longer a triangle congruent with the one at ZDG. In short, there is a very complex pattern of ways in which substitutions and rotations can combine and ways that they cannot. It becomes a second-order combinatoric problem, above

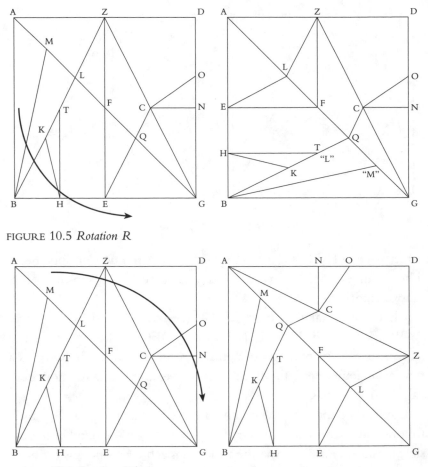

FIGURE 10.5 *Rotation R*

FIGURE 10.6 *Rotation R★*

and beyond fitting the fourteen pieces together, the problem is fitting the substitutions and rotations together. This kind of complexity, with combinations and combinations-of-combinations, very often arises in discrete mathematics.

There is another complication. We saw that some substitutions and rotations rule each other out, but others *cancel* each other out. To see this, let us consider a very simple case. One possible rotation, as we saw, is rotation R: turning the triangle ABG around the imaginary

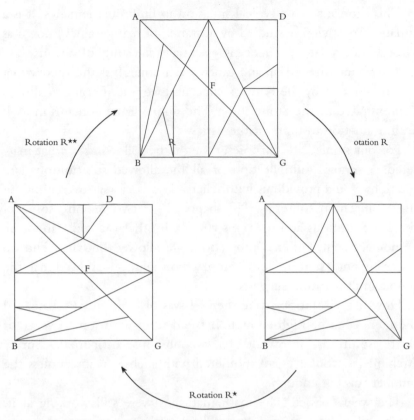

FIGURE 10.7 *The three rotations R, R* and R**, combined, end up canceling each other: we're back to the original square*

axis FB. Another possible rotation, of course, is what we may call rotation R★: turning the triangle AGD around the imaginary axis FD (see fig. 10.6). What happens if we apply both rotations R and R★? We end up having rotated the entire square. Nothing in the internal arrangement has changed. In this sense, the two rotations cancel each other out. Worse still, if we add in another allowed rotation, call it R★★, where we rotate the *entire* square around the imaginary axis DFB, then the effect of the combination of the three rotations R, R★ and R★★ is to cancel each other out. Having applied them all, we return to exactly the same starting position (see fig. 10.7).

This is once again a typical situation in finite mathematics. It is a situation most closely studied by a branch of mathematics known as Group Theory. Group Theory is, essentially, the study of various ways that permutations add up and cancel each other. It is this theory that is demonstrated by the Rubik's cube, and we find that it can also be demonstrated by the Stomachion. The simple game contains in itself an introduction to finite mathematics.

For our immediate purposes, though, the following is what mattered. A simple multiplication of all the allowed substitutions and rotations would provide us with what is known as an "overcount" of the Stomachion solutions. This happens for two reasons: some of these substitutions and rotations rule each other out and cannot be combined; while other combinations are allowed but then end up canceling out. There are fewer Stomachion solutions allowed than the simple multiplication suggests.

How many solutions were there? I was on tenterhooks. I needed the number to be high enough. If I ended up with some twenty or thirty solutions, it would be an obvious anticlimax. Surely Archimedes wouldn't have bothered with such a treatise unless the number was big enough.

The weeks passed. The mathematicians were still working at it. Meanwhile, I kept going back to my hard drive, adding to the transcription, each time a few more characters. Gradually, word by word, it made more and more sense. In a way, it was the mathematicians who helped me the most in the reading. This is how readings take place: you can make a reading only after you have formed some kind of guess as to the possible meanings of the text to be read. This, above all, was why Heiberg had not succeeded in reading the infinity passage in the *Method* or in reading the *Stomachion*. He had expected neither actual infinity nor combinatorics.

I began to make sense of the small theorem we had, right after the introduction. The mathematicians made clear that a major simplification resulted from the fact that certain pieces were "glued together." It could be proved, geometrically, that no substitution or rotation could ever separate, for instance, the two pieces AMB, MLB. There is no legitimate way the two can fit inside the square unless they are glued to each other along the side MB. In effect, it is as if we had just one piece—ALB—with the line MB forming a kind of decorative pattern, no more. Applying such reasoning in two other places, it could be shown that the problem amounts to a puzzle with eleven effective pieces, not fourteen. This, indeed, was a major simplification. And it became clear that the first small theorem was likely to make a contribution toward this kind of geometrical analysis.

Better still, the analysis of the structure of substitutions and rotations seemed to make sense of the second, and last, paragraph of the introduction—the one that Heiberg had been unable to read. I could now, finally, offer a reading and one that was even supported by Nigel Wilson. This was crucial, Nigel had not been privy to the mathematical discussions. While those discussions were indeed requisite for my *own* formulation of the text, it was important to see that the reading was there even without any knowledge of the mathematics. And so the text that we put together went like this:

> So then, there is not a small number of figures made of them,
> because of it being possible to rotate them into another place of
> an equal and equiangular figure, transposed to hold another
> position; and again also with two figures, taken together, being
> equal and similar to a single figure, and two figures taken
> together being equal and similar to two figures taken together—
> then, out of the transposition, many figures are put together.

It appeared as if Archimedes was discussing precisely this phenomenon of rotations and substitutions.

But at an even more elementary level, the most crucial thing for scholars, at this point, was that the new reading was inconsistent with the "elephant and warrior" interpretation. This treatise was *not* about how many *different* figures could be composed. We know this, now, because of the repeated insistence on *congruity* of different pieces and piece-combinations. For the sake of moving pieces about, as you do when putting together a warrior or an elephant, such insistence was irrelevant. But it was absolutely to the point, if the goal was to compose different combinations *within the same square*. Those different combinations arise precisely from the fact that one can substitute one piece for another (or one combination of pieces for another) because *the two are congruent.*

We were thus confident that Archimedes' treatise dealt with the problem of the combinations for constructing the square from the given fourteen pieces. And we could say even more. The clear emphasis of the introduction was on one small statement to which the first paragraph led and from which the second paragraph took off. It appeared that this statement asserted the very point of the treatise. So here was what Heiberg could not read: " . . . There is not a small number of figures made of them . . ."

This is what Archimedes was doing in this treatise—*counting a big number*. The operative word—"number"—is in fact the very same word, *plethos*, which was so crucial in the reading of the infinity passage in the *Method*. (In the context of abstract proportion theory, *plethos* is usually translated as "multitude," but in this counting-based context the best translation is "number.") In both cases, Archimedes, surprisingly looking at big numbers—those of infinity, in the infinity passage, and those of combinatorics, in the *Stomachion*.

But was the number really that big? This we still did not know. I knew that the various back-of-the-envelope calculations people were producing at first all involved an overcount because of the problems previously mentioned. How many remained? I just did not know. As the days passed, I began to worry that my problem, which at first I thought might have been too trivial, might in fact be too complicated. If modern mathematicians couldn't solve this straight away, perhaps I was wrong in believing Archimedes would have tackled it.

I finally scribbled my thank you note to Marasco, mentioning that the Stomachion might be even more interesting than it appeared at first sight. He promptly showed up at Stanford. It turned out that Marasco was a retired businessman from the computer industry with a PhD in physics. He understood very well the mathematical issues, and he also had the business experience and the contacts to suggest one further avenue for progress. We needed to spread the word among computer scientists, offering a small reward for the first person that came up with a solution to the Stomachion puzzle. He thought $100 would be enough, which he then put up. It became the informal Marasco Stomachion Award.

My mathematical friends had now decided that they needed to get their minds around it, too. Persi Diaconis and Susan Holmes had already brought in another renowned combinatorics couple, Ron Graham and Fan Chung from UC, San Diego. They had already been conversing by phone and email for a few weeks, but at some point they decided they needed to take a more hands-on approach. Persi and Susan traveled to San Diego and, for a long weekend, the four of them did nothing but draw diagrams and study the combinatoric principles underlying the Stomachion puzzle. At the end of it, they came up with what they were quite sure was the final count.

At the same time, Bill Cutler, a computer scientist from Illinois found a way of defining the problem in computer algorithm terms. He described to the computer how to put together a Stomachion square and then wrote a program that went systematically through all the potential arrangements. Many of them aborted. The program then counted all potential arrangements that *did* work. In this way, it counted all of the actual solutions to the Stomachion. The software came in first: Bill Cutler won the Marasco Award!

The answer was 17,152. Specifically, there were 17,152 different ways of arranging the pieces and still getting a square. In figure 10.8, you can see part of the printout produced by Cutler's software. And to think, I had been surprised to find out that there was more than a single solution!

Mercifully, the group of mathematicians found the same number. And while they could not claim first place, they did something extra that was crucial for our understanding of the problem. Cutler's software was based on counting all the possibilities one by one, a process that in

FIGURE 10.8 *Some of the solutions found by Bill Cutler's software*

principle can only be done by a computer. Archimedes certainly did not do it that way. However, the group of mathematicians found their number with "pencil and paper," which would have been Archimedes' method (only he would have used papyrus and a reed pen). They literally did not use any computers for their work. Nor did they rely on any high-powered mathematics that were not available to Archimedes.

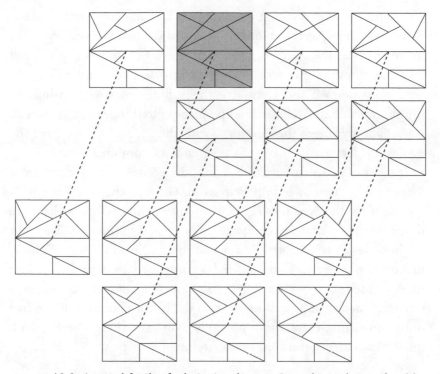

FIGURE 10.9 *A typical family of substitutions between Stomachion solutions, found by the group of mathematicians that solved Archimedes' puzzle*

Instead, what they did was produce an ingenious "map" of the possibilities (see fig. 10.9). The various solutions to the puzzle were arranged into twenty-four basic "families," depending on a certain arrangement of the main constituents. Inside each of the twenty-four families was a list of the basic possible solutions drawn with lines connecting any two solutions that could be transformed into each other by simple substitutions and rotations. At this stage the study had produced 536 basic solutions. Finally, certain simple rotations, which did not involve any substitutions, were applied independently to the rest to generate from each basic solution thirty-two rotations. This finally gave rise to the 17,152 solutions found by the mathematicians.

We now had everything in place. We had the historical context, thanks to Fabio Acerbi's pioneering work. We had the reading, confirmed by Nigel Wilson. We had the mathematical solution, produced by a distinguished group of mathematicians and confirmed by computer software. We also knew that this solution was well within the means available to Archimedes. The pieces fitted together. We had an watertight argument showing that, with the *Stomachion*, we have the earliest evidence, anywhere, of the science of combinatorics.

It was early December 2003. I announced our new discoveries at a conference at snowbound Princeton. Gina Kolata, science correspondent for the *New York Times*, was present and two weeks later we found ourselves on the front page of the *Sunday New York Times*. "In Archimedes Puzzle, a New Eureka Moment," read the title. Which, indeed, it was. We had now gained a completely new understanding of Archimedes, as well as the process of the making of Western science. Once again, we had rewritten the history books. And we had done something extra, more precious than everything else. We had, quite by accident, stumbled upon Archimedes at play.

11

New Light on an Old Subject

The autumn of 2003 might have been a high point for Reviel, but it was a low point for everybody else. The new interpretation of *Stomachion* was thrilling, but you could still look at the Palimpsest 17,152 ways and, even after three and a half years, it was not completely disbound. And however many ways you looked at the images, they were just not good enough—at least not good enough for Mr. B. He was not satisfied with our progress, and he told me so in no uncertain terms. Worse than that, Reviel agreed with him. There were passages on folios already imaged that he still could not read. And they were important passages. The very first folio of the Palimpsest, for example, was *Floating Bodies*. Heiberg had not read it; it had never been transcribed; and Reviel and Nigel were making very little headway with it. Most challenging, of course, were the folios containing the forgeries. The pseudocolor and ultraviolet were of almost no use on these folios. And very little progress was being made on the pages of the Palimpsest that contained texts from other palimpsested manuscripts. The pressure to decipher these grew to a new pitch after Hyperides was discovered, but we were having little success.

I told them I was happy to look for other solutions. I was lying. I was exhausted, and I really didn't think we could do any better. Mike Toth told me that there was no point in sending out a new Request for Proposals across the country. Since September 11, 2001, most imagers had been working on lucrative government contracts developing systems to locate and identify terrorists. He should know, I thought. Mike and I have a "don't ask, can't tell" policy. I don't ask, because he can't tell. Just staying the course was a daunting prospect for me, for Abigail, and for Roger. The forgeries, in particular, seemed entirely beyond us. I had no idea what to do.

A Meeting of Minds

Inevitably it was Mike who came up with ways forward. His first idea was to get us to the heart of the intelligence effort at the CIA, to the wizards of Langley. Mike even got me into CIA headquarters, which was quite a feat so soon after the attacks of 9/11. We toured the CIA museum with its curator and met Charlie the Catfish. Charlie really looks like a catfish, and he swims like a catfish, too. He's actually a mechanical gadget and his mission is still classified. Not sure he will be of much use in Afghanistan or Iraq. I also saw a bug, literally and figuratively—a remotely controlled dragonfly that can steal sound. Unlike Charlie, she had never been operational. She was too easily blown off course by the wind. After leaving the museum we went into the elevator and up several floors. I was introduced to Dr. Don Kerr, who was the Deputy Director of the CIA for Science and Technology. I presented him with images of Archimedes' *Floating Bodies* to hang on his wall. It was, after all, the government that had invented multi-spectral imaging. The imagers spent two hours in briefings and conversations with the experts at the CIA; they clearly knew far more than they were allowed to say. It was interesting, but we did not come away with the radically new approach to our problem that we so clearly needed.

Program managers sometimes take a bad rap as unimaginative bean counters. Not mine. Turning 180 degrees away from his secret resources, Mike decided to take full advantage of the press. Archimedes had always found his friends through the press. It was because of the *Washington Post* that Mike had gotten in touch with us, and Keith, Roger, and Bill had known the manuscript was at the Walters. The subsequent success of the project had secured more airtime. Within a few days of the publication of Will Peakin's article in the *Sunday Times,* I had a chat and a quick bite with John Lynch of the BBC at Washington Union Station. John told me that he had produced a science program that recounted the story of Andrew Wiles's single-handed effort to prove Fermat's Last Theorem. I had seen and marveled at this program. I agreed to make a documentary with the BBC's flagship science series *Horizon.* The director of "Archimedes' Secret," as the program on the Palimpsest was called, was Liz Tucker. It aired on March 14, 2002 and attracted 2.9 million viewers—over 13 percent of the UK viewing audience that evening. The project to retrieve the unique texts of Archimedes was now world famous. Surely, ambitious and cutting-edge imaging scientists would want to be in on this act? Let's cut to the chase, Mike said. Let's have these guys thrash out solutions to the most difficult imaging problem in the history of science.

Mike told me that I should not waste anybody's time—least of all mine. I didn't have to bother with a full scale RFP. I just had to send out a short summary of our problem: we needed to read text that had been written on animal skin in about 970 AD; erased shortly before April 14, 1229; written over; scraped off again; and covered in paintings. Anyone who responded to the challenge would not have to write thorough, wordy proposals just a brief summary of 500 words. To any credible proposal, I would give a good sample of our data, as well as information on how we had collected and processed it, and tell them that they were welcome to improve upon it. Mike told me to make it clear that I was not looking for science experiments, but rather practical propositions that could be made to work within six months. He then told me to invite the best ten suggestions to a summit at the Walters. This was, Mike insisted, an efficient and quick way to explore a variety of new approaches. It would also be inexpensive. Mike insisted on this point; we do not pay these people anything. The best

of them, he said, would not come for money; they would come for
Archimedes.

And come they did. This was thanks in no small part to Keith,
Roger, and Bill, who searched for anyone who might help. Kirk
Martinez, whom Bill and Keith had been to see in London a year
earlier, came from the University of Southampton. From the
University of Rutgers, Bill conscripted the delightful Professor of
Chemistry, Gene Hall, and from Bartlesville, Oklahoma, he pulled
in Bob Morton and Jason Gislason who both work for
ConocoPhillips. Andy Johnston, who worked on the Archimedes
database, brought in the late John Hillman from the University of
Maryland and his colleague Bill Blass from the University of
Tennessee. They had recently imaged the "Star-Spangled Banner."
Abigail found Emanuele Salerno. Emanuele came from Pisa and
represented the Easyreadit consortium, a European advanced
image-processing collaboration with representatives in the
Netherlands, Italy, the United Kingdom, and France. She also contacted Mike Attas and Doug Golz from the University of Winnipeg,
Canada. Finally Uwe Bergmann came from Stanford. His mother
Ingrid, who lives in Karlsruhe, Germany, subscribes to *GEO* magazine. Uwe was visiting her from California, where he is a scientist
at the Stanford Linear Accelerator Center. Although Ingrid did not
know much about his work, she thought he might be interested in
an article on the placebo effect in the magazine. So she left it on his
bedside table. He picked it up, read it, and happened to look at the
next article too. It was by Katja Trippel, and it was an excellent
piece on the Archimedes Palimpsest. It caught Uwe's imagination,
and he thought he could help. He emailed us at exactly the right
time.

The summit started on Thursday, April 1, 2004, which I thought
was most appropriate. In my undying skepticism, I asked Mr. B to
attend. I did not want to try to convince him of something I almost

certainly would not believe in and probably would not understand. If he decided to support anything that a scientist suggested, he needed to know precisely what he was getting into, both in terms of time and money. He came and watched the conference unfold. Everybody played his or her part, and it was intense. We didn't have the time to be genteel. We wanted clarity, we wanted proposals, and we wanted them both fast. Tempers flared as eminent scientists advocated their proposals and criticized their opponents, their equipment, and their competence. Under these circumstances, my generous hospitality budget became important, as drinks were passed well into the night. On Sunday morning Mr. B, Abigail, Roger, Mike, and I met in closed session. Then and there Mr. B approved the funding of three new approaches to the task.

New Approaches

OPTICAL CHARACTER RECOGNITION

Could a computer guess Greek characters better than Reviel Netz and Nigel Wilson? Mr. B thought that it would be an interesting experiment to try. So did Reviel. I think, like the chess player Gary Kasparov, he wanted a computer to beat. I kept my thoughts to myself. I wasn't particularly concerned. Computer processing would not interfere with the campaign as a whole. It would not involve the manuscript itself, because the computer would work best from the pseudocolor images that we had already generated. In terms of workflow, Mike assured me that Optical Character Recognition by a computer was a breeze.

There were several impressive OCR proposals, but they all seemed a long way from implementation given the time period required. Mike, once again, came up with an idea to get the desired result. We would hold a competition. The goal of the competition would be for the imaging scientists to produce something that would help Reviel read the text. The machine that got closest to Reviel's transcription of two designated pseudocolor folios would triumph, and Mr. B would pay $10,000 to the winner. Whether or not you think $10,000 is a lot of money depends upon who you are. To design a machine for Reviel, a professor might not think it is a lot of money. And clearly they didn't, because we didn't get machines from them. But to Derek Walvoord, a graduate student of Roger Easton's at RIT, $10,000 seemed like a lot of cash. Six months later, he delivered his product.

Derek set himself the task of identifying characters by comparing them to a known alphabet. His machine was effective and very simple to operate. It worked on any PC. You pulled up a pseudocolor image of the folio you wanted to work on and selected a "Region of Interest," normally a partially obscured character. Then you ran the software and watched as the machine did its number crunching. It produced a list of characters in order of likelihood. It worked, too. You could click on a partially obscured theta, and the machine would display a theta as the closest matching character. Amazing. The only problem was that we already knew it was a theta. The letters we wanted the computer to recognize were precisely the ones that were so obscured that the human eye could not recognize them.

Derek's machine was affectionately called DEREK. DEREK was impressive. But it wasn't Deep Blue, and it couldn't beat the ten giga-neurone computer inside Reviel's skull. But it showed enough promise for Mr. B to give the go ahead for DEREK II. DEREK II is much more powerful, because it combines optical recognition of the characters with a statistical approach to the Greek alphabet and Archimedes' vocabulary. This will be useful in helping the scholars see possible combinations of letters and words in the parts of the text that have been completely eaten away by the mold. It is being tested as this book goes to the press.

EL GRECO

There were several multi-spectral-imaging proposals at the conference. We could, in theory, have invited any of these contributors to
image the Palimpsest. Emanuele Salerno had worked extremely hard
with the data that we had sent him, but he concluded that no better
results could be achieved with that data. Like other participants, he
wanted to collect more data. There is virtually no limit to the amount
of slices that you can add to your data-cube; if you image with
enough wavelengths, you are called a hyper-spectral imager. But Mr.
B concluded that it was not worth the investment to essentially revisit
techniques that we had already tried.

Bill Christens-Barry was on the inside track, of course. He knew
that Mr. B was no longer seriously invested in multi-spectral imaging.
Bill came to the conference with a *very* inexpensive method to
address all the problems that the scholars had found in the early trials.
His solution would give a far more finely sliced data-cube than was
possible with the push-button processing Keith had used to process
the pseudocolor images. So, he put his idea forward. A year or two
earlier, he and Keith had visited the National Gallery in London to
see a multi-spectral imaging apparatus called VASARI. Giorgio Vasari
was a sixteenth-century Italian painter, but now VASARI was an
acronym for Visual Arts System for Archiving and Retrieval of
Images. VASARI interested Bill and Keith because it did not filter the
light in front of the camera. Instead it used light sources of very particular wavelengths, and thus avoided filters altogether. This approach
largely eliminated the registration problems that beset Keith and
Roger when they compiled their dense data-cubes. The problem
then was that narrowband light sources of sufficient intensity were
very expensive. But technology is always on the move and in 2004
Bill realized he had an extraordinarily cheap way to generate light at
specific wavelengths. He could use Light Emitting Diodes or LEDs.
LEDs are the lights that you can find all over the dashboard of your
car, and have been able to for some time. But only in recent years

have they become available at many different wavelengths. LEDs are so cheap that they are almost throwaways. Bill's thought was to attach them to fiber-optic cables and illuminate the parchment in various wavelengths of light.

Mr. B agreed to fund Bill's proposal, so Bill put his machine together and we tagged the experiment on to our last production-imaging session at the end of 2004. Roger brought the monochrome scientific camera from RIT that he had used with Keith in his initial experiments. To achieve the same resolution as the Kodak camera, forty images needed to be taken of each folio. Bill's machine looked like a wonderful gadget, and Bill had automated the controls so that it could take a great number of images quickly. LEDs are easy to build into electronic circuitry and have no moving parts, so the automation of the system was very simple. This was effective hyper-spectral imaging on the cheap. Although the idea stemmed from VASARI, Bill's imaging machine looked nothing like it and a different technology was used. We christened it EL GRECO, the nickname of the great painter Domenico Theotokopoulos, as a nod to the Greek text that it was designed to capture.

Using EL GRECO, Bill avoided the registration issues that had plagued the initial trials, and he had the narrowband light that he needed to slice his data-cube more finely. Bill found that the most effective post-processing technique for the EL GRECO data was the algorithm that Keith had written for the push-button processing. In fact, time and again during this experimental phase, we realized how effective the push-button processing was at retrieving Archimedes' text. The EL GRECO images of the Archimedes text were slightly better than the standard images that we had been distributing to the scholars. More importantly, EL GRECO gave us the chance to tailor-make our wavelengths for the different texts in the manuscript. The standard pseudocolor worked better for the Archimedes text than it did for the Hyperides and the Aristotle commentary. By using different LED sources for the various palimpsested codices, we hope in the future to make significant strides.

EL GRECO was an improvement, but it was no better at reading through gold than the standard techniques that we had been using. To do this we needed a very different technology.

X–RAYS

Gene Hall, Professor of Chemistry at Rutgers University, calls himself the "Paper Detective." He specializes in identifying and dating forgeries of all sorts, but particularly letters and banknotes. He does this by examining their chemical composition using X-ray fluorescence. X-rays, just like visible light, consist of photons, but the photons of X-rays have a much shorter wavelength (hundredths of nanometers, rather than the hundreds of nanometers in visible light) and a much greater energy. The human eye cannot see them but other detectors can. These detectors can convert the information into a form that we can see. We are all familiar with X-rays because of the dentist. But the X-ray images of our teeth are generated by transmitted X-rays. X-rays are zapped through our jaw and received by an emulsion plate on the other side. Gene wasn't interested in the transmitted X-rays. He was interested in the X-rays that do not get through. These interact with the material that stops them, and they cause this material to send out other X-rays at very particular wavelengths. These emitted X-rays contain crucial information—if you can get it.

Now here is the important part. While the photons of visible light give you color information, X-ray photons give you elemental information. This is because they interact with atoms differently. In the early 1920s, Niels Bohr and his colleagues thought of the atom as containing a nucleus of protons and neutrons. Electrons were found around this nucleus, orbiting in shells at various distances from the nucleus. This may well be how you think of an atom; it is one of the very last creations of classical physics and it will serve our purposes. Bohr labeled each shell with a letter, the one closest to the nucleus being letter "K." (The reason that these distances were designated with letters from the middle of the alphabet is simply that when scientists first probed the makeup of the atom, they were not sure how many shells they would find so they left room at either end of the sequence.) Photons of visible light interact with electrons found in Bohr's outer shells. Since they are further from the nucleus, less energy is needed to change the state of these electrons. Higher-energy, shorter-wavelength X-ray photons interact with electrons found on Bohr's inner shell, K, where more energy is needed to change the state of the electron. When I say that X-ray photons change the state of electrons on the inner shell, I actually mean that they knock them from the shell entirely. However, at the same moment that the electron "on" shell K is displaced, an electron from the next shell, L, replaces it. The electron on shell L makes a quantum leap to the inner shell. As it does so, it loses a lot of energy and it emits an X-ray photon. Since the atoms of each element have their own distinctive arrangement of electrons, the precise wavelength of this emitted X-ray corresponds to the energy difference of the electrons involved. Hence it will be specific to the element of the atom hit by the incident X-ray. If you can detect this emitted X-ray, you can determine which element it came from.

Gene's thought was that his instrument should be able to detect the X-ray photons given off by the iron in the ink of the palimpsested texts. It was a clever idea, and it was the idea that Gene had very briefly put into practice in his lab with a forged leaf from the Palimpsest before the conference. But the results were inconclusive.

Another participant in the conference was convinced that Gene's idea was a good one. His name was Bob Morton, and he was a research scientist at the petroleum company ConocoPhillips. Bob is not normal. He does not have a measurable IQ because he does not belong to the population for which the test was devised. He is one of the most intelligent, alarming, funny and inventive people I have ever met, and I say this without ever having been to one of his fabled Fourth of July parties in Bartlesville, Oklahoma. He came to the conference with his minder, Jason Gislason, who interpreted Bob for the rest of us until we got used to him. Bob's presentation was, frankly, amazing. It wasn't about Archimedes at all; it was about fossils. Using the same machine as Gene, Bob had looked at fossils from the famous Burgess Shale. He had mapped the distribution of elements in the fossils. More than this, he had mapped the elemental composition of the stone beside the fossilized bones, so that he could determine the chemical makeup of the soft tissue of the fossil. He called the results EXAMS—"Elemental X-ray Area Maps." His images of the fossils were far clearer than normal photographs. His final image stole the show. He called it a SEXI—a "Stereo Elemental X-ray Image." It was a 3-D image of the fossil *Marrella splendens*, made out of various EXAMs in silicon, iron, and potassium. He had made this by taking two EXAMs of the same fossil at a slightly different angle—actually 7.5 degrees. This is the difference in angle at which your two eyes see the same object at a distance of 4.2 feet. He then overlaid the two images on top of one another and color-coded them so they could be seen separately by your eyes when wearing 3-D glasses. The result was truly amazing. Not only did you see the fossil in startling 3-D clarity, you also saw its elemental composition. Not surprisingly, I wanted Bob and Jason on my X-ray imaging team and so did Mr. B.

Both Gene and Bob used an EDAX Eagle II Micro X-ray Fluorescence imaging instrument. Inside a chamber is an X-Y stage (a calibrated moving platform) controlled by a computer. The stage moves the sample beneath an X-ray generating tube and an X-ray detector. The software on the EDAX machine is very clever. The detector actually picks up a wide range of X-rays. The result is a data-cube of information analogous to the data-cube collected by the multi-spectral imagers. However, since this is a data-cube of X-rays, it contains elemental information rather than color information. As the sample is scanned, the computer automatically produces EXAMs extracted from the data-cube, each of which displays the distribution of a particular element across the area of the scan. EDAX probes cost in the low hundreds of thousands of dollars. Mr. B was all for buying one, but we thought we had better try it out more vigorously first.

So we got in touch with EDAX, specifically Tara Nylese and Bruce Scruggs. We asked if we could come to their offices in New Jersey for a week and try out their machine with two folios of the Palimpsest. So Abigail, Bob, Gene, and I went to their office in New Jersey and occupied it for a week. Tara, Bruce, and the entire EDAX team opened their doors.

We brought with us one of the toughest of all the challenges, folio 81. We intended to image the recto page. It was not a particularly important part of the Palimpsest. It contained part of Archimedes' *Equilibrium of Planes*, the text of which was well known through Codex A. It was also in good physical shape. But it was almost entirely covered by a forgery. Our first scans were not very successful. But with Bruce, Bob, and Gene in consultation, we refined our parameters. We doubled our dwell-time (the amount of time that the detector stayed over a particular area), so that we could pick up a bigger signal. We also increased our resolution (the granularity of the recorded image in dots per inch) and reduced the area that we scanned. We concentrated on just one line where we thought Archimedes text might be present. Fifteen hours later, we had a whole bundle of maps. We had a large number of maps that contained elements from the forgeries. We had a gold map (blank across the folio), a zinc map, a barium map, and a copper map, all of which brought out different parts of the forgery. But we also had an iron map. I emailed the iron map to Reviel; he could read the words: *para eutheian*. We had read through the gold.

There was only one fly in the ointment. In fifteen hours, we had scanned half a line of Archimedes text. There were approximately thirty-five lines of text on any given forged folio. If we worked on all four forgeries, it would take us 4,200 hours. Bob had always warned me that time was the biggest factor in X-ray imaging. If we went ahead with this procedure, I would be retired by the time we had finished imaging the Palimpsest.

Beamtime

The conclusion was clear. Since we didn't have the time, we needed a more energetic source for our X-rays. This was when Uwe Bergmann showed his stuff. He also gave a presentation at the conference suggesting that X-rays could be used to retrieve Archimedes text. While Gene and Bob proposed to do their work on an EDAX Eagle machine, which is the size of a small refrigerator, Uwe Bergmann proposed to use a machine the size of a soccer field—the SPEAR (Stanford Positron Electron Accelerating Ring). It is part of the Stanford Linear Accelerator Center or SLAC in California. SPEAR was built as an atom smasher—more technically, a synchrotron, which is an oval particle accelerator. The particles, electrons, and their positively charged equivalents, positrons, are accelerated to very, very, very nearly the speed of light. The electrons travel in one direction around the ring and the positrons travel in the opposite direction. When they collide, they create new particles and particle physicists analyze the results. It was at SPEAR that Burton Richter discovered the charm quark in 1974 and Martin Perl the Tau lepton in 1976. This is very cool. It is, in fact, so very cool that I was rather determined to get Archimedes there, even if it meant transporting him across the United States.

The SPEAR is not used as an atom smasher anymore, and anyway, we didn't want to hit Archimedes with particles traveling at 99.999999986 percent of the speed of light. Rather, we wanted to hit it with light itself, and now SPEAR is used as the world's greatest light bulb. To explain this, we need to go back to two of Isaac Newton's famous Laws of Motion. His first law states that every object in a state of uniform motion tends to remain in that state of motion unless an external force is applied to it. Even though the electrons in the synchrotron are traveling at a uniform (extremely high) speed, their state of motion is not uniform; they are not traveling in a straight line. Actually, they are bent by very powerful magnets. The third law states that for every action there is an equal and opposite reaction. So what happens when the highly energetic electrons are swerved? What's the reaction? Well, electromagnetic radiation—lots and lots of it—spun off the ring like tomatoes off the back of a truck turning a corner at high speed.

To the particle physicists this synchrotron radiation was wasted energy, an inconvenient by-product of the atom-smashing process. But one day in the mid-1970s someone summoned up the courage to ask the particle physicists if they could literally "tap" the ring and capture the synchrotron radiation that it was emitting. For several years at SPEAR, X-ray scientists, like parasites, harnessed the synchrotron radiation provided by the ring that was primarily there to serve the atom smashers. Eventually the high-energy physicists moved on to bigger machines. Since 1990, SPEAR has been dedicated to the generation of synchrotron radiation. A synchrotron X-ray beam is intense (there are an awful lot of photons), collimated (all the photons point in the same direction), and polarized (the electromagnetic field of all the photons swings in a well-defined plane). In other words, you have a colossal army of X-rays, all marching to the same drum, and the experimenter can call the tune. The Stanford Synchrotron Radiation Laboratory (SSRL) is one of the most advanced light sources in the world. Today, more than fifty synchrotrons are operated around the world and many more are under construction. They have names like BESSY, Boomerang, Diamond, Soleil, SPring-8, and SPEAR3—the newest upgrade of the ring at the Stanford Synchrotron Radiation Laboratory.

A number of "beam lines" run off the synchrotron to little independent labs. We were designated beam line 6–2. Many beam lines have two hutches, so that while one experiment is being run, another can be set up. There is no downtime for beams at SSRL, because "beamtime" is a precious commodity. The hutches are lead-lined and while the experiment is running, no one can enter the hutch. It is not a good idea to be zapped by the beam. This is all you get when you get beamtime at SSRL—a beam line and a hutch. While the EDAX Eagle probe is a commercial machine with an awful lot of software attached, designed for a wide variety of applications, the synchrotron is just a light source. Uwe had to build the machine.

Unlike the EDAX machine, which sends out X-rays at many different wavelengths, Uwe could tune his beam precisely to the best wavelength to look at iron or any other element. Uwe and Abigail got Greg Young of the Canadian Conservation Institute to do exhaustive tests on an old parchment document of Abigail's to make sure that his experiment would not damage the parchment. Having conducted these tests, Uwe realized that he could indeed raise the intensity of his beam at the wavelength that responded to iron. Uwe attenuated his beam using especially designed filters. He fine-tuned it with a filter of Reynolds Wrap, which he assured me was good enough for the job. He designed his X-Y stage and carefully calculated the distance between the sample and the detector. He constructed a humidity chamber, so that the humidity would remain constant and the folio of the Palimpsest would not change shape while the scan was running. All the computers and workstations were positioned outside of the hutch. Each of the several computers did different things One computer recorded the position of the beam and another recorded the position of the sample on the X-Y stage. If the stage stopped moving, the experiment automatically shut down so as not to damage the parchment. Another computer recorded the data in the scan and a final computer was used to convert the files into a format that we could use in the post-processing software and distribute to the scholars.

To help him, Uwe had Martin George write the software for the computers, which had to meet two very different criteria: it had to be advanced enough to precisely capture the data and it had to be easy enough for Mike, Abigail, and me to use. The three of us would have to take turns with Uwe running the scans, keeping an eye on the Palimpsest, and even fine-tuning the beam. The reason we had to do this was that the experiment would run for seven days, twenty-four hours a day, and in shifts.

It didn't look like a professional set-up. Inside the hutch the guts of the machinery were scattered all over the place and outside of the hutch it looked like an electronics junk yard. I soon realized that this is precisely what serious professional operations look like, because looks don't matter. Essentially, new machines are tailor-made for very different operations every day in this extraordinary place.

Uwe estimated that the scanning of one of the two columns of folio 81r, the forged page, would take thirty hours—approximately seventeen times faster than at the EDAX machine. Abigail put the folio on to the X-Y stage and the scanning started. It was utterly mesmerizing. Back and forth the scan would go, and slowly the iron map would appear that brought out the Archimedes text. We had to be constantly watchful for a fading signal, because the position and strength of the beam changed over time. (The electrons got topped up three times a day). If it did change, we had to "nudge" the beam. We couldn't scan large sections because the resulting files would be too big. So Mike wrote down the novice's guide to the synchrotron and stuck it on a computer: "Press STOP; Open hutch; Turn on light; Check humidity; check ARCHIE; Turn off light; Close hutch; flick SAFETY switch; press EXIT PLOTTER; Press EXIT RASTER; Check FILE save in Dir/*.*; Select RASTER; press RETURN; Change XY coordinates; press APPLY; flick SHUTTER 3 switch; select RASPLOT; choose pixel 1; press START."

Thirty hours later we had a column of text to show Reviel. And Reviel read it. We had achieved our objective. We assured Uwe that we would be back, and when we came we would bring the most important pages of text containing the most difficult challenges.

March 2006

We returned to SLAC for two weeks in March 2006. This time we took more people with us. We needed more people to staff the beam, but we also needed the talent. Uwe spent all of his time optimizing the experiment that only he understood. Bob lent his years of experience on imaging with X-ray fluorescence. Keith and Roger processed the images. Jennifer Giaccai, the conservation scientist at the Walters, joined Abigail. And Mike and I lent a hand when we could.

This time we also brought out the very first page of the manuscript. This was the page that Reviel and Natalie had first recognized as *On Floating Bodies* in April 2001. It was the one that also contained the inscription by the scribe of the prayer book with the date April 14, 1229. The page really was a wreck and the pseudocolor images had revealed nothing.

From the moment the scanning started, it was clear that something extraordinary was happening. The charred, stained, and worm-eaten parchment in the hutch appeared on the screen as a dense lattice of Greek characters. I knew that we were seeing, pixel by pixel, line by line, at the Stanford syncrotron, a map of the iron on the page that would give us the previously unknown Greek version of Archimedes' *On Floating Bodies*. Keith Knox sent the first images to Reviel by email. He received this reply:

From: Reviel Netz
Sent: Mon 3/13/2006 12:32 AM
To: Keith Knox
Cc: Nigel Wilson; Mike Toth; Uwe Bergmann; Roger Easton; William Noel
Subject: folio 1v col.1

Thanks Keith for the images.
XRF for 1v col. 1 is sensational. I attach the transcription of

1v col. 1 lines 2–11. Previously, with very hard work, I squeezed some 3.5 lines out of the old pseudocolor, but now I fairly easily read effectively the entire text, noting a couple of errors, too, in my old pseudocolor based reading.

Reviel

This leaf comes from the very long final proposition of *On Floating Bodies*, which is, by common consent the most complex proposition ever written by Archimedes. It concerns the conditions under which a conic section, somewhat similar in appearance to the hull of a boat, will or will not be stable when immersed in water. It is significantly different from the Latin text that Heiberg derived from Moerbeke and a group of diagrams appear where none were suspected. This unique surviving Greek text of Archimedes' *On Floating Bodies* was finally revealed on March 13, 2006—777 years after it had been erased and overwritten.

The Gift-Giver

The colophon from which John Lowden had so painstakingly extracted the date on which the scribe of the prayer book had dated his work as April 14, 1229, was also on this same page. I sent out the following email:

> All: We attach two images of the lower section of fol. 1v. "Before" was taken when the Palimpsest arrived at WAM. "After" was taken today: it's an X-ray fluorescence image taken at SLAC; after Abigail Quandt conserved it. It contains some text written on April 14, 1229. But can anyone now give us any more details?

My friend Georgi Parpulov was the first to reply:

From: Georgi Parpulov
Sent: Tue 3/14/2006 4:39 AM

To: William Noel
Subject: colophon

Hi, Will,
+[This] was written by the hand of presbyter John Pogonatos (?) on the 14th day of the month of April, a Saturday, of the year 6737, indiction 2.
Wait till you hear from Nigel Wilson: he will be able to read it with much greater precision.

Before we heard from Nigel, we heard from John Lowden:

From: Lowden, John
Sent: Thu 3/16/2006 10:31 AM
To: William Noel; Georgi Parpulov; Nigel Wilson, Reviel Netz
Subject: RE: colophon
Have just received this on return from Dublin. The improved legibility is astonishing.
First impression is that the name (refining GP) is Iw(annou) iere(os) tou Murwna
I would check Ioannes Myronas iereus as scribe.
But maybe I should check first and communicate after!
Yours (too hastily?)
    John

And then finally, on the Sunday, we got confirmation from Nigel:

From: Nigel Wilson
Sent: Sun 3/19/2006 7:32 AM
To: William Noel; Georgi Parpulov; John Lowden; Reviel Netz
Subject: Re: colophon

Dear Will, John, Reviel et al.,

I agree with John's suggestion and that Myronas is probably the name; the last letter could be alpha and has an accent. I have asked a Greek student of mine to check in the telephone directories to see if it is still a name in Greece. (Mylonas is well attested.)

Best wishes,

Nigel

There we are then. The case is nearly closed. Finally we know who preserved the texts of Archimedes, Hyperides, and the rest. The priest Ioannes (John) Myronas finished his work on April 14, 1229. In that year, April 14 was the day before Easter Sunday. Traditionally, it was a day upon which people made gifts to religious institutions for the good of their souls. What an extraordinary gift this was. Ioannes did not just redeem himself. On the anniversary of Christ's Resurrection, Ioannes Myronas gave the world its greatest palimpsest and saved the secrets of Archimedes.

"The Vast Book of the Universe"

Moonlighting for Archimedes

This is not typical university work. The Archimedes Palimpsest seems to insist on being unique and the project of its decipherment has few parallels. Remarkably much has been achieved in less than ten years. Remarkably, too, nearly all of this was achieved by weekend warriors, summoned by the thrill and glory of working for Archimedes. We all had our day jobs. Will Noel was curating manuscript exhibitions at the Walters, I was teaching Greek science at Stanford, while Roger Easton was teaching imaging science at Rochester, and Nigel Wilson was editing the works of Aristophanes for the Oxford Classical Texts series. I am not sure what Mike Toth was doing. In fact, only one individual got the Archimedes Palimpsest as a day job—and this underlines the priorities of manuscript studies. Abigail Quandt put aside most of her other obligations to concentrate, day after day, on the disbinding and conservation of the manuscript. Her hands were the busiest.

And all of us did this for one simple reason: we are in awe of one individual who lived, some 2,250 years ago, on a triangular island in the middle of the Mediterranean. That we succeeded in doing so much for him is, in my view, due to three individuals. They deserve our thanks.

The Patron

That so much has been accomplished so quickly is primarily a tribute to the owner of the Palimpsest. The team of scholars and scientists working on the project have something which is, today, very rare: our work is led by *a rich patron*. There was a time when this was standard. Science in Alexandria—as well as in Syracuse—was pursued under the patronage of Hellenistic kings. No doubt a rich patron commissioned the Archimedes manuscript in the tenth century. Most Renaissance artists and scholars worked for rich patrons. However, since at least the Middle Ages, scholarship has often been pursued within public institutions. The Church is the most obvious example, and it is due to her that most manuscripts survive. Today most manuscripts are held by a different kind of public institution—the state or its universities. Almost all the important manuscripts of the world can now be found in such institutions and, at first, everyone's feeling was that this manuscript should belong to the public. We were proved wrong. In retrospect, it was a stroke of luck that the manuscript found itself in private hands. No public institution could have acted so flexibly, with such generous and well-thought application of resources. Think of it; the owner did something rather outrageous. He entrusted it to Will Noel, who is by now a world expert on the Archimedes Palimpsest but eight years ago could not tell Archimedes from Pythagoras. The owner then more or less told Will Noel to do with the manuscript as he pleased. The owner implicitly promised to pay along the way as necessary. (I say "implicitly" because, I am told, the owner is not a man of many words.) It turns out this was the clever thing to do. Had the manuscript been housed at a university, the academic politics of its research would have been much more difficult and each expense along the way would have had to be accounted for in a much more tedious, haphazard, and time-consuming fashion. In short, the owner saved us the disadvantages of public institutions. Not that private owners are to be preferred in principle. In my own view, private owners are, in general, not the best custodians of world treasures. After all, it was the Greek Church that saved the manuscript for a millennium and then it was private owners that, through the course of the twentieth century, nearly destroyed it. With the current owner we have been lucky. He has not merely done well by Archimedes; he did all that he could.

The Philologist

I do not know the owner of the Palimpsest all that well, however Will Noel does. Almost daily, he is in email correspondence with him discussing the way to move forward with the Palimpsest project. My own daily correspondence is even more virtual. It is all in my head. And it is with another great benefactor of this project without whom all of this would have been impossible. In my thoughts, I always converse with Johan Ludwig Heiberg.

Right down to the last pages, we have been critical toward him throughout this book—the gaps he left, the false guesses he made, the diagrams with which he never bothered. Now is the time to admit the truth. Without Heiberg, we could have never made it. We would look at the text and see at first just a jumble of meaningless traces. We would interpret a few of them. We would conjecture a sense. We would end up at a dead end. Then we would check Heiberg and, low and behold, he had already made sense of it. He had even read further! Only then, looking back at the page, do we see those traces that provided Heiberg with his reading. And then, finally, based on Heiberg's foundations, we can go further and add to his readings.

The transcription project was rather like an expedition to a lost island. You believe you face what no one has ever witnessed. And then, time and again, you have the same uncanny experience. You suddenly realize that the previous explorer—Heiberg—had already been there. I was excited when I saw symbols for circles emerging out of Abigail's treatment of the Palimpsest. I took it for granted that they were new.

But no, Heiberg had seen them too and had noted them in his critical edition. Again and again, Heiberg took me by surprise.

Let us put it this way. There is a long tradition of readers of Archimedes, from scholars such as Hero of Alexandria, Eutocius of Ascalon, and Leo the Geometer from Byzantium, to the present day. No one in this tradition will ever rival the authority of Heiberg. We are extraordinarily lucky that he, and no one else, was in Istanbul in 1906 and studied this manuscript for that brief historical moment. No one else would have made so much out of the manuscript. Heiberg almost single-handedly saved the text of Archimedes. It is only thanks to the most modern technology that we can now go beyond his reading. And for this, I suggest, our gratitude should go to Archimedes himself.

The Founder's Tools

I started this book by saying that Archimedes was the most important scientist who ever lived. We can now see how: in the tools he created—and in the way in which later science was shaped by Archimedes' blueprint for science. Archimedes, more than anyone else, shaped the history of the calculus—the essential study for the measurement of curves. And he also, incredibly, was the founder of combinatorics—the science underlying our own theory of probability. These two—the calculus and the theory of probability— underlie contemporary imaging science. The imaging scientists working on the Archimedes Palimpsest applied a science that was fundamentally Archimedean.

To illustrate this, I now concentrate on a relatively standard tool used by imaging scientists—the equalization of probability curves. While standard, it is a useful introduction, because it brings into focus the main concept of imaging science, namely that of *information*.

We have often mentioned the term "information" in this book. We have discussed the way that books move from one information storage system to another and how changes in information technologies impact the transmission of knowledge. It is time to come clean and explain that "information" is not some kind of vague, metaphorical concept. Information is a technical term possessing a clear, subtle mathematical definition. Most importantly, in contemporary science, information can be *measured*.

The fundamental intuition can be articulated as follows. We look at an array of numbers and we ask, "how predictable is it?" Suppose the array of numbers is as follows:

255, 255, 255 . . . 255

All of the numbers are exactly 255. There is a clear intuition that this is very predictable and so it is also very uninformative. On the other hand, an array that is as follows:

127, 45, 254, 11, 6, 189 . . . 39

is much less predictable and contains more "information."

Now, let us review the arrays of numbers:

255, 255, 255 . . . 255   127, 45, 254, 11, 6, 189 . . . 39

What do they mean in terms of image science? As Will Noel has already explained, imaging scientists do not think of images as faces or flowers. They think of images as two-dimensional (sometimes many-dimensional) arrays of integer values. Each of the integers in an array represents the properties of a pixel. Typically, they consider the grey level of a pixel in a black-and-white picture. In a black-and-white picture each pixel is assigned a level of grey that usually ranges from 0 (least light—that is, black) to 255 (most light—that is, white). The 255, 255, 255 . . . 255 array, therefore, is correlated with a perfectly blank image—one that is totally white. The 127, 45, 254, 11, 6, 189 . . . 39 array, on the other hand, is associated with a complex pattern of light and shade. The perfectly blank image is completely predictable (totally white), therefore totally uninformative. The complex pattern of light and shade is much less predictable and therefore also much more informative.

At this point, it can be mathematically shown that: the most informative image is the one in which all the levels of grey are equally probable.

In the perfectly blank image, a single level of grey was the most probable—the totally white one. All of the rest had no probability of occurring. In the complex pattern of light and shade, however, all levels of grey were equally probable. And this is the underlying mathematical reason why the complex pattern of light and grey is the more informative.

The goal of imaging science is to make images as informative as possible so that, for instance, scholars can use them to read the words of Archimedes. The mathematical result implicitly suggests a certain possible technological application. In order to make an image more informative, let us equalize its distribution of probabilities. We should try to make all the levels of grey equally probable.

How do we do this? We need a new mathematical conceptualization. We need to return to the image and consider it not merely as an array of numbers but, instead, as a curve. We draw a two-dimensional matrix with the familiar x and y-axes; x horizontally and y vertically. We make the x-axis stand for the possible grey levels—from 0, the perfect black, to 255, the perfect white. For each of the 256 levels of grey, we draw on the y-vector each times it occurs. So, for instance, the perfectly blank image has a very simple appearance in such a matrix; it is empty everywhere except for a single, tall column standing at 255 at the rightmost end of the x-axis (see fig. 12.1). A complex pattern of light and shade, on the other hand, has a more complex appearance (see fig. 12.2).

To simplify it a bit: most images appear as a kind of bell-curve, with most pixels somewhere in the middle between black and white and the rest somewhat less probable (more black or white) as we move away from the center.

Now recall our aim—to make the image as informative as possible—is to make the distribution of probabilities *as equal as possible*. That is to say since the most informative image appears as a "flat" curve or rather like a rectangle—one where all levels of grey occur equally often (see fig. 12.3)—we wish to take a curve such as the bell-curve in the figure and turn it into a flat, rectangular shape.

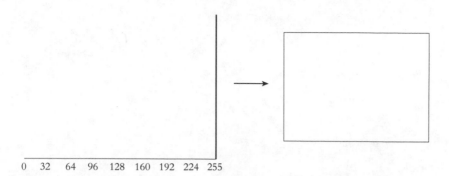

0   32   64   96   128   160   192   224   255

FIGURE 12.1 *A distribution of pixels where all pixels have 255 level of light corresponds to the perfectly blank image.*

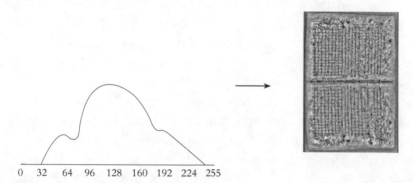

0   32   64   96   128   160   192   224   255

FIGURE 12.2 *A normal image has associated with it a curve that has a roughly bell-like shape.*

Now Archimedean science kicks in again. For this operation, the transformation of a bell-curve into a rectangle, is simply the measurement of a curvilinear object by a rectilinear one. When Archimedes was measuring his parabolas, showing how they were equal to two-thirds a given rectangle, he was doing *precisely* the kind of operation we need to do right now. (Indeed, some of the curves we need to measure may take the form of a parabola.) And what contemporary scientists do, at this stage, is apply the tools of the calculus—i.e. of the science arising out of Archimedes' measurement of curvilinear objects—in order to "flatten" the curve correctly.

287

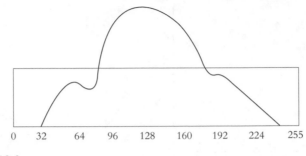

0   32   64   96   128   160   192   224   255

FIGURE 12.3

We applied the theory of probability to develop the notion of "information" and to discover that the most informative image is the one associated with an equal distribution of probabilities of grey levels. We then applied the calculus to transform the curve of the actual distribution of probabilities into the desired "flat" shape associated with the equal distribution of probabilities. The end result was no more and no less than the simultaneous application of probability and the calculus. This is just an example of what imaging scientists do, but also a representative one (if you wish, an *informative* one)—though, of course, to develop the images used for reading the Palimpsest, much more than this was required. But this is precisely the type of mathematical technique applied. Probability and the calculus are what imaging science is made of. And so, without Archimedes, we would not have the science to read him.

Archimedes' Blueprint for Science

Even more important than the contents of Archimedes' science was his spirit—his blueprint for science. After all, his combinatorics were lost when Ioannes Myronas decided not to use all of the parchment in front of him and to only use a single leaf of the *Stomachion*. It remained for seventeenth-century mathematicians to reinvent the science of combinatorics and therefore to create probability. They would have done so even without Archimedes having written the *Stomachion*. And yet, without Archimedes' example, I doubt that we would have the kind of science we have today. We can see how it goes back to Archimedes' invention of applying mathematical, abstract models to the physical world.

Let us take as our starting point, once again, the mathematical notion of *information*. Imaging science and the computer sciences, as well as many other disciplines of the digital revolution, are all essentially based on this concept. As mathematical concepts go, this is a very recent one. A mathematician working at Bell Laboratories named Claude Shannon introduced it in the year 1948. He was working on making telephone lines function better, and it occurred to him that there could be a mathematical theory associated with the amount of information traveling through such lines. His inspiration came directly out of physics, and the concept of information, as found by Shannon, is inherently a concept of mathematical physics.

What Shannon did was to take the concept of *entropy*, defined in mathematical physics, and to apply it to the flow of information in, for instance, telephone lines. What is entropy? It is a measure of how "probable" a given physical state is. A physical state can be very likely, in which case its entropy is high, or it can be very unlikely, in which case its entropy is low. We can therefore see where Shannon took his inspiration: information is (to simplify a bit) *reverse entropy*.

One of the deepest observations ever made by science is that— hold your breath—*probable things happen more often*. So that, more often than not, physical systems move from unlikely states—with low entropy—to more likely states—with high entropy. Wait long enough and *the amount of entropy in the universe must increase* (or, as we may put this after Shannon, *the amount of information in the universe must decrease*, which is also the reason why reception on our cell phones is so bad). I am completely serious about saying that this is one of the deepest observations ever made by science. It is a beautiful example of how, by the power of pure thought, we can work out how the universe *must* behave. It is a tautology, that probable things happen more often;

and because of this tautology, which we came to by pure thought alone, we can see also that *the amount of entropy in the universe must increase.* This is known as the second law of thermodynamics, and it ranks as one of the most fundamental discoveries of physics.

This becomes especially significant the moment we can calculate which physical systems have more entropy and which have less. This was the reason the concept of entropy was introduced in the first place in 1872 by a German physicist named Boltzmann. He produced a mathematical approach for measuring the amount of entropy in a physical state. Suppose we take as our physical system a certain gas composed of many gas molecules. Then Boltzmann could show that the more rapidly, on average, the gas molecules were moving the less entropy the system had; or that the slower, on average, the gas molecules were moving the more entropy the system had. In short, Boltzmann could show that higher entropy is associated with the slower motion of molecules. Based on the second law of thermodynamics—showing that entropy must increase—Boltzmann could also show that gases must eventually move from faster states to slower states.

Now, it is also established that what we call "heat" is really a measurement of the speed of molecules in the physical system. A "warm" system is really one where the molecules move faster, a "cool" one is where they move slower. And so Boltzmann shows, based on the second law of thermodynamics, that all systems must, eventually, became *colder.*

This is magic—belonging right up there in the pantheon next to Archimedes. Applying pure thought alone, Boltzmann proved in 1872 that *everything must, eventually, become colder.* But the comparison with Archimedes can be sustained further.

Why did Boltzmann produce his mathematical theory in 1872? The behavior of heat was the urgent scientific problem of his time. So much else in science was already understood in mathematical terms but not heat. In the two centuries prior to Boltzmann, scientists were working hard on extending Newton's achievement.

Newton determined, on purely mathematical grounds, how the planets must behave. The universe was made of points—centers of gravity—exerting the force of gravity on each other. This was a unified theory of motion, where everything was reduced to basic tools of geometry and calculation. The theory was published in 1687 in Newton's *Principia*. And from 1687 onward, scientists tried to emulate Newton's achievement—to produce mathematical theories to which one could reduce various physical phenomena. In the early nineteenth century electricity followed gravity, analyzed by mathematical techniques somewhat comparable to those of Newton. By 1872 the central physical phenomenon still resisting mathematical treatment was heat. Boltzmann, in his study, made a fundamental contribution to the mathematization of physical science. He was essentially completing Newton's program.

Only it wasn't Newton's—it was Archimedes' as Newton would be the first to admit. Newton, in 1687, was himself heir to a long tradition. His great predecessor was Galileo. Both Newton and Galileo aspired, above all, to return science to its Archimedean heights. They wished to take Archimedes' mathematical tools and to make such tools deduce as much of physics as one could. The Newtonian program of reducing physical systems to geometrical representations obeying mathematical laws was taken from the Archimedean blueprint for science. And so, without Archimedes, there would be neither Galileo nor Newton. And for that matter, there would be no Boltzmann or Shannon either. Nor, for that matter, contemporary imaging science.

The "Vast Book"

"Philosophy is written in this vast book, which lies continuously open before our eyes (I mean the universe). But it cannot be understood unless you have first learned to understand the language and recognize the characters in which it is written. It is written in the language of mathematics, and the characters are triangles, circles, and

291

other geometrical figures. Without such means it is impossible for us humans to understand a word of it, and to be without them is to wander around in vain through a dark labyrinth."

So Galileo wrote, in 1623, recovering the spirit of the science of Archimedes. This metaphor of the vast book of the universe is still with us. We do think of the universe as a "book" whose secrets we try to uncover, and we still use mathematics to do so. The importance of Archimedes to the history of science is his having shown how this metaphor could literally work. The book of the universe was first deciphered by him—and it was found to be written in the language of mathematics.

In 1623, when Galileo came to write down these words, all the manuscripts of Archimedes were already gone. Codex B was lost some time in the fourteenth century; Codex A was lost some time in the sixteenth century, probably when Galileo was still a child. Only one copy remained but it was hidden from sight. The monks who used it never did learn to read its triangles, circles, and other geometrical figures.

In 1687, when Isaac Newton's *Principia* was published, this codex—the Archimedes Palimpsest—was still in the Holy Land, still hidden from sight. It was worlds away from the British scientist cloistered in his lodgings at Trinity College, Cambridge.

In 1872, when Ludwig Boltzmann published his study on the second law of thermodynamics the Archimedes Palimpsest was already in Istanbul. It was about to be discovered, however briefly, by Heiberg. By 1948 it was lost again. When Shannon produced his mathematical definition of information, the manuscript was probably already lying mutilated in a Paris apartment.

Fifty years later it walked on stage. And now, science was ready. The science inspired by Archimedes came full circle to be able to recover nearly all of his words. And now, finally, we get a sense of the full measure of the man.

A final word of caution should be added. We have not gotten everything. There are still gaps in our reading. But we remain optimistic. Even now, as I write, I am studying the latest SLAC images of the forgery pages, and I can see that Heiberg's transcription of *Method* proposition 1 needs significant revision. The science inspired by Archimedes never stands still. The process extends without end: science steps back from physical reality to consider its mathematical underpinnings and, this way, more and more is always found. Archimedean science keeps making progress, and, in time, it will catch up with Archimedes.

Acknowledgements

Reading the Archimedes Palimpsest was a far more complicated undertaking than the narrative encompassed in these pages might indicate. Indeed, we do not know all the people who helped. Choosing just a few may alienate many, but the contributions of some have been so substantial that we cannot conclude this book without listing them. Knowing that this list is incomplete, we nonetheless extend our thanks to all who have so generously contributed to the project. A lot of the work was done at night, on weekends, and during vacations, and we have also to thank the project's many widows and orphans, particularly Carol Christens-Barry, Dale Stewart, Daniel and Donald Potter, Elisabetta Gaiani and Sofia Bergmann, Hanneke Wilson, and Lucretia Toth. Deep gratitude is owed to Uwe Bergmann, Serafina Cuomo, Patricia Easterling, Roger Easton, Jr, László Horváth, Geoffrey Lloyd, Abigail Quandt, Ken Saito, and Nigel Wilson for their expert assistance in the writing of this book. All mistakes of fact and interpretation are our own. Many friends helped us make ourselves clearer, including Richard Ash, Christopher Collison, Charlie Duff, Susan Elderkin, Guy Deutscher, Kathryn Gerry, Richard Leson, Amanda Mann, Audrey Scanlon-Teller, and Jean-François Vilain. Success depends upon good editors, and we had the wonderful Francine Brody at Weidenfeld and Nicolson, the sagacious Robert Pigeon at Da Capo, and the heroic William McLean at the Walters.

MANAGEMENT AND
ADMINISTRATION
Ken Dean
Barbara Fegley
Kirstin Lavin
Richard Leson
Griffith Mann
Amy Mannarino
Joan Elisabeth Reid
Harold Stevens
Mike Toth
Gary Vikan
Lynn Wolfe

CONSERVATION AND
HANDLING
Kevin Auer
George Chang
Jane Down
Gil Furoy
Jennifer Giaccai
Paul Hepworth
Erin Loftus
Amy Lubick
Maureen McDonald
Mike McKee
Elizabeth Moffatt
Elissa O'Loughlin
Abigail Quandt
Jane Sirois
Scott Williams
Gregory Young
Anthea Zeltzman

SCIENCE AND IMAGING
Allyson Aranda
Mike Attas
Uwe Bergmann
Bill Christens-Barry
David Day
Charles Dickinson
Roger Easton, Jr
Alex Garchtchenko
Martin George
Jason Gislason
Douglas Golz
Gene Hall
Tom Hostetler
Keith Knox
Matthew Latimer
Bob Morton
Nick Morton
Tara Nylese
Emanuele Salerno
Bruce Scruggs
Derek Walvoord

DATA AND INFORMATION
TECHNOLOGY
Martina Bagnoli
Diane Bockrath
Doug Emery
Cathleen Fleck
Andy Johnston
Joe McCourt
Carl Malamud

SCHOLARSHIP
Fabio Acerbi
Colin Austin
Chris Carey
Persi Diaconis
Patricia Easterling
Mike Edwards
Zoltán Farkas
Eric Handley
Jud Herrman
Susan Holmes
László Horváth
John Lowden
Gyula Mayer
Henry Mendell
Stephen Menn
Tamás Mészáros
Stefano Parenti
Georgi Parpulov
Erik Petersen
Marwan Rashed
Peter Rhodes
Ken Saito
Robert Sharples
Richard Sorabji
Natalie Tchernetska
Stephen Todd
Nigel Wilson
David Whitehead

Further Reading

Those interested in finding out more about the Archimedes Palimpsest, its imaging, conservation, and scholarly study, should visit the website www.archimedespalimpsest.org, and follow the links. It is our hope to present all our data on the web at www.archimedespalimpsest.net, and we have already made a start at this. Other than this, readers might like to consult the following publications.

ENCYCLOPEDIAS
Gillispie, C. C. (ed.), *Dictionary of Scientific Biography* (New York, 1975).
Hornblower, S. and A. Spawforth (eds.), *Oxford Classical Dictionary* (Oxford, 1996).
The Catholic Encyclopedia, at www.newadvent.org.

ANCIENT MATHEMATICS
Those interested in learning more about ancient Greek science would best start with these very readable books:
Lloyd, G. E. R., *Early Greek Science: Thales to Aristotle* (London, 1970).
———, *Greek Science after Aristotle* (London, 1973).

Those interested more specifically in the achievements of Greek geometry should start with:
Knorr, W. R., *The Ancient Tradition of Geometric Problems* (New York, 1986).

ARCHIMEDES
The best general book on Archimedes' scientific achievement is likely to remain for many years to come:
Dijksterhuis, E. J., *Archimedes* (1956; revised edn, Princeton, 1987).

The following is a three-volume publication, written in Greek, with Latin translation and introduction. It may be difficult to read. Still, we thought we should mention this; we have referred to its two authors quite frequently:
Heiberg, J. L., *Archimedes, Opera Omnia* (Leipzig, 1910–15).

Those interested in the early history of the calculus and its concepts should still read:
Boyer, C. B., *The History of the Calculus and its Conceptual Development* (New York, 1959).

HYPERIDES
The speeches of Hyperides known before their discovery in the Archimedes Palimpsest are edited with a translation in the Loeb Classical Library:
Burtt, J. O., *Minor Attic Orators*, vol. II (Cambridge, MA, 1954).

MANUSCRIPT TRANSMISSION OF THE CLASSICS
For the transition from roll to codex:
Roberts, C. H. and T. C. Skeat, *The Birth of the Codex* (London, 1983).

For those interested in Greek scripts, the following are good introductions:
Barbour, R., *Greek Literary Hands AD 400—1600* (Oxford, 1981).
Easterling, P. and C. Handley (eds.), *Greek Scripts: An Illustrated Introduction* (London, 2001).
Metzger, B. M., *Manuscripts of the Greek Bible: An Introduction to Greek Paleography* (New York, 1981).

★

For a broad survey of the history of writing, readers might try:

Sirat, C., *Writing as Handwork: A History of Handwriting in Mediterranean and Western Culture* (Turnhout, 2006).

There are many technical studies on the making of manuscripts. A useful basic text, with bibliography, is:

Brown, M. P., *Understanding Medieval Manuscripts: A Guide to Technical Terms* (Malibu, CA, 1994).

Not at all relevant to Archimedes, but for readers who would like to know more about the wonderful world of medieval manuscripts, the best general introduction available is:

De Hamel, C., *A History of Illuminated Manuscripts* (London, 1987).

For those interested in the transmission of ancient texts through to the age of printing, the following are indispensable:

Reynolds, L. D. and N. G. Wilson, *Scribes and Scholars*, 3rd edn (Oxford, 1991).

Wilson, N. G., *Scholars of Byzantium* (London, 1983).

A major scholarly feat, focused on the history of the text of Archimedes in Latin-speaking Europe, is:

Clagett, M., *Archimedes in the Middle Ages* (Madison, WI, 1964–84).

IMAGING AND IMAGING PROCESSING

Roger Easton recommends:

Baxes, G. A., *Digital Image Processing: Principles and Applications* (New York, 1994).

Falk, D. R., D. R. Brill and D. G. Stork, *Seeing the Light: Optics in Nature, Photography, Color, Vision, and Holography* (New York, 1986).

For advanced light sources, such as the Stanford Linear Accelerator Center, check out http://www.lightsources.org.

THE PALIMPSEST

The main publications on the Archimedes Palimpsest since September 1998 are listed below, alphabetically by author:

Christens-Barry, W. A., J. R. Bernstein and M. Blackburn, "Imaging the Third Dimension of the Archimedes Palimpsest," *Proceedings of IS & T PICS Conference* (Montreal, 2001), pp. 202–5.

Christie's, New York, "The Archimedes Palimpsest," sale catalogue 9058, Thursday, 29 October 1998.

Down, J. L., G. S. Young, R. S. Williams and M. A. MacDonald, "Analysis of the Archimedes Palimpsest," in V. Daniels, A. Donnithorne and P. Smith (eds.), *Works of Art on Paper, Books, Documents and Photographs*, The International Institute for Conservation, Contributions to the Baltimore Congress, 2–6 September 2002 (London, 2002), pp. 52–8.

Easton, R. L., Jr, and W. Noel, "The Multispectral Imaging of the Archimedes Palimpsest," *Gazette du Livre Médiévale*, 45, 2004, pp. 39–49.

Handley, E., "Eureka? The conservation, imaging and study of the Archimedes Palimpsest," exhibition pamphlet, Trinity College, Cambridge, 21–2 and 25–9 July 2005.

Knox, K., C. Dickinson, L. Wei, R. L. Easton, Jr, and R. Johnston, "Multispectral Imaging of the Archimedes Palimpsest," *Proceedings of IS & T PICS Conference* (Montreal, 2001), pp. 206–10.

Lowden, J., "Archimedes into Icon: Forging an Image of Byzantium," in A. Eastmond and L. James (eds.), *Icon and Word: The Power of Images in Byzantium* (London, 2003), pp. 233–60.

Netz, R., *Archimedes: Translation and Commentary, with a Critical Edition of the Diagrams and a Translation of Eutocius' Commentaries*, vol. I: "The Sphere and the Cylinder" (Cambridge, 2004).

———, *Archimedes: Translation and Commentary, with a Critical Edition of the Diagrams and a Translation of Eutocius' Commentaries*, vol. II: "Advanced Geometrical Works" (Cambridge [forthcoming]).

————, *Archimedes: Translation and Commentary, with a Critical Edition of the Diagrams and a Translation of Eutocius' Commentaries*, vol. III: "The Mathematical-Physical Works" (Cambridge [forthcoming]).

————, "Archimedes and Mar Saba: a Preliminary Notice," in J. Patrich (ed.), *The Sabaite Heritage: The Sabaite Factor in the Orthodox Church: Monastic Life, Liturgy, Theology, Literature, Art and Archaeology* (2002), pp. 195–9.

————, "The Origin of Mathematical Physics: New Light on an Old Question," *Physics Today* , June 2000, pp. 31–6.

Netz, R., F. Acerbi and N. Wilson, "Towards a Reconstruction of Archimedes' Stomachion," *Sciamus*, 5, 2004, pp. 67–99.

Netz, R., K. Saito and N. Tchernetska, "A New Reading of Method Proposition 14: Preliminary Evidence from the Archimedes Palimpsest (Part 1)," *Sciamus*, 2, 2001, pp. 9–29.

————, "A New Reading of Method Proposition 14: Preliminary Evidence from the Archimedes Palimpsest (Part 2)," *Sciamus*, 3, 2002, pp. 109–25.

Noel, W., "The Archimedes Palimpsest, Old Science Meets New Science," *Proceedings of IS & T PICS Conference* (Montreal, 2001), pp. 199–201.

Parenti, S., "The Liturgical Tradition of the Euchologion 'of Archimedes'" *Bollettino della Badia Greca di Grottaferrata*, IIIs. 2 (2005) [but actually 2006], pp. 69–87.

Quandt, A., "The Archimedes Palimpsest: Conservation Treatment, Digital Imaging and Transcription of a Rare Mediaeval Manuscript," in V. Daniels, A. Donnithorne and P. Smith (eds.), *Works of Art on Paper: Books, Documents and Photographs*, The International Institute for Conservation, Contributions to the Baltimore Congress, 2–6 September 2002 (London, 2002), pp. 165–70.

Tchernetska, N., "New Fragments of Hyperides from the Archimedes Palimpsest," *Zeitschrift für Papyrologie und Epigraphik*, vol. 154, 2005, pp. 1–6.

Wilson, Nigel, "Archimedes: the Palimpsest and the Tradition," *Byzantinische Zeitschrift*, 92, 1999, pp. 89–101.

———, "The Archimedes Palimpsest: A Progress Report," in "A Catalogue of Greek Manuscripts at the Walters Art Museum and Essays in Honor of Gary Vikan," *Journal of the Walters Art Museum*, 62, 2004, pp. 61–8.

———, "The Secrets of Palimpsests," *L'Erasmo*, 25, 2005, pp. 70–5.

———, *Archimedes' "On Floating Bodies" I.1–2*, edited with an English translation (Oxford, 2004).

Young, G., "Quantitative Image Analysis in Microscopical Thermal Stability Measurements," Canadian Conservation Institute Newsletter, 31 June 2003, pp. 10–11.

Index